D1138071

Challenging
Blank Minds and Sticky Moments
in Counselling

Challenging

Blank Minds and Sticky Moments

in Counselling

Graham Dexter
&
Janice Russell

© 1997 Graham Dexter and Janice Russell

The right of Graham Dexter and Janice Russell to be identified as authors of this work has been asserted by them in accordance with the Copyright, Designs and Patents Act 1988.

All rights reserved. No part of this publication may be reproduced or transmitted in any form or by any means, electronic or mechanical, including photocopying, recording or any information storage and retrieval system, without permission in writing from the authors or under licence from the Copyright Licensing Agency limited. Further details of such licences (for reprographic reproduction) may be obtained from the Copyright Licensing Agency Limited, of 90 Tottenham Court Road, London W1P 9HE.

A catalogue record for this book is available from the British Library.

ISBN 0-907769-25-X

Set in 10 on 11 Bookman Old Style

Designed and printed by Winckley Press, 5 Winckley Street, Preston PR1 2AA.

Printed and bound in Great Britain

Acknowledgements

As is traditional and befitting, we would like to express our appreciation and respect to all those people who have been our students, our clients, our supervisees, and our teachers. We continue to learn from all of them and their willingness to share their experiences, their confusions, their learnings and their ideas. This holds as true for those we engaged with twenty years ago, as it does to those we work with today.

A book, after all, begins as an idea, stimulated by thought, discussion and influence. Inevitably, the writing of a joint work on interpersonal relationships, which counselling essentially is, entails a considerable challenge to the authors' interpersonal relationship and their ability to negotiate on issues of content, style and control. We would therefore like to acknowledge this process, and to say that what you will read is a synthesis of our individual experience and our joint negotiation.

As we decided to publish this book ourselves, we were heavily dependent on those who helped us by reading the work in its complete form. Each of the four people who did so, deserve special mention.

Judi Irving commented on an early draft of this work in her own inimitable style. Judi is one of the most creative and enabling people that we have the pleasure to work with. She's the sort of person who makes opportunities turn into accomplishments, and who encourages free thinking. Judi has the enviable and unpretentious knack of saying honestly what she thinks, and so her feedback has been invaluable.

Ralph Benson read the penultimate manuscript with a rigour and thoroughness that took determination and energy, especially since he was so doubtful about the tone of our work! Ralph offered us a wonderful perspective which was heavily informed by his considerable intellect. Our hope is that he acknowledges his intellectual and personal worth as strongly as we do.

Paul Smith deserves thanks for a number of reasons. He offered us his astute and respected opinion, and we knew that he would offer no platitudes. He brought to his reading that essentially human ability he has to express both thought and emotion in a straightforward manner. Visions erupt for us of snooker halls, singing, mime and just good heart, hidden depths, and good fun.

Linda Garbutt listened to a reading of this book for us and offered us a unique and much valued perspective. Linda is an extremely experienced counsellor and trainer , and her comments were really very encouraging for us. Linda has an ability to see in her mind's eye that which a lot of us miss, so we were privileged to have her help.

All four readers are people whom we trusted to be respectful, genuine, sensitive, discerning and hard-hitting, so thank you all very much.

For the cartoons, we must thank Leddy and Lindsey, who did us a magnificent job in a very short time. It really is wonderful to be able to represent ideas and comments through pictures, and Leddy and Lindsey really got into the spirit which we want to convey. Thanks also to Ron for co-ordinating us to their direction.

A special and gratuitous mention for Kez and Sam, really because they have been acknowledged now in three books, and would like to go for a world record. Time also to publicly acknowledge Alex and James and to stake their claim to fame. The presence of all four of you is constantly fulfilling and challenging, in no particular order! And finally, the writing of this book has been much aided by our eldest daughter Samantha Watson, who has provided us with several tranquil opportunities to reflect and write. Sam has also given us food for thought and great pleasure in recognising the hidden influence of genetics. All five of our children are important influences.

An introduction to Blank Minds and Sticky Moments

Welcome to Blank Minds and Sticky Moments, a book on counselling for counsellors, supervisors, trainers, students and basically anyone who has the remotest interest in this cult called counselling which has swept the western world of late. We hope that you are looking to be stimulated and enlivened, that you have interest in what makes counselling tick, and that you are willing to be entertained. If we can achieve this, and if you take out of it some educative principles as well, as we have, then we guess that your money will be well spent.

Who are we? A question that burns for many people, I guess. We are two people who have lived and worked in areas of communication and counselling for a lot of years. We both encountered families when we were small, went through the school system, experienced various trauma, experienced highs, and learned how to create our own paths through the maze of life. Like the average person, in fact, we learned how to communicate and to solve our problems as best we could at the time. We both went into 'helping' people, one through social work, the other through psychiatric nursing. We both moved towards counselling and undertook a wide range of ventures to learn and practice our art. We both returned to higher education as mature students, and began to critique that which we had learned. We provided families, love and trauma for our own five children to learn how best to make out. And now we counsel, supervise, train, consult, research, write; we go to the cinema, keep pigeons, play the cello, dance, read, on Fridays we go shopping, and oh yes, we go to the lavatory...

We are, then, pretty ordinary. Our perspective on counselling is that it draws on ordinary, non-mystical activity and skills in a principled manner. Over the last twenty years, you will have noticed that there has been an emergence of professionalisation of counselling. Currently, however, definitions cannot be agreed, competence measures are not yet established, there is argument about whether competence can ever be tested, and the demands on counsellors under the guise of personal development has become so ridiculous that many courses now insist that their trainees have counselling in order to be counsellors. In other words, the profession is in a bit of a mess, with a tendency to mysticise the whole process. Current moves are to make a register of counsellors; it will be interesting to see how this is policed, given that counselling depends upon human interactive skills and activities - would helping people problem solve over dinner parties be illegal? Could people be outlawed for empathising during pillow talk, on the grounds that it has elicited self-disclosure beyond that which the partner had wanted to engage in (but of course only realised this retrospectively)? The mind boggles.

Not surprising, then, that practitioners of counselling have somewhat mixed perspectives on what they are supposed to be doing. While this has always been the case, and indeed led to the innovative aspects of counselling, we have noticed lately an increasing shift away from the pioneer approach of what *could* be done in counselling, where counsellors had a spirit of adventure and discovery, towards a trend for counsellors to ask what they *should* be doing. While the purposes and principles of counselling seem to be more blurred, there seems to be more caution about *how* specific ends are met, and notions of success and failure seem to haunt even the most experienced practitioners.

At the end of the day, we believe that counselling is about an approach, and an attitude. The adoption of each has resulted in the construction of a number of skills and techniques which reflect the nature of this approach, and which achieve the desired outcome. However, such skills and techniques are merely footprints made on the road to fulfil the attitude; just because one person walked this way, we don't all have to. There is no one right way to do it, and there is no proficiency in technique without the attitude and approach of inquiry. We essentially understand counselling to be a dynamic process of negotiation which purports to create opportunities for self-determined change for the client.

The overall purpose of this book, then, is to address the principles and issues associated with the complexities of counselling, whether for the 'pure' counsellor, the student counsellor, or for workers who use counselling as one part of their job, e.g. mental health workers, psychiatric social workers. We recognise that people arrive at the role of counsellor through very different routes, some through academic courses, and others through practice- based learning augmented by short courses. When the idea for the book was conceived, we decided we would like it to be accessible to a varied audience if possible, so that it has academic credibility but is not exclusive. In other words, we want to reach the practitioner, not just the academic student.

The idea for the book began from our own practice in counselling, training and our supervision of practitioners. It has become apparent that whatever the level of training and experience, counsellors come across issues or moments in the counselling relationship when they feel stuck. They either don't know what to do, do not have the confidence to try out their own ideas or suspect that they may be about to infringe some taboo or other. It seems that certain themes, issues or 'skill gaps' emerge consistently. We wanted a book which would address these areas in reasonable detail, with reference to pragmatic experience and to current available literature, and which would suggest further specialist reading and training opportunities for those interested to pursue any one area.

In our experience as trainers, we find that the "blank minds" and "sticky moments" that happen from time to time are not usually addressed in training courses or supervision, despite there being a strong call from practitioners that they should be. We want to identify some of the common issues or scenarios which seem to confuse or baffle counsellors, and to look at a range of intervention techniques to help them deal with them. The book is not only concerned with 'techniques', however, and attempts to acknowledge some of the deeper intra and interpersonal issues which are provoked within the counselling relationship.

The philosophy of the book is very much concerned with empowering the counsellor to free themselves up to be more imaginative, creative and flexible. Much counselling literature is caught up with what *should* be done, whereas the intention of this book is to encourage counsellors to think of what *could* be done within a framework of purposeful and ethical practice. Moreover, while theory is a useful adjunct to counselling, we adopt a somewhat realist and relativist view that all psychological theories are merely informed speculation. Who said that the self is like a layered onion? Who dictates what is the 'real' experience, the 'core' of the self? How can we measure emotion and meaning on an elevation scale using 'depth', and 'levels'? Part of the thrust of the work is to demystify some of the more 'precious' aspects of counselling which can be frightening to the counsellor and ultimately diminish their trust in the client. We would also like to regain some humility for the profession which assumes and theorises so much about human nature, on very flimsy evidence.

The inception of this book is underpinned by some strong personal views, experiences and philosophy. We made the original proposal to our existing publishers, back in 1994. As publishers do, they sent it out to two high ranking counselling academics who expressed severe reservations. One was that the subject matter was not appropriate to be treated humorously, while another was that it seemed a very pragmatic and eclectic approach which was not currently in vogue. Since we believe that counselling needs to be developed towards the interests of the *client* first, we were stuck with the pragmatic, wanted to be light hearted here and there, and so decided to publish ourselves. We trust that you will find what follows both helpful and provocative, and a contribution to the rich debate of counselling which will no doubt continue for many years to come.

Overview

The book is organised into two sections, which are inherently interdependent. The first section will focus on pragmatic issues, and will include some ideas and approaches, even some skills, which might be helpful to the practitioner who experiences blank minds and sticky moments. Chapter One will outline some examples of what such moments might look like. Chapter Two will examine such moments grouped together as intra-personal issues - what is going on for the counsellor as they do their work, before they do it, after they do it? Chapter Three will look at interpersonal issues, with four major headings which incorporate intimacy, sexuality, friendship and culture. Chapter Four offers a dynamic approach to the skills and attitudes of challenging clients, to help them move on in their lives rather than become embroiled in their own blank minds and sticky moments for ever. Chapter Five will outline perspectives on working creatively with clients who do not respond well to 'traditional' communication methods. Chapter Six will look at the context of counselling in relation to the counsellor and the agency, and will act as a bridge to the second section of the book.

The second section of the book will be exploring the more general context of counselling. Chapter Seven will draw on a broader perspective of the place that counselling plays in society. Chapter Eight will look at what counselling is in theoretical terms, and outline some of the current debates. Chapter Nine will look at some of the paradoxes within counselling, such as the impossibility of accurate empathy, the limitations of unconditional positive regard and other generalised assumptions which inform counselling.

Finally, Chapter Ten will reiterate the principles of counselling practice in the form of a four stage model. We hope that by this time your interest will have been pursued, captured and liberated to further your own practice and your own arguments. We hope that this will provide a theoretically informed practical book which is of use within and after training.

Contents

Chapter Four. Challenging : do I really have to sit here and listen to anything, even when I think it's drivel?...................................... 69

Chapter Five. Tight Lips but Heavy Hearts.... 106

Chapter Six. Let's get all this counselling stuff into perspective: We can only do what we can do.. 123

Chapter Nine. Philosophy, Psychology, Faith, and Goodwill: Aimless prattle or just common sense? 174

Chapter Ten. Blank Minds - Hardly Ever Sticky Moments - Not any more! 201

Chapter One. Blank minds and sticky moments

Introduction

This chapter overviews some examples of blank minds and sticky moments that can happen in practice. They can be very different from each other, yet each offers a learning opportunity which will be different for each person. We will describe a wide range of examples of blank minds and sticky moments that the reader may recognise or be alerted to, based on some of our own experiences and our data collection. These will be linked where appropriate to theoretical explanation, bearing in mind that these are only useful as long as they are enabling, and are never so rigid as to be right!

'Er . . . er . . . der . . .??!!**'

At the end of the chapter notions of counsellor development will be discussed.

Over the years, we've begun to identify a series of typical examples of blank minds or sticky moments. We might add that some of our personal worst moments in counselling have taught us best, and we can now look back at these with humour and take the learning with us. They are many and varied, some more ridiculous than others, some more dramatic, some more serious. We hope then that as you read this chapter, you will dare to feel amused, reassured even, and perhaps a little freed up.

A fine example of a sticky moment occurred for one counsellor we know who used to use a rocking chair when counselling. She had no idea just how engaged she was with the client, until she leaned back so far, and so carelessly, being engrossed in the story, that she rocked all the way over and landed with legs akimbo. Fortunately, both parties found this to be hilarious, and at least the counsellor can say that she remained 'genuine' throughout the ungainly exercise of putting skirts down, dusting herself off, and resuming counselling.

'That told him, he'll definitely come back for more of that.'

On a more serious note, however, another example of a blank mind left one of us with much food for thought about what harm might have been done. As a novice counsellor we were working with a heterosexual couple. The man frequently beat his wife, and they were trying some marital therapy. One day, he came on his own. When asked where his wife was, he laughed and said that he'd given her a good slap, and she was too bruised to come out. The counsellor went completely blank, and with no sense of purpose, issued him with several challenges which reflected the counsellor's emotion of anger, but which were sadly lacking in any skill. An argument ensued to the point where the man was told not to bother coming back on his own, at which point he left. Walking out of the counselling room, the counsellor felt exhilarated, and proud of 'not putting up with any nonsense' - for about two minutes. Emerging from the complete blank regarding the client needs and outcomes, realisation dawned that the counsellor might have acted in such a way that the man's wife was more at risk. The contract had been completely blown, and neither party ever came back. A salutary lesson, and we shall never know how serious those mistakes were.

These are notable examples, and on a more regular basis we know that blank minds and sticky moments are usually more mundane and that some common themes begin to occur. What is more, the nature of blank minds and sticky moments might change over time in relation to the experience and the developmental stage of the counsellor. For example, as practitioners develop, their ideas and values towards issues such as sexuality, abuse, death, or politics may change radically. It would be naïve of us to ignore the influence of such development on their practice, and more specifically, their reluctance or willingness to take on certain types of clients.

This chapter is organised in two main parts, then. In the first, we will offer a range of examples of blank minds and sticky moments which we have come across in our experience and research. We will then identify six stages of counsellor development which might influence the counsellor's approach and blind spots.

Clients turning the table [getting control] - Feedback to me instead of me to them

Client feedback is usually, and theoretically, a useful event. Without it, how many of us would know if our counselling relationships are productive. On occasion, however, the client might use their feedback, wittingly or otherwise, as a means of gaining control.

Consider the following situation. Moira, fresh from her first year of her Diploma course, is counselling Janet. Janet is a single parent, lonely, has a history of abuse, is finding life a strain. Currently, she co-habits with Paul, who frequently threatens her, sometimes hits her, and will not give her the kind of support she wants. Janet is frustrated. What is more, she feels so isolated that when she has the opportunity to talk about her problems, she 'gushes' with story and emotion. Moira is sympathetic to Janet. She was at one time in a similar situation and is keen to show her understanding. What is more, she is apprehensive of taking control of the process and interrupting her client 'in full flow'. Inexperience leads her to believe that this would be disrespectful. Thus she is not as challenging as she might be to Janet.

It is only a matter of time before Janet is letting Moira know in no uncertain terms how little she is helping. Janet expects more - 'I've been for four sessions now, and you hardly say anything. I'd expected you to be more helpful, to do more somehow. I'm not really sure whether you can do anything for me or not. I feel worse now than when we started'. Moira feels uncertain and a little defensive - what is it that Janet expects? Did she make explicit her role in the first place - and if so did she stick to it? In supervision, Moira is so concerned with her own feelings of incompetence that she feels she has lost the plot with Janet, and doubts whether she can help. Moira is, in fact, feeling very clientish! In this scenario, the counsellor's personal fears and anxieties have sabotaged movement within the counselling process, and the counsellor is left feeling slightly bruised.

I know just how you feel

Identification can lead to all sorts of unhelpful responses. Recently, one of us (Janice) had the experience of being diagnosed as having cancer of the breast. She felt lucky to receive enormous support from close friends and family, and from colleagues, and indeed, moved to be supported by people whose concern surprised her. People were generally at pains to understand how she felt and to help her in all sorts of ways.

Amongst the understanding, however, were one or two comments which slightly grated, despite the kind intentions of those who made them. These were the comments which were prefaced by other people's stories, and the conclusion 'so I guess I know how you must be feeling right now'. Experiencing a sense of discomfort when hearing this kind of message, and feeling far from understood, she realised how her circumstances had tapped into other people's experiences and emotions. They felt sure that they recognised or identified with her story. While this might have been the case, such strong identification meant that there was no room for understanding her emotions.

This experience was not problematic to Janice: people were not counselling her, they were demonstrating the wide range of genuine responses which we would offer to friends and colleagues. Moreover, such responses came from people who perhaps were still very involved with their own emotions rather than someone elses. However, this really is a pitfall for counsellors to be aware of.

Rarely would a counsellor offer the client their own story in this way. Yet often they try the impossible task of trying to identify precisely how the client feels, along with exercising the myth of unconditional positive regard. Moreover, often counsellors come up against accounts of experiences which are similar to experiences that they have had themselves. This double barrelled experience can mean that the counsellor hijacks the client by listening to their own emotions, rather than the clients. Thus they can go for the 'quick and dirty' way of demonstrating empathy, which is rarely useful or uncontaminated.

Sorry, what did you say your name was?

Sometimes, counsellors become anxious when they don't remember the details of the client's story. Some counsellors take copious notes after a session to remind them of the ins and outs of each part of the scenario. They may become anxious about not knowing the name of a son, or the age of an aunt. And at times, whilst in the counselling session, they might forget a detail or even get it wrong.

Fear of forgetting, or even actually forgetting factual information, creates a wonderful vicious circle. Anxiety creates conscious attempts to remember - but who for? For the counsellor, in order to reduce their anxiety. As soon as this becomes a primary motivator, if only temporarily, then it interferes with the ability to listen whole-heartedly to the meaning of what the client is telling themselves and you. Counsellors can become brilliant at eliciting flawless case histories - which of course the client already knew.

Forgetting factual information is not a hanging offence. Indeed, often it illustrates that the counsellor is more concerned with the client's process than the content of their stories. There is of course a neat little paradox which then begins to operate. The person who is not anxious about forgetting factual details, who is not embarrassed to check something which they have not remembered, is often likely to be the person who, through paying careful attention to the client, rather than themselves, does in fact remember!

'Oh, have we met somewhere before?'

'Yes, wasn't it when you counselled me about my bad back?'

Isn't it great to be a guru?

Early on in her counselling career, one of us, (Janice) worked with a client through a traumatic period of her life. The client achieved an outcome which she evaluated very positively. In the final session, she said , amongst other things:

> 'Jan, this has been so useful. I don't know what you've done, but whatever it was, it was wonderful. You really have helped me more than anybody ever and I don't know what I'd have done without you. I shall recommend you to my friends, if ever I'm stuck I know where to come!'

The counsellor went home with a rosy glow, knowing the hard work that had been done, and appreciating the enjoyment of that work. And lo! to be so marvellous into the bargain was just the icing on the cake. To have been so indispensable, so magical, to have such powers....

Over a period of time, as this accolade was reflected upon, a growing sense of unease descended. It was those small statements *I don't know what you've done,* and *I don't know what I'd have done without you.* Two things struck home - who had done what, to whom, and had it been done by the counsellor alone? These comments afforded a marvellous stimulus to reflect on issues surrounding the greatness of the Guru!

Further experience generated the opportunity for somewhat humbler and more gratified feelings, when two pieces of client feedback occurred in quick succession.

The first was from a woman who was, by trade, a photographer. She said , amongst other things, that the counselling had helped her to clarify her perspectives and emotions, that she had felt validated, and that she could see how the utilisation of skills and qualities had helped her to feel empowered. She now felt that she could do much more of that for herself. She requested that in the final session, she should have ten minutes in which she could take photographs so that she had the opportunity to demonstrate *her* expertise.

The second opportunity for feedback came from a piece of work with a man who was facing the loss of someone he loved dearly, who was terminally ill. Having worked very intensively and very purposefully, he came to recognise that there was nothing like the real valuing of time to help to focus wants and preferences. After the death of his beloved friend, he returned three or four times, in which it was a privilege to share in his grief and to participate in his evaluation of events. In terms of the counselling, the client and counsellor went through what had been done together, and in reviewing the process, with reference to sources where appropriate, the client excitedly correlated theory to the practice which he had experienced. He went away with a method for coping with future problems and concerns, and he knew not only what the counsellor had done, but what *he* and the counsellor had done together, and, most crucially, how he had achieved what he wanted in this most challenging situation. This was a delightful outcome. To achieve it, the counsellor needs to hang up the magician's hat and be comfortable to be sorcerers' apprentices together.

Haven't we met before somewhere?

It is quite common for counsellors and clients to experience aspects of a relationship which Freud conceptualised as transference and countertransference. Transference and countertransference are quite simple concepts to describe a process which might occur in any relationship, and sometimes, therefore, happens in counselling. Transference is used of the client when they relate to the counsellor as if s/he were some other significant person in the client's life. Countertransference is used to describe the same process occurring for the counsellor. Quite literally, feelings which were evoked in the previous relationship are 'transferred' to current situation.

For example, one of us, (Graham) counselled a woman who was the same age as his mother, and who had offspring the same age as him. She described problems regarding assertiveness with her family, and presented herself as quite a victim in the family. Her pattern of behaviour was somewhat martyrish, often performing tasks which she didn't want to, and then bemoaning the family for taking her for granted.

At some point in the counselling process, Graham became very aware of a strong feeling of irritation towards his client, and soon identified that this martyrish behaviour reminded him of his mother's tendency to behave in this way. The irritation that he felt was actually what he felt toward his mother when she was like this. Once identified, he could use this constructively to both better understand and to challenge the client into new understandings.

I can be whatever you want

Sometimes, the client brings their ways of relating very powerfully into the counselling relationship. This is vividly illustrated when the client is used to being victimised in some way. This may be overtly, through repeated episodes of physical/sexual abuse, or more subtly, feeling picked on, reprimanded and judged. The expectation of the client has sometimes become that all other people are in some way her/his oppressor.

This can be difficult and challenging for the counsellor, and one possible response is to relate to the client much as other 'oppressors' have. For example, an individual who is used to being related to sexually might act in a way which is sexually provocative, and this may evoke a sexual response from the counsellor. A client who is used to people being irritated by them might have developed a whiny or apologetic interpersonal style, which the counsellor becomes irritated with. Before they know it, the counsellor might actively internalise the proffered role of being irritated, and begin to behave accordingly.

Theoretically, this is the syndrome which is usually described as projective identification. The client projects their notion of what people do to them, the counsellor complies by identifying with those people. In other words, we might simply see this as a form of self-fulfilling prophecy. You be wingey, I'll be critical. You be seductive, I'll be seduced. Unspotted, this can lead the way for some very unhelpful and at times exploitative or destructive practice.

I haven't got a clue how you feel!

From time to time, counsellors will encounter the extreme where they find it very difficult to recognise any aspects of the client's story, feelings or strongly held values, and where they just cannot identify with situations or behaviours. This may occur when the type of behaviour or situation is very alien from their own experience. For example, a counsellor working with an individual who has vivid sexual fantasies about children might be at a loss to understand how this really feels, or why it might be arousing.[2] They might find the behaviour quite alien, and outside of their realm of experience.

Equally, it might be difficult to identify with a client's value systems. One client of ours had very strong religious beliefs, so that his extreme unhappiness within his marriage was held in tension alongside his love for his god whom he sought to obey. One of the measures of such obedience was to stay within the marriage, com-

'I don't even know what sealions think about, let alone how they feel!'

mitted for better or for worse, and until death. It was difficult to understand such commitment to a set of values which were so restricting of this man's potential, and not to be tempted to see the religious belief as an 'excuse' rather than a 'valid' reason for keeping the situation the same.

Such non-recognition may also occur with the ordinary and predictable aspects of life when the counsellor has never dealt with a specific situation before. This may be a situation where someone is revealing childhood abuse, current abuse, bereavement, or some other form of post-traumatic stress disorder. It is easy to confuse a new theme with unnecessary difficulties. Counsellors sometimes become anxious if they've never dealt with sexual abuse, say, or with depressive clients. It is useful to remember that clients are whole people, for whom the named problem is one aspect of their experience.

When we worked in Kuwait in 1993, helping to train counsellors to deal with some of the aftermath of the Iraqi invasion, we were faced with a number of quite new situations. We were advised to read various books in order to orientate ourselves and understand, but chose instead to go 'cold' into the situation. Perhaps going cold should be reframed as 'warm' - we went with open hearts and humility, and learned our way through confidence in our ethos and a willingness to negotiate issues and situations. Our overriding belief system was perhaps that the commonalities in our humanity were greater than the differences, and so the 'new situations', the 'new culture', were a forum for learning and sharing, rather than an inhibitor.

If we'd just met elsewhere, I know we'd be friends

One of our supervisees recently made a confession. She is counselling a woman with whom she feels a tremendous rapport. She is an empathic, challenging, creative, highly experienced counsellor, and said 'I so much enjoy this client, that what I really want to say to her, what I have said, is "sometimes I feel like saying oh sod the counselling, let's go down the pub" '. She went on to say that had she met her client in other circumstances, they would have got on like a house on fire, and become really good friends.

Now, this supervisee is aware enough to know the pitfalls of such a belief. Hence she has not actually suggested that they go to the pub, and she has used her immediacy as part of the counselling relationship. Further, she is reflecting on the issue in supervision. But what of that assumption, that 'if we met in other circumstances we could have been friends' ? The answer, of course, is that we'll never know, but our general perspective is that this is largely a fallacy. Consider the situation.

One person in this dyad (the client) has revealed her story, her emotions, her hopes and her fears. Something has occurred between you which has resulted in a close rapport. You feel so strongly for this client, that you really would like to help them, and you know they have such potential, and you understand their feelings so well. Hmm. As yet, she does not know your feelings, your potential, or your hopes and fears. She sees someone who always listens, who understands, and who is positive in all respects. She does not know your 'weaknesses', your failings, your values.

Now then, being human, it is possible that of all the clients who we meet, some of them might be our 'type', in terms of friendship. It is equally possible however that we don't always identify those who would be most likely, for often the bits we hear in counselling are the bits that clients *don't* tell their friends. We offer a contract which guarantees to try to make the conditions for intimacy to occur. Would we really like our friendships to be the same?

And of course we have the whole debate about who is being intimate with whom in the counselling relationship. Georg Simmel once said that in order for true intimacy to occur, then each party must offer some *unique* aspect of self to the other, i.e. some information or mode of being which is for them alone. While the client may do this, it is quite clear that the counsellor does not, however open or genuine they might be. These are after all conditions which they offer to *all* clients.

Feeling friendly with the client may be a smokescreen as well for feeling flattered. The trap is that you can be lulled into an inability to be challenging - after all, how can you challenge if you're seen as really nice? At its worst, this may even be, intentionally or unintentionally, a part of a manipulative behaviour pattern by the client.

It's difficult, isn't it? As we write this, we are aware of how impoverished it can be to reduce all counselling relationships to a series of pitfalls and portraits of unhelpful behavioural patterns. This is not the intention here, and of course it is possible that some of the clients you meet, should you have met in other circumstances, might have developed into friends.[3] But they might not, and since we'll never know, it seems a lot more pragmatic to us to have a perspective which enables us to work effectively and fruitfully, and to recognise our different roles within the relationship.[4]

My client has resistance

Resistance is one of those nice theoretical terms that, should we choose to, we can nominalise and make an attribute of the client. Counsellors talk about 'the resistance', working with 'it'. What on earth are they really referring to?

We believe that resistance is used to cover a number of dynamic situations. What the counsellor really means is that the client is not willing at this point to confront some area of counselling work. Now this can have a number of possible explanations. It may be that they are afraid. It may be that they are ambivalent about whether or not they really want any exposure or change at this stage. Or it may be that the counsellor is so naff, that the client would rather tell their cat about their troubles and the intimate details of their life.

Have you ever had a client who, having poured out a story of distress and dissatisfaction, comes back the following week to de-clare, no, I didn't do the homework, but I feel much better. And of course it may be that enough change has occurred to satisfy their wishes. Or it may be that they have some inner conflict wherein they both do and don't want to make changes. There are numer-ous possibilities.

What we can be sure of, however, is that resistance is not some concrete entity. Its only usefulness as a concept is if it is used to describe the fact that at this particular moment, or period, the client is choosing to resist the counselling process as conceptual-ised by the counsellor. Although this may seem obvious, to demys-tify resistance in this way opens up possibilities and limitations of the work. In other words, this is something that the client is doing responsively. And the challenge for the counsellor is to examine what *they* are doing, or not doing, which may be part of this dy-namic.

Consider the following. A counsellor who attended a workshop of ours asked if we could help her with a resistant client. This was a young man of fifteen who had been sexually abused. She could not help him through the trauma, she said, as he had tremendous resistance. She wondered if one of us would see him. It was agreed and some time later the client rang and made an appointment. In the subsequent session, he talked about how distressing he found it to talk about the abuse. He had been to court, and publicly testified against the abuser. He now wanted two things: one was to go to college, and the second was to stand up to his rather strong-minded father. No resistance at all. It was simply that the helper had not accurately negotiated the direction of the work.

This is a sharp edged example. More subtle variations occur which may only be noticed in hindsight. For example, have you ever noticed that when you do some work on a theme, such as bereavement, sexual abuse, your clients tell you more about such issues just as you become more open to hearing about them? Often this is because clients will previously have gently tested the waters as to how open a counsellor is, perhaps not even consciously, and if the counsellor has resisted listening carefully, then the client will say no more.

■ If a client is 'resisting', what is it then that I, the counsellor, am imposing?

■ Or what am I missing that would enable more work to be done?

It is far more useful to ask these questions than to attribute some 'thing' called resistance to the client. *Those activities in which we are engaged,* can be changed. Those mysterious occurrences which we dub resistance will trap us in their net!

And ultimately, of course, some clients have genuine difficulty in doing work that they want to do, but which causes apprehension or ambivalence. Challenging such ambivalence is perfectly legitimate and helpful, within a crucible of rapport and empathy. And certainly, some clients do not yet (or ever) want to make changes. All of these situations need to be respected.

Here, my dear, have a nice cup of tea

Sharing emotion is a habit which we are sometimes not used to. While it seems obvious that we must allow client distress, sometimes the process by which counsellors deny distress can operate quite subtly, or in a way which confuses even the experienced. Sometimes the hug, the offering of a tissue, the symbolic nice cup of tea, the urge to have the client stable by the end of the session, all may help the client to suppress as well as to experience emotion. What we don't always recognise is that the blandness of the nice cup of tea approach can also mean that we suppress the real experience of joy, of excitement, of anticipation, of love, or of enthusiasm.

Sympathetic responses often indicate very powerfully to the recipient that the sympathiser is not keen to hear strong emotion. The reason this happens is obvious - by giving out this sort of message we protect ourselves from having to hear about some distressing experience, and we spare the other person from the (imagined) distress of talking about it! The illusion of a helpful transaction is complete. Practitioners who adopt this type of interaction will suppress emotion, and in this vacuum wonder why they have become - STUCK.

Strong emotion can be frightening. However, not having trust in the client can be restricting. Several years ago, one of us remembers watching a client leave a session still in the throws of uncontrollable sobs, and feeling really very concerned as we watched her cross the road. The following week, the client declared that she had sobbed for most of three days, and that this had been the most helpful experience she had had for years. So while it is easy to be frightened, and to offer the nice cup of tea, it can be a way of avoiding a sticky moment for the counsellor, rather than helping the client.

I know just the theory to confuse us

Introducing theory at a critical moment may be tempting when your mind has gone blank. Sometimes, the introduction of well-timed theoretical understanding is helpful, if it might help the client to gain insight within their frame of reference. However, it can also be used when the counsellor wants to challenge the client into a new understanding, but isn't quite sure how to. Thus a little theoretical knowledge is grasped at to fill the blank;

Have thought, must share it.

Counsellor: 'Well yes, Clara client, you see what's happening in T.A. terms is that you're playing the part of the victim. Laura your lover is persecuting, and your mother keeps on coming in and rescuing'.

Clara client: 'Oh, that's really useful. I thought it was just that I keep on feeling really inferior and helpless, Laura gets fed up with me and punishes me, and my mum keeps encouraging me to go home to get out of the situation. But now I know what's really going on'.

This of course is rarely useful, although it does add yet another way of staying in the present and making no changes. Clara client can now go home with a new hanger to hang her woes on - I'm like this because I'm in Victim role/because I was abused as a child/because I was bullied.

What can go awfully wrong is when suddenly unplanned in the session, a distant memory of some dim and somewhat unclear theoretical proposition is triggered by what the client has said. 'Yes, Yes, I remember', you suddenly blurt out, 'Fred Bloggs wrote a paper on this, I remember something about..... ' Just as quickly as it overtook you, the idea retreats from your grasp. This leaves you feeling a complete nurgbrain , and the client is left open mouthed waiting for the pearl of wisdom which is about to change their life. It would be true to say that at this point, rapport with the client is lost as all the counsellor's attention is on their own memory. The challenge to a new perspective is never made.

Let's dance

Challenging generally is one of the trickier areas of counselling, and instead of pursuing it, counsellors and clients are notorious for their taking up dancing instead. This can be productive; they dance the dance of intimacy - moving closer, drawing away, twirling around, touching, backing off; they dance their way onwards and through time, learning new movements, dancing into the sunset. Sometimes, however, their dance takes them round and round the mulberry bush - a lovely movement, very enlivening, and getting nowhere fast.

Dancing round the mulberry bush is easy. People can enjoy talking about themselves *immensely.* Have you ever had that experience where someone is actually listening carefully to what you have to say? You may feel that your issues are important, your emotions valid, and your perspective worthwhile. For many people, this

'Well, if we're going nowhere – let's go in style'

is an uncommon occurrence in their everyday life, and is extremely enriching. Thus it can be tempting, when in the client seat, to repeatedly add on to the story in "and another thing" vein. And if the counsellor is curious, sympathetic, unassertive, or into diagnosis, they will become stuck for a strategy to 'move the client on'. When they move towards the future, the client will tell them more of what they don't want, more of what they've always had. One of the most common pleas which we hear from trainees in particular, and supervisees to some extent, is - we're getting nowhere, how do we move on?   And while a sense of plateau to integrate change is no bad thing, the clue to the mulberry bush is the never ending repetition, the endless new aspects to the story. A sure sign to introduce a change of music.

The concept of stages of counsellor development

The scenarios painted above represent some examples of the kind of blank minds and sticky moments which we and others have experienced, and we guess that these are, in some form or another, familiar to you. Roughly speaking, they cluster under the headings of intrapersonal issues, interpersonal issues, and the art of challenging. The next three chapters address these three headings.

It is also our experience that the type of difficulties encountered might change over a period of time and over a trajectory of counselling experience. At the beginning of this chapter, we suggested that the concept of counsellor development might have some use. This concept has previously been usefully identified in relation to supervision. The developmental increments which are usually identified span a spectrum where concern with the client's story or issues are at one end, with heightened self-awareness and focus on the internal world of the supervisee at the other.

There is also work available on counsellor's general development, and what influences them. As we all know, counsellor training, whether in-house or on a course, is often only the beginning of a career, not the end. A lot happens between training and death - we hope! And of course not all counsellors are formally trained. Most of us wend a winding road of development which influences our work. To complete this chapter, we would like to offer a six stage framework of practitioner development which illustrates the different possibilities.

Enthusiastic: Bright eyed, bushy tailed and lamps burning brightly

Many of us begin to study counselling and psychotherapy with an enthusiasm not dissimilar to converts to a new religion. We have discovered 'therapy' through having it, seeing it done successfully, reading about it or through going on a course . The enthusiasm is often excessive, either because we have grown disillusioned by our current profession or because we are seeking newer, fresher anti-dotes for the ailing world we live in. It is not surprising then that the new recruit passes through this stage avidly reading, practis-ing, and debating. Finding and attending all possible workshops is symptomatic of this phase, as is practising skills on unsuspect-ing friends and family; relationship problems take a high profile here! The lamp shining so brightly does not, however, always make for the best therapy, and blank minds and sticky moments are often concerned with 'what do I do now I've tried an approach?'

To illustrate the case, let us follow the journey of Francesca. Francesca started off her helping career in social work. Young , idealistic and radical, she had dreams of changing the world. Her motivation, so she thought, was entirely altruistic, and her insight into her own needs or the motivation for her passionate concern for the underdog was near the zilch end of the continuum. Her social work training and basic counselling course had equipped her with an introduction to some therapeutic techniques. At that stage they were most definitely techniques and not skills. She was particularly keen to help a family with serious problems regarding care, communication and control. She had learned family sculpt-ing in class, and was keen to try it. Every Thursday night, for six weeks, she visited the family, sculpted them, and left. No real con-text, no sense of ultimate purpose, but it seemed a good idea at the time. She has wondered from time to time what they might have thought of her, and when she does, she remembers one of her favourite cartoons from Case Con, which shows a couple sitting on the sofa, with the door bell ringing, and the husband saying "Try to be non-judgmental, Doris, that'll be the social worker". The lamp certainly shone brightly, but she had no idea of which way she was trying to light.

Despondency: I'll never get the hang of this!

At some point the new recruit becomes a working practitioner. Whether this is simply working with other students on a course, or working with 'real' clients under supervision, the lack of clarity and the under-developed skills may lead the student into a potentially depressive phase. The overt symptoms of this phase include anxiety and panic attacks, especially before sessions. It is not uncommon to feel stuck, bewildered or to frequently feel blank. Questions range from 'what should I do now', and 'are you sure that I'll ever be able to do that' to 'why do I have to do that at all'. Occasionally within this stage students will be overheard to remark 'I'm sure this is the same as I was doing it before' or 'I can't see why this is better than the way I was doing it'. Other positions adopted by students are the 'Can't I just hint at what they (the client) should do' or 'If they (the client) can't think of a strategy can I tell them what I would do?'.

All of these overt expressions of discouragement, frustration and mistrust are of course equally symptomatic of covert feelings of self doubt. Inside the exploding mind of the student, the effort to paraphrase, reflect, empathise, summarise, clarify and challenge, as well as having some sense of purpose and direction, *and* to practice self-awareness, is overwhelming. The student is like the learner driver, feeling that they will never get the hang of changing gear, declutching, steering, looking in the mirror, indicating and manoeuvring simultaneously, even though they can do each bit on their own - and as for following a route into the bargain, well!

Francesca's second bash at counselling was at a clinic offering contraceptive and pregnancy counselling for young people. She trained in behavioural sex therapy but realised that while she knew how to make behavioural programmes she had little real skill in responding appropriately to the nuances which she picked up. Whilst the blank mind of the previous example was mostly revolving around what to do when the family were sculpted, the sticky moments in this second stage are exemplified by the couple who "We've done the squeeze, and it hasn't worked. What can you recommend?". Francesca had a choice of basic counselling skills and behavioural programmes, but could not quite yet put them together consistently in a purposeful manner. Thus her response to the sticky moment would be ad hoc; it might be a combination of some empathy with yet more behavioural advice "That's a little disappointing, have you tried squeezing harder", or it might be downright suggestion born of frustration - "couldn't you just find a spot and rub it?"

Competent and restless: This is OK but let's get on with the sexy stuff!

Almost imperceptibly, the transition from despondent inconsistency changes almost overnight to 'Yes now I've got it - what's next?' It is almost as if the 'therapy' fairy calls during the night and sprinkles competency dust over the student. There is no doubt that they have come a long way in a short space of time, but it always surprises us just how quickly the 'now competent' student wants to move on to the 'sexy stuff'.

It seems to us, that just as some of the hard work of learning skills, adjusting attitudes, and operationalising the values and philosophy of therapy could begin to pay off, the student becomes bored and wants to move on. Zealous searches for magic, not dissimilar to stage one, are heralded by the typical question - 'How does Personal Construct Theory, (or Neuro-Linguistic Programming, or Jungian Psychology, or Hypnotherapy, or Transactional Analysis, or whatever the current 'in' approach is) fit in to counselling?' Foundation skills are experienced as mundane.

Such searching may take months or years, and for some it never ends. Some practitioners never pass through this stage, and are always looking for the 'new' way, the way that will be 'easier', 'quicker', 'more interesting', 'deeper', 'better', 'cheaper', 'posher', 'slicker' and so on. This is both useful and healthy to some degree, and learning and developing should be a life long activity for all practitioners. However, it is perhaps not too useful when it becomes a *substitute* for using what skills you do have to be helpful. Sticky moments and blank minds might then occur when the practitioner is more bound up with trying to fit what they are hearing into their theoretical framework, rather than really listening with an open mind. It is likely that all approaches will have some merit, but all require some hard work to master, and all need to be employed gainfully and responsively with clients before consolidation of learning can occur.

Francesca, to illustrate, remained enthusiastic. She read Egan and Rogers, liked them, and integrated them into her counselling approach. She had consciously acquired more active skills, and her unconditional positive regard was an asset to be proud of! The next few years saw her take a flit round the theories. Social work had focused on ideas of functional and dysfunctional families and on systems theory. Subsequent years in counselling had her working a lot with abused women, and focusing on feminist theory. She was a member of a Gestalt group for a year, and was keen to encourage her own clients to speak to empty chairs, and to express their anger in a way which she approved of. Her own personal life and history was under review. She was able to blame much sexual abuse on 'the patriarchy'. She was hitting some intra personal issues which were stimulated through the work, and was attracted to the work through the intrapersonal issues. Blank minds and sticky moments occurred when her preferred theories did not quite do the trick, or when her intra or interpersonal issues were impinging on the work; she didn't get on with a client, she felt angry at a client's story, she liked a client too much, a client didn't like her. Awareness changed again.

Cynical: Yes but is this any use to the starving millions in Africa?

Once the practitioner becomes competent, experienced and insightful, there often follows a phase of disenchantment, or discontent. They are inevitably going to be faced with some problems that may be considered trivial, and some which may seem overwhelming. The 'trivial' problems, although important to the client, may induce a feeling that some of the most powerful techniques are being 'wasted' on such simple issues, or conversely that the techniques available are of little benefit when faced with some immense social problems. A common complaint heard from counsellors who have reached or are going through this phase is 'yes, counselling is OK, but it doesn't really address some of the bigger issues. There are very few homeless, starving people in war zones asking for counselling - they're all too busy trying to find food and survive'.

Although we have some sympathy for this view, it is a little akin to saying the skills of a cardio-vascular surgeon are pathetically inadequate when they are faced with the problem of an undug garden. Abraham Maslow's hierarchy of need can help here. A person's problem will always be contextualised by their current situation, and where that individual is within the hierarchy will determine their priorities. In other words, the baseline of the hierarchy is to take care of the physiological needs of the person. Thus a starving person will not be yet thinking about their safety or belongingness needs until food is found. It is only when a person has secured their physiological and security needs that they may be interested in progressing further up the hierarchy and attempting to meet their social (belongingness) needs. As counselling and psychotherapy are largely concerned with even 'higher' needs such as self esteem, and self fulfilment, it is often the case that counselling will not be in great demand to individuals struggling to meet the baseline needs. Recognition of such differentials may lead us to devalue our work and to see counselling as an indulgence.

For Francesca, it was certainly the case that issues arose for her which were more concerned with challenges to her values than to her skills, and perhaps to the clients. Feminist theories could lead to a sense of despair that unless patriarchal values were challenged, the work was useless. Similarly, counselling suddenly seemed a rather bourgeois individualist activity, which helped to make private troubles of public issues. Blank minds and sticky moments took another turn again, more to do with her own frustration regarding large issues.

Arrogant: I'm so brilliant - do I really need to bother with that empathy stuff?

Perhaps an inevitable, yet undesirable stage of development for most practitioners who choose to continue is the 'proud and ready for a fall' stage. We have worked with many experienced and creative practitioners who say that they are stuck, only to find the reason is that they have forgotten or neglected the basics. The use of good old fashioned empathy has gone; there is no clear contract of what client and counsellor expect and can offer. Instead, there is the preferred fashionable process, technique or theory that is not working. Instead of asking what am I doing wrong, or why aren't I getting anywhere with this client (despite my brilliant supersonic skills) the practitioner often projects onto the client - the client is resistant, or not working hard enough, or doesn't really want to change. Although all of these are possibilities, it is often useful to explore our own potential for arrogance and laziness first. With experience and success it is easy to arrive at a view of yourself as infallible. So keep taking the humble pills - both we and our clients will be better off!

So what of Francesca? She emerged from her heady days of radicalism, having taken a break from counselling, and re-entered the profession from a different perspective again. She realised that her theories were flawed, did not and could not explain everything, and that her own agenda needed to be clearer. When she was frustrated with clients for not understanding her, she realised that it was likely that she was not understanding them. She developed her own framework for helping people, trying to retain a sense of purpose, of realism, of joint enterprise, and of a future orientation. She no longer wanted to be superwoman: she counselled less, and supported herself more. Simple genuineness, and enthusiasm, re-emerged as crucial assets. She became more adept at helping to challenge clients in the sense of helping them to find different and more helpful ways of experiencing their world and taking some control. When blank or sticky moments occur, they are more likely to be a matter of her awareness and how can she increase her flexibility in how she works and what approaches she offers, a sort of ongoing and gentle self-monitoring. Her aspirations as a counsellor are humble. She has now reached what we would regard as the sixth stage of counsellor development.

Outcome based and professional: I'd love to help, and it will take some time, some hard work and unless you really want to change you'd be better off spending your time and money somewhere else!

Somewhere after the arrogant stage, but so close that it may sometimes be mistaken for it, is the end professional stage. This is the consummate professional who knows their limitations, what exactly they can do, what service they are providing, and exactly what the client and counsellor must have attitudinally and behaviourally to make the contract worthwhile for both parties. At this end stage it is still easy to slip back into arrogance or complacency, and thus continued supervision is very helpful, but there are no longer intrusive self doubts, false modesty, or unrealistic expectations of self or potential client outcomes.

This is the stage when the practitioner realises that they can only be at the service of the client if they are realistic, honest and up front with their clients. Competence requires an ability to say -'I can only help in certain ways, I can only help if you will work hard with me, there are no magic pills and very few secret recipes, but I have some skills, techniques and processes which I will share with you, and if we both work very hard your life can change for the better. The amount of change, the specifics of the change, and the success of the change are all controlled by you, I take neither responsibility nor credit for any changes you make in your life, only for the way I practice my profession'.

Summary

In this chapter, then, we have outlined a series of examples of blank minds and sticky moments. These have revolved around intra personal issues for the counsellor, interpersonal issues and the inability to make effective challenge. We have suggested a context of six stages of counsellor development which might generate different types of blanks and stickys; this is a conceptual template, not a rigid stage model. The next four chapters will address the clusters of issues which we have suggested; intrapersonal, interpersonal, ability to challenge, and context of counselling.

Endnotes

1. We will be contending that it is impossible to know precisely how anyone else feels, and that the best that can be hoped for is a negotiated, close approximation, which is enough to enable purposeful counselling. This is after all the function of demonstrating empathy.

2. This example is chosen to be useful, rather than to imply that counsellors typically cannot identify with this. Indeed, it may be just as problematic when they do, and this will be discussed further in Chapter Two.

3. Two comments are noteworthy here. One is that many counsellors, including ourselves, do make careful counselling contracts with friends from time to time. Secondly, we are aware that the term 'friend' represents a whole load of understandings. Some people regard as friends those with whom they share humour and experience of some situations, while others go through a lifetime regarding themselves as having a very small number of friends, those with whom they offer a unique intimacy..

4. See for example Ingram (1991) for a clear exposition on roles.

Chapter Two. The Inside Story - or trapped and alone with the couch . . .

Introduction

The life of a counsellor can be pretty tough and pretty lonely. The tendency to isolation can be seriously underestimated by bright and sparkly-eyed candidates on an introduction to counselling course. After all, counselling is about working with people, learning with people, so that at first sight it might seem like a very interactive job. However, those of you who have spent some time in the profession will recognise various experiences which belie the simplicity of this belief. Counselling is interactive, yet in a very specific way which is different from the usual rules of personal encounters. It does have a certain status, it does initially provoke appreciation from successful clients, and it can result in a certain glow of self esteem when we appreciate ourselves. However, such rewards are neither continuous nor great enough to overcome some of the 'bad days', and the more surprising experiences of isolation which can occur

The nature of counselling entails high levels of confidentiality. This in itself may lead to a sense of aloneness. A counsellor may develop a sense of isolation if they 'box off' their work into 'no go' areas. For example, in 'normal life' and relationships the common question "what did you do at work today dear" gives an opportunity for the worker to share some of their experiences of the day within their close relationships. If this question and similar opportunities are met with "I'm sorry I can't talk to you about that", then there is an increasing possibility that the other in the relationship feels excluded from an important area of their loved one's life. For the counsellor, it can become a burden when their day's work has had effects on them personally, whether to do with graphic accounts of powerful experiences, or to do with some aspect of self-reflection into which we are so relentlessly encouraged. When such effects are screened off within normally intimate relationships, then, *distancing* may occur for one party in the relationship, and *isolation* for the other.

The potential for isolation is exacerbated when the counsellor is also working without agency support, for example, when s/he works as an independent or as a single worker without a team. Any sense of frustration, helplessness, or that 'locked in' feeling can be overpowering and debilitating. This is exemplified by the acknowledgement that one of the necessary benefits of supervision is the great relief felt when one is able to 'tell someone'. The burden of confidentiality can weigh heavy, not always because of the impact of the content of the disclosure one holds inside, but simply because it has to remain inside. The 'trapped and alone' syndrome can be made worse on occasions when you may feel that you are not helping 'enough', that perhaps someone else could be 'helping more', that there seems to be no way forward, or simply that you are 'upset' by what you are hearing.

Moreover, counsellors are asked to do something as part of their *job* which is reasonably unique, i.e. to 'self-develop' towards self-knowledge and authenticity. We might challenge this imperative; can counselling be done by an actor who knows how to operate certain communication styles at any one time? Do we really have to be 'ahead' of our clients? Are we in danger of positioning the counsellor as some sort of idealised self, some role model for the rest of humanity to aspire to?[1] Such arguments aside, however, the reality is that currently, counselling imposes an imperative to counsellors to try to 'work themselves out', or at the very least to monitor themselves for 'what's going on', and how it affects the client. The effect of this can be a very strong self-preoccupation which can be rather absorbing, and which can be extremely demanding, so that the counsellor begins to see the world only in relation to them. How exhausting!

All of these types of feelings have been disclosed to us in supervision and we hope that by simply noting them, we may be helping you to realise that you are not alone. The regular declarations of such feelings amongst counsellors in supervision, and indeed to friends or loved ones, are seldom aired in public. It would appear that there are no books that deal adequately with the internal mental life of the counsellor, or indeed, on how the work may affect the counsellors' interpersonal relationships.[2] The best one can hope for is that through counselling training or supervision, awareness to this phenomenon is raised. Through such media, you may be advised to go to personal counselling when or if the nature of the work distresses you. This is only one strategy however, one which continues to focus on your internal life. Useful at times, but we can't emphasise enough that it's equally useful to go on holiday, cut down hours, talk to a friend, have a dirty weekend away, get engrossed in music, film, books, sailing, dancing - whatever you find relaxing, and whatever has a different focus. Often, the degree of isolation felt can be paradoxically connected to how involved you are in the 'counselling world', and in intense self-exploration.

So, our point is that counsellors sometimes will feel trapped and alone. This may be within the counselling relationship, it may be within the general work context, or it may be to do with effects or demands of the work on self. We would suggest then that counsellors review some of the principles which they adhere to in the light of the following questions:

- Are my contracts of confidentiality with my clients honest and realistic? Part of one of our contracts now is that the counsellor will discuss aspects of their work with their supervisor, with an occasional consultant, but also with a trusted friend/lover, albeit with anonymity.

- Am I as in touch with other people as I want to be? Do I have a network of people who I can turn to simply to have a chat about the nature of the work?

- Do I see the number of clients who I really want to, or are they disproportionate to the rest of my life?

- Have I got a life, or is it all wrapped up in striving to personally develop, in my therapy sessions, in my reflective meditation, in my quest for self-knowledge ? Do I step back and see counselling as only one part of a much wider existence? Is there life without counselling?

In the rest of this chapter, we will try to elucidate some of the more common responses to and effects of the counselling work. In addition to examining the effects that the counsellor's intra-personal issue can have on the process of counselling, we hope to present a realistic picture of what is and isn't humanly possible in counselling. Our experience is that counsellors can set such incredible expectations that they are bound to be struggling. To offer more than a simple description of what happens, we also include some thoughts on coping with the more unpleasant aspects of the work.

Firstly we look at *identification,* and how it may lead to contamination of understanding, to advice giving, and controlling of the clients' material. Secondly the issue of *voyeurism,* or how 'curiosity killed the counselling' occurs. Thirdly, the chapter focuses on *anxiety,* what causes it, maintains it, and how it can be controlled or dissipated. This section also looks at what we call 'the saviour syndrome'[3] and the issues of stress and over work which have become known as 'burnout'.[4] Finally we consider a list of possible *distractions* and categorise these into physiological, emotional / psychological, and physical. Some possible antidotes or strategies worth pursuing are considered. We would emphasise at this point that all of the suggestions we make in regard to intra-personal issues are included to stimulate thought rather than direct you to our particular prescription of what should be done. We do however use statements of principle as a means of differentiating counselling from other activities. Where these occur, they may be seen as a guiding light, or resound as a motto to be remembered or simply an additional thought which stands alone. It is our wish to enable practitioners to address the principles of practice.

Identification: I know just how you feel and I want you to get better . . .

It is important to try to remember who has the problem. Clients' issues can be disabling and distressing if you identify with them, or indeed the source of a vicarious pleasure when they 'do well' . This may seem obvious, but it is surprising how many counsellors disclose issues of identification which they are finding troublesome. It is almost as if they have brought the issue to supervision for permission to refer clients on. The fact is that if clients disclose bereavements, separations, abuse, betrayal, anger and confusion, and you too are in a comparable circumstance or situation, it is not surprising that difficulties can arise. Counsellors are human beings with the same repertoire of emotions and potential for distress as their clients.

Although, for some, counselling training is helpful in order to resist potential 'infections' of emotions, it is unlikely that you have become immune. When it is considered that counselling training is mostly engineered to enable the trainee to become more sensitive to emotion, it could be anticipated that it will not prepare students to avoid contamination from the clients' distressed world, especially when similarities emerge. As a student nurse, I (Graham) remember being extremely distressed when working in an operating theatre. As the 'scrub' nurse I had just received an anaesthetized 22 year old male patient with testicular cancer. The surgeon remarked that the patient was riddled with secondaries in the lungs and would not be seeing another Christmas. The powerful effect of such certainty of death for this young patient who was the same age and gender as me was enough to create an extremely powerful identification. The subsequent emotions were both personally overwhelming and debilitating to my professional practice. Although this state was quite temporary it was sufficient to render me completely ineffective in my role (who wants a sobbing scrub nurse to assist the surgeon).

Principle: Remember who has the problem

Potential effects of Identification

Identification is a common occurrence, and may arise with issues or feelings which are live for the counsellor, or which are rooted in their past. The chances are that the fervour with which identification takes place will affect what the counsellor might want to change it to, and how they might do that. This means that there is a whole range of possibilities open; sometimes simply acknowledging an identification is enough, while sometimes more active strategies are needed, and sometimes it is desirable to terminate the counselling relationship. It may be useful to briefly explain the reasoning for avoiding counselling the client with whom you have identified, or are potentially likely to identify with.

Contamination

Identification may give rise to the inability to separate the emotions of the counsellor from those of the client. For example the quality of listening offered to a bereaved client talking about the death of *their* mother, may be contaminated by the feeling the counsellor had about their mother's death. One counsellor we know made the classic error of 'sympathising' with his client about the death of her mother, stating that "it must be a lonely and empty life for you now". This, of course, was the counsellor's experience of his mother's death, not necessarily the client's. Weeks later the client was able to reveal that the real truth of the matter was that she felt guilty at being so happy that her tyrannical mother was dead. It can be clearly seen from this example that the counsellor not only could not differentiate between his own feelings and that of the client's, but he also projected his feelings onto the client. This had the effect of making it more difficult for the client to disclose her real feelings to him. It could also be argued that he placed an opinion or judgement onto the situation - i.e. You *should feel* lonely and empty after your mother's death.

Interestingly, discussion of contamination is often limited to the identification with the 'negative' emotions or feelings of clients, those which might consciously distress or disturb the counsellor in some way. Equally, the counsellor might become enthusiastic for a particular 'positive' statement or desire of the client, because it's one that they have or have once had. One common theme which has occurred in our experience is that of planned separation from a relationship which seems unsatisfactory or disabling. Many female counsellors we know are aware enough to declare that they have been secretly cheering for female clients getting out of such a relationship, particularly when they have once done that themselves, or, even more insidious perhaps, would love to but haven't quite managed it! This sort of subtle identification is more likely to be communicated through implicit 'well dones', under the guise of validation and empowerment.

Principle: a problem contaminated is a problem complicated

Finally, contamination through identification is not a one way process. A counsellor who is listening to distressful stories which echo for them will be exacerbating their own pain. This is not conducive to good health and good spirit, and when it occurs, then there is a message to be listened to. If counselling is complicating the counsellor's life, then perhaps it is time for a review.

Advice Giving

Identifying with the client's situation or experience may in some cases lead to an irresistible impulse to give guidance and advise. The fact that you have experienced the same or similar event or situation may lead you to into believing that you know what is the best course of action for the client. Although these suggestions are invariably made with the best intentions, the result is commonly that some client self determination is lost.   The client's freedom and self reliance has been interfered with by the sharing of the counsellor's ideas, and the identification of the client's resources and strategies has been neglected.

Whenever advice or guidance is resorted to the client is short changed in terms of empowerment and independence. When counsellors give advice they increase the potential for dependency and decrease the potential learning from any client experiment. A really good antidote to falling into this practice of advice giving is to remember that there are usually only two possible reactions from the client:

I. The advice is useful, thus the client is grateful and more dependent.

II. The advice is unhelpful, so the client blames and resents the counsellor.

In either case the client has been robbed of the opportunity to develop insight into his/her own resources and problem solving, and the counsellor must assume much greater responsibility for the client's outcomes.

This rather tight way of construing advice is currently the common wisdom of counselling. However, recently this approach, which makes counselling a bedrock of non-directiveness, preservation of self determination and strict avoidance of advice has been questioned by some.[5] Some pragmatic counsellors see that it is possible to 'blur' the role of counsellor and include a little therapy, guidance, direction, befriending and advice. It is our view that these are all proper though different ways of helping, and are appropriate in different contexts.

However, we would argue that if counselling has been *purposefully* chosen as a particular approach, then this implies some justification or reason. Why did the client want counselling? Why did the counsellor agree that this was appropriate and desirable? To change to some other approach must equally have some rationale. It would seem to us that if you are to change tack, then ethically, you would be required to share these reasons with your client and seek their agreement. In other words we would assert that if there is some reason for 'doing counselling' rather than 'eclectic helping' then the differentiations have to be made clear to the client.

Principle: Trust your client to find their own advice

Controlling the content and emotions of the client

Strong feelings of identification may also lead to the suppression of the client's emotions. It may be that the unconscious avoidance of the strong unpleasant feelings that the counsellor has identified with, may result in the counsellor being unable to 'hear' certain parts of the client's story and certain emotions within it. It is easily possible, for example, for counsellors who have a personal history of being sexually abused to 'unconsciously' miss parts of a client's story subtly alluding to a similar past history. Strong emotions of guilt or sadness in a client's story of their bereavement may not be overtly reflected if they resemble the counsellor's own emotions which are currently being repressed. These are fairly common examples, often debriefed in supervision, of the counsellor's sudden awareness of themselves suppressing client material, indicating that they had little realisation of this type of contamination during the actual counselling.

Conversely it is possible that identification may lead to the emphasis of certain emotions and content that has more relevance or impact on the counsellor than the client. For example, if the counsellor has experienced a similar situation to their client, it is possible that whatever the counsellor experienced as the most insightful aspect of the experience is what may be emphasized or quickly returned to in the clients' story. To elucidate further, one supervisee told one of us that his greatest distress in the death of his mother was his guilt at "never telling her that he loved her". In subsequent interactions with clients disclosing difficulty in their relationships with their parents, he would insist upon returning to points in the story that would allow him to probe into the precise nature of disclosed emotions between them. This type of control over the content of the story is unacceptable in regard to respecting self determination.

Principle: Control the process, never the content.
This is not to deny the possibility of purposeful self-disclosure as a tentative challenging skill. Testing out a hunch as to what the client feels, what seems to be important, is perfectly legitimate if offered genuinely. However, it needs to be distinguished from any 'knowing best' what emotions and stages of the story should be elicited (cf. Chapters Three and Four). Otherwise, once counsellors begin to employ different helping strategies which have a greater potential for dependency, exert greater influence and limit self determination, they have moved toward the therapy end of the helping continuum. When this occurs the therapist must assume greater responsibility for the clients' outcomes. Counsellors who take this approach either consciously or unconsciously have changed from counselling to therapy or teaching. Both of these are appropriate helping strategies, but have different names because they are different activities and have different outcomes.

Most of us of course will identify to a certain extent with what is written here, and this is no cause for discouragement We need to be realistic about counselling, and acknowledge that while it is possible to keep *largely* within the purpose and principles of non-directiveness, with honesty and critical judgement, it may well be argued that there is strong evidence to suggest that there is no possibility of total non-directiveness, and that even the most non directive person centred counselling is strongly influenced by the values and attitudes of the counsellor.[6]

It would seem that the best we can do is to see counselling as one very important and helpful approach for some clients. It then becomes clearer that counselling is not the panacea for all ills, and that other approaches are acceptable. Our point here is that to know what counselling is and isn't may help you be more conscious of what you are doing. When this is the case then you are in a better position to determine what may be more helpful for your client. Thus we are suggesting no magical antidote at this point, other than for you to remain conscious of what it is you are doing. As a rule of thumb remember that whenever your own point of view, experience or preference is indicated to the client consciously or unconsciously, then in counselling terms *undue influence has been exerted.* At this point you are guilty of nothing more than moving along the helping continuum further towards therapy, which represents no problem other than the need to raise your awareness to you having now a greater responsibility for the clients' outcomes.

In summary, it can be seen that it is important, in order to remain professional, that identification detrimentally affecting counselling, clearly indicates the necessity for immediate attention. The subsequent action will be determined by the intensity and the lasting nature of the identification. Obviously to be temporarily overwhelmed by emotion is one thing, while to be incapacitated for the whole and subsequent sessions is quite another. Various possibilities then exist:

- Note the identification experienced and move on.
- Discuss how strongly you are identifying in supervision, and make sense of it for you.
- Suspend the counselling if you continue to struggle, and seek whatever help or support you need to minimise your tendency to identify.
- Make a re-referral It serves little purpose for counsellors to become embarrassed or feel it necessary to seek permission to refer the client to someone else. It is not a matter of letting the client down by referring on, but a requirement to enable the client to receive the appropriate help. The bottom line is that the counsellor should not be working with a client if identification is creating contamination of roles, decreasing effectiveness or reducing the counsellor's ability to be optimally helpful.

In order to remain ethical, counsellors are required to identify their own personal problems and issues and carefully consider what action to take if they have clients that are presenting with similar problems. This, of course, may not always be as easy as it sounds, for sometimes clients can present with one initial problem which later turns out to be quite different. Moreover, counsellors' issues may be unconscious until stimulated to awareness. Therefore knowing the full potential for identification may be extremely difficult! Consequently it is necessary to be alert and sensitive to one's vulnerability in this regard and take the appropriate action when necessary. This reinforces our view that *effective*[7] client centred supervision is essential for healthy counselling practice. It is this issue and similar issues that are often picked up in supervision, as supervision offers opportunities for counsellors to listen carefully to themselves in regard to what they think, feel, and do in their practice. Without these opportunities to 'get off the treadmill and reflect', ineffective and potentially unethical practice may thrive.

Pass me those binoculars, they go with my mac . . .

So have you ever found yourself just really interested, intrigued, captivated by the story of the client in front of you? Such interest just might trigger the capacity for voyeurism, or perhaps curiosity, which we all have. The tendency for individuals to be curious about their clients is quite *normal.* An interest in people is, after all, a facet of the attraction to counselling.

Unfortunately, however, clients are not really there to fulfil our curiosity, and indeed "Curiosity killed the counselling" is an observation which both of us have made over many years. Counsellors, then, need to keep a spirit of inquiry into what the client is doing and how they want to change, while resisting their natural curiosity regarding the 'content' of the story. Unfortu-

Blimey, look at the story in that!

nately, especially to the unskilled eye, a healthy interest in the client and an interrogation may look similar. Have you ever witnessed a session where the questions flow – how often did you do that, what was the position, when did you say your grandma entered the room, where did you say you bought the book?

One of the difficulties in discerning the difference between healthy interest and crippling curiosity is that clients will co-operate equally with both processes. Often the client is delighted to supply endless amounts of information requested by the counsellor. How many children do they have, their precise relationship that exists between themselves and their great aunt Cecily, or the rough approximation of their monthly sexual activities, will be easily forthcoming from the client. Why? Simple - the client believes that supplying this information will be helpful to the counsellor. The client believes that with this knowledge the counsellor will be able to tell them what to do! Thus this type of interrogation paves the way for advice giving. We would suggest that the partial or entire reason for your curiosity and your questions is to aid your analysis of the client's problem and work out your solution to it. The client is of course quite accustomed to this; it is after all what all other professionals, neighbours and friends have done for years. The client understands that this is the precursor to the advice that they expect, and it is their hope that this time your advice will be better than the others!

The reader may suppose that this is unduly cynical, but having spent many hours listening to many tapes of real counselling interviews, we can assert unequivocally that many counsellors, both experienced and inexperienced, fall into the trap of subtle direction and disguised advice giving. Often it is quite difficult to observe, only showing itself as an occasional digressive 'curiosity question' sprinkled amongst the orthodox high level counselling skills, and thus by its very nature it is difficult to detect by the practitioner without careful scrutiny of a taped session. The skilled counsellor has been trained to ask well phrased and subtle questions, therefore any hidden agenda or any solutions generated may be delivered gently and gradually, directing the client towards your solution – sometimes without either party noticing! The proffering of questions as a substitute for empathy is often the first sign of the counsellor beginning to control the content of the session. Although purposeful open questions can legitimately control the **process of** counselling, questions that direct the **content** of the session are unacceptable if the principle of self determination is be respected.

Thus curiosity kills the counselling!

So how do we counter this potential? The antidotes are simple, but require considerable self discipline:

- Beware of asking two questions concurrently, unless for clarification. This would mean you are interrogating. It would mean that you have neglected to reflect back the content of the answer to your first question, or the second question had to be asked because your first one was so poorly constructed.

- Consider asking no questions at all! Or at least for periods of time, perhaps up to 15 minutes. This will help you to concentrate on thorough listening to the client's agenda and to switch off yours. This invariably strengthens your empathic skills. We often employ this tactic in counselling training programmes to demonstrate how questions can destroy effective, non directive listening. It is amazing how quickly even the best of counsellors become dependent on questions to 'bale them out of trouble' in **sticky moments or when their mind has gone blank.**

- Think about taping your sessions and spending some time counting the amount of questions you asked.

- You could decide to examine each question asked and test it for motive. Why did I ask that? Be honest, why did you ask how many children she has? Does it help you to have the full picture so you can diagnose and prescribe some action from your expertise? Or is it really your honest attempt to challenge the client to bring to consciousness something she is not aware of? Questions asked should help the client to determine for themselves areas of thought which may be helpful in developing insight. One can't help but wonder what sort of clients would forget how many children they have!

- It may be helpful to check that your questions are open and do not carry a hidden agenda. For example, the question 'What would you like your future to be like?' has only the agenda of directing the process not the content. But consider whose agenda is addressed by a question like 'have you talked to your children about this?'

Voyeurism sometimes takes another form. The content of the client's story may be of a nature that intrigues the counsellor. In this event the counsellor can be hooked into the perspective of "I must know what comes next". The counsellor in this circumstance is waiting with baited breath for the next instalment. Some clients become quite expert at story telling to the extent that they capture the interest of the counsellor almost permanently. This ensures that the next appointment is likely to be sooner rather than later, and that the motivation to move on past the problem to constructive change is largely negated.

Occasionally counsellors are brave enough to admit that the material that the client is disclosing is arousing. It is important that the reader understands that to be aroused by the nature of the client's material is not uncommon. It is sometimes difficult to accept that counsellors are human, and the nature of being human is that they will react to stimuli from time to time according to their nature. Of course, the congruent reactions such as rage when told of exploitation of vulnerable people is much more easy to accept than the counsellor becoming sexually aroused when listening to the disclosure of some sexual encounter. Even worse to contemplate is the incongruous arousal that might occur when the client describes, for example, a rape, or some other sadistic act. Because such reactions are not usually considered consistent with a sensitive, caring human being, then they must clearly be inconsistent with an appropriate counsellor's reaction. The temptation is therefore to conclude that if we are aroused by such descriptions then we must be abnormal, perverted and definitely not fit to be a counsellor. This of course is a classic example of the counsellor being able to be non judgemental to others but experiencing great difficulty addressing the concept to themselves.

Principle: Apply a non-judgemental approach - that means, to you too!

Once having discovered that you the counsellor are human and therefore vulnerable to experiencing arousal, the next step may be to try to suppress the arousal or deny that it occurred. This seems rather a shame to us; we would suggest that the important aspect of this discussion in regard to the loneliness of the counsellor, is that secret hidden aspects of the self which can affect effectiveness need to be debriefed. The moral rights and wrongs of becoming aroused are to some extent irrelevant, the fact that the counsellor is distracted from the purpose of counselling is the central point. Whether the distraction occurs because of a judgement that to have such thoughts is monstrous, or by the arousal itself, is incidental. Much more important than the moral implications are the ways forward to effective practice. Preventing distraction, marshalling self discipline and summoning determination to concentrate and get on with the task of effective counselling is a much more valuable goal than self deprecation.

On this theme, a particularly disappointing anecdote was recounted to us a few years ago. A social worker who had summoned the courage to disclose to his supervisor the feelings of arousal that he felt when interviewing a female client in a sexual abuse inquiry, was immediately suspended and subsequently dismissed. This response to a courageous professional who was prepared to recount real emotions which he had identified as potentially problematic, should not in our opinion be punished but given constructive help. It is interesting to note that some people have great difficulty in differentiating between what is *fantasy* and what is a conscious *intent* to act out. It would seem to us that it is far safer to have counsellors relating their real and potentially problematic arousal states to their supervisors than suppress their emotions and be distracted by their secret fantasies.

The antidote to the voyeuristic nature of human kind is of course not easy to suggest. The nature of our species, and particularly those of us who are drawn towards the 'caring professions' is such that we are interested in other human beings. Thus we suggest that you consider the following possibilities:

- Learn to listen to yourself; become more aware of your emotions during sessions and ask the question - is this an appropriate reaction? This question deserves to be asked at a human level not just as 'a trained counsellor'.

- Determine what is a realistic level of interest for you to have in your client and at what level it ceases to be non directive.

- Assess the level of distraction that occurs due to your intrigue or arousal, and ask whether it detracts from the service that you profess to offer the client?

- If you believe there is any possibility of acting upon your arousal, then seriously consider the most appropriate way to discontinue working with the client.

- Review emotional arousal with yourself and with your supervisor.

Anxiety

Whether you are a novice or an experienced counsellor, we would hazard a guess that you will have suffered low level anxiety or something approaching a panic attack from time to time in regard to certain clients. As novice counsellors we both suffered the 'normal' anxiety of the first real client, and even now we occasionally get a flutter of butterflies with certain clients or referrals of new ones. No matter how long you have been counselling there will be times in your life when your confidence deserts you and when those creeping 'self doubts' allow the demon anxiety to get you. The most extreme of these anxieties are often associated with or precluded by those thoughts in one's head saying "do I know what to do?" "What if?" "I know I'll get it all wrong" "I can't concentrate, I'll forget what they've said, I'm sure I'll blow it". Or there may be anxiety connected to the status of the client - can I really counsel this eminent managing director, this important playwright, this famous musician?

For the novice counsellor those messages in your head may suggest that "you're not ready, you're a fraud, you'll make it worse for the client, or you'll make the client commit suicide".

'Oh my god, I think I've got a real live client'

This type of anxiety is often associated with the feeling that you are trapped and alone. Your supervisor or trainer can't be with you, you have to do it on your own, and because you have a contract with the client and you care about them, you can't let them down. The overwhelming feeling of wanting to be beamed up, go back to bed and pull the covers over you, or feign illness are all tempting alternatives to 'going through with it'. We hope that by graphically describing the process that many of us have gone through or continually go through, you won't feel quite so alone again.

A particular type of anxiety syndrome is created by what we call the 'saviour syndrome'. This is the immediate sense of impending doom that rapidly approaches when you feel that a client is not being helped enough. It sometimes occurs when a client asks for an urgent appointment and you think you should say no even as you say yes! The 'no' may have very good reasons attached to it, like the client is becoming dependent, or you are so over worked that your concentration is lapsing; nonetheless the temptation to say yes is too strong to resist. When this occurs you are in grave danger of acquiring the 'saviour syndrome' and its accompanying stress. This is a particularly nasty syndrome as it has its roots in both the noblest and basest of motives. The noblest of motives are those which arise from the earnest wish to be helpful to another human being, with no selfish purpose or hope for reward; the basest arise from the arrogance and self serving nature within most of us - the part that wants to be recognised and exalted as indispensable. In either case, the impact of the saviour syndrome is somewhat deleterious for both parties. The syndrome invariably results in the client receiving so much support that they become dependent. This can create a climate where the principle of self-determination and independence is no longer fostered, and is occasionally destroyed - hence counselling has ceased. In this case the counsellor loses humility, cannot see alternatives to being always available, and experiences stress syndromes, damage to personal relationships and the awesome burden of responsibility for other peoples' lives.

Instant attention to the client can also result in a form of manipulation by the client which is negative to both parties. We are sometimes amazed at how available counsellors make themselves, and the excesses of manipulative behaviour which they will put up with (cf Chapter Six). Not so amazed however that we cannot remember our own sorry learning points; for one of us, it was only on the *third* occasion that a client put a suicide note through the door of our own home on a Saturday afternoon that we finally realised that being a Rapid Response Agent was not conducive to client or counsellor! At this stage, anxiety about how much our dependability was *not* helping overrode the initial anxiety of 'What if she kills herself?'

Antidotes and strategies to anxiety and their associated problems are many. However, a few we think worth considering are as follows:

- The absolute antidote to anxiety is relaxation. It is impossible to remain anxious and relaxed. This may be obvious but it is surprising how many ways there are which enable you to be more relaxed. Try to remember what they are and employ the suitable strategies when appropriate.

- Debrief is also essential. It may be necessary to contract with one other person who you trust that you can contact them at any time to simply blurt out your most secret and horrible fears. Ventilating these often attenuates them, in other words when spoken out loud you can hear how silly they really are. Your debrief partner may not even need to respond other than by listening.

- Regular supervision with a person who is enabling, who can assist you to focus on your professional goals and challenge any unrealistic demands you or your client places upon you, is invaluable.

- In regard to the 'saviour syndrome', we recommend that you take a daily dose of humble pills. This entails saying regularly to yourself - I'm not the only one that can help. Its particularly helpful if you can learn to believe it!

- Try to remember that 'nobody does it right', because in truth there is no absolute right way of helping. As there is always a minimum of thirteen possible choices of response, you won't always choose the most beneficial one. What is more, it's almost impossible to evaluate which of the thirteen would have been best anyway![8] For once any of the responses has been selected then none of the other possibilities could be evaluated to see if they would have been better, as that particular opportunity has gone.

- Finally, try to remember and genuinely subscribe to the perception that you are only responsible for your part of the counselling contract with your client, not for the rest of their lives. Counselling is only a small part of the client's life; by all means maximise its impact, but don't be deluded into overestimating your importance.

Distractions

Finally, a note on distractions. Everyone gets distracted. We know of no one who can routinely give one hundred per cent attention to the client for an entire session. Some common distractions are categorised into three main divisions and are listed below:

Physiological	Psychological/ Emotional	Physical
Tummy Rumbling		Too hot
Nauseous	Anxious	Too cold
Headache	Depressed	Tired
Indigestion	Sad	Uncomfortable
Hung over	Excited	Noise
Ill - flu colds	Affected by client's story	Quiet - fear of being overheard
Hard of hearing	Curiosity	
Visually impaired	Concerned about someone	Incidents/activity
Memory difficulties		outside
Need to urinate/defecate		

There would appear to be little chance that a mere human being would be able to avoid all of these possible distractions all of the time. To go further we would say that not only is complete concentration impractical but perhaps even undesirable. Most of the clients that we have counselled have had a need to see that we, the helpers, are real and human. To be completely focused on the client without ceasing, totally concentrated and unrelenting in your attention, may be at the very least off putting and possibly intimidating to some clients. So it could be argued that to apologise for momentary lapses of concentration, to admit to the occasional distractions may add value to the process and relationship formation. This is part of the negotiation which exists in the counselling interaction.

Again, although this sounds obvious, it is surprising how, especially within the early phases of counselling, practitioners can be really reluctant to manage distractions, for fear of being thought disrespectful. To excuse oneself to the bathroom, to turn a fire on or off, takes on an unrealistic magnitude. We remind you yet again that we're all just human beings at the end of the day, with needs to be fulfilled. Some of these are really very basic, and if we are comfortable, then our clients are likely to be comfortable too. So take time to eat, to relax between sessions, to service your body in whatever way it needs, to negotiate temperature, acknowledge the pneumatic drill which has started up outside, or the window cleaner who is smiling cheerily at you as you determinedly try to empathise!

Summary

The thrust of this chapter has been very much to underline that doing counselling may affect you intrapersonally. This may be because of the way the job works and the ethics attached to it, because of the content of the client's work and its effect upon the counsellor with their own personality and history, and because of the demands, right or wrong, toward self-exploration and awareness. The overall message is to look after yourself and to make careful decisions as to what work you want to be doing, and what work you are capable of doing appropriately. We believe that such a maxim is in the interests of both counsellor and client.

Endnotes:

1. Alex Howard (1996) disputes the impossible ideals foisted upon counsellors in his book Challenges to Counselling and Psychotherapy, while Alasdair MacIntyre draws attention to the role of Therapist as a kind of 'ideal type' in Western Society, along with the Ascetic and the Manager, in his work After Virtue. Gerard Egan (1994) regularly supplies a list of the qualities of the ideal helper in each new edition of The Skilled Helper, which we would guess is over and above the attributes of most of us more modest earthlings.

2. Dexter (1997) reports that one effect of training in counselling is considerable unfavourable reconstruing of family and friends. Dexter, L. G. "A critical review of the effect of counselling training on trainees" Unpublished Ph.D. thesis, University of Durham, 1997.

3. For a more detailed debate on this syndrome see Berry, (1991)

4. Burnout is considered in greater detail by some authors in regard to the personality types drawn to the helping profession. It is not our intention to explore these issue here, but interested readers may find the following texts useful: Maslach, C. (1982) Grosch, W. N. & Olsen, D. C. (1994)

5. Michael Carroll (1996), who has written much on the use of counselling in the workplace, focuses on the effectiveness of counselling, and the pragmatics of approaches without great concern for the preciousness of some of the underpinning philosophy or principles.

6. Strong (1968) suggests that the social influence process operates in all human interactions and there are no exceptions. B. F. Skinner in his analysis of Rogers' practice identified many behavioural reinforcing expressions, gestures, and verbal statements which could be seen as directive.

7. The word *effective* is used advisedly here. In practice, we believe that people's supervision needs are greatly varied, and that legislating for some norm of supervision is somewhat questionable. However, it is a useful guideline to have the capacity for supervision, by self or others, and to learn to use it when and if necessary.

8. These are the traditional or classic skills usually associated with counselling skills. (An empathic response; a clarification response; a simple paraphrase; a simple reflection; a summary; some self disclosure; an immediacy response; an information giving response; advanced accurate empathy; a challenge to a discrepancy, smokescreen or game; a paradoxical challenge; a summary as a challenge; or a question.) In addition to these there are all the non verbal skills and all the specific skills which accompany the various particular counselling approaches. All in all if these are all taken as potential variables which could be used in combinations with each other, then the potential responses available to the counsellor could be seen as almost limitless.

Chapter Three. Me and You, You and Me: Interpersonal Issues

Introduction

While the last chapter was concerned with the inner life of the counsellor, the concern of this chapter is to explore some of the issues and thinking around interpersonal relationships in counselling. We know that it is difficult to define or code exactly what goes on between people, or what exactly constitutes an 'interpersonal relationship'. Within counselling, it seems that there is a real pull between two distinct philosophies regarding the counsellor/client relationship. One suggests that interpersonal exploration should have no boundaries, as the very exploration is therapeutic; the other suggests that the interpersonal aspect to counselling be monitored, boundaried and directed to purposeful ends.

It is our view that the interpersonal side of counselling demands an awareness and a direction to a purposeful end. As far as is humanly possible, it is the responsibility of the counsellor to use their knowledge and awareness to minimise the chances of psychological harm from the interpersonal relationship, and to maximise the benefits. This is achieved through a constant process of negotiation of meaning and intent. And even as we write this, we feel the lid being taken off a particular can of worms which provokes uncertainties and dissents.

The nature of the therapeutic relationship has then attracted much discussion.[1] This chapter will explore some of the areas of interpersonal relationship which are fundamental to counselling from a slightly wider perspective. Our interest is to try to locate the nature of the interpersonal relationship into a discursive frame; in other words, we are interested in how they are built up and perpetuated through beliefs and practices. We will then try to elicit some principles which help the practitioner to ensure, as far as possible, ethical and effective practice. In particular, we will address issues of intimacy, self-disclosure, sexuality, friendship and culture.

Keeping Our Distance:
Boundaried Intimacy

Before exploring specific issues pertaining to influential factors on the counselling relationship, it is worth spending just a little time noting some of the assumptions regarding counselling as a relationship of intimacy. As stated above, there is a curious paradox which seems to operate in relation to intimacy within counselling. On the one hand, intimacy is seen as desirable within the counselling relationship, while on the other, it is made clear that there are certain rules to be obeyed regarding its nature. The whole area, then, is very uncertain.

In a recent piece of research carried out by one of us (Janice), several key points emerged which are salient to issues of interpersonal relationships within counselling;

- Intimacy is commonly assumed by counsellors to be a desirable part of the counselling relationship. and as offering fulfilment of the highest value.[2]

- There is no consensual concept of intimacy within counselling discourse.

- No specific reason can be given as to why intimacy is desirable, other than reasons of faith that it is a 'good thing'.

- Many counsellors believe that the counselling relationship may be the first time that the client is experiencing intimacy, and therefore take upon themselves an obligation to 'model' an intimate relationship.

- Within counselling culture generally, intimacy is generally viewed as a positive concept in terms of making for successful counselling.[3]

We believe, however, that the insistence on intimacy, and the value attributed to its achievement within relationships, is questionable. In practice, there is no evidence that intimacy enhances the chances of a 'good' relationship. Within marital therapy, for example, it has even been suggested that marital therapists might be better to dispute the notion of intimacy as being crucial to the good relationship. A recent article in a popular women's magazine suggests that sex within intimate couple relationships is adversely affected by the high degree of intimacy because the partners become so close that they feel almost familial; one study suggests that sixty per cent of American marriages are affected by a lack of lust associated with over-familiarity, and an inability to see part-

'Don't be getting intimate Mavis, I want this marriage to last.'

ners as other and different from self.[4]

Intimacy can of course lead to experiences which are evaluated as destructive, or intrusive. Interestingly, the research cited above showed that where clients described 'negative' intimate relationships, the counsellors concluded that this was not then 'proper' intimacy. Their implicit definitions then revolved around the notion of intimacy as both beneficial and constructive . This kind of well-intentioned arrogance denies thousands of years of philosophical inquiry and human experience, to fit in with a modernist notion of the self wherein 'open' equals 'healthy'. Our own brand of well-intentioned arrogance causes us to caution strongly against such naïveté!

Further, there is no evidence that the counselling relationship *must* be intimate in order to succeed. It is our view that this is the kind of over-generalisation which inhibits a useful definition of counselling being made. Counselling can be differentiated from other relationships by its *purpose* and its *principles*. Currently, argument is sometimes made regarding the 'unique, interpersonal nature' of each counselling relationship as evidence that we cannot define what we do. We would say that this is not the case. Psychiatrists, teachers, social workers, all need an effective working relationship to succeed, yet this does not lead to grand claims regarding the preciousness or the precise nature of that relationship. A major principle underlying the relationship aspect of counselling is that:

Principle: The nature of the relationship in counselling must be instrumental to the purpose; it is not itself the purpose

To forget this fundamental principle is to do something other than counselling, and may have repercussions for the client or the counsellor which are unexpected and unhelpful. The counsellor might become obsessed with the client's life, rather than concerned to offer the best possible service in the time available. The client might feel exposed, or have expectations of a specialness between them and the counsellor which are unrealistic. We do well then to be somewhat challenging to the claims made for intimacy per se. The counselling profession owes it to clients and to the profession alike to examine its fundamental philosophies somewhat more carefully before building on shallow foundations. So while we cannot then 'prescribe' the level of intimacy necessary to effective counselling, we can make some useful observations.

Production of intimacy

A central observation regarding intimacy is that the counselling relationship is one which is actively and deliberately produced . In other words, it is not accidental. We do not begin work with clients and leave it to chance as to whether we 'get on with them' or not. We endeavour to offer some qualities and mechanisms of relating which will be useful. Where these are not useful, or even dangerous, or where the purpose of 'relating' is not therapeutic, the client will not be best served. This observation is highlighted by some accounts of intimacy within the counselling relationship which represent experiences which were conceptualised as inappropriately intimate.[5] There are then three key points to be made pertaining to the deliberate nature of the counselling relationship.

- When intimacy occurs within counselling, it has a *situational* aspect to it. Thus the intimacy which might be found within the counselling room, or session, may not be replicated outside the contracted time/space. Within this, there is a notion of intimacy which is appropriate to the situation.

- The notion of appropriateness, or 'propriety', is engaging. It seems that practitioners must establish with their clients a sort of optimum condition, whereby anything can be said or done, providing it is 'appropriate' to the situation. In this sense, counselling may be seen as being a defined *role*. The view that counselling may be seen as a form of 'role' relationship is compatible with notions of authenticity: I can be 'real' with you, and acknowledge that you are originally attracted to me because of my role as counsellor, my perceived expertise and authority.

- Where intimacy in counselling occurs, it has a rather different emphasis from relationships of attraction. In other words, there need be no mutual attraction between counsellor and client. The client is attracted to the role, the promise of help, rather than the person, and the counsellor need feel no attraction to the client in any way in order to pursue activities which are

'You mean some people do it with clothes ON!'

geared toward generating intimacy. This renders it available to analysis not in the tradition of relationship as chemistry, as in courtship or marriage, but in the paradigm of the production of intimacy as an active social process.

The conditions for intimacy to occur, then, are deliberately produced or engineered through the qualities and skills which the counsellor offers. This leads us to our second principle regarding interpersonal relationships in counselling, namely:

Principle: Interpersonal intimacy within counselling is functional only to the extent that it helps the client with self-knowledge

However, this is not always a popular perspective, and many counsellors believe that the intimacy within the counselling relationship is a two way process - both must be intimate for useful change to occur. To this end, counselling is conceived of as using enough elements of self to constitute a mutually intimate experience. We would like to dispute this in the next section.

The Myth of Mutual Self-Disclosure
I really feel this with you

What implications, then, do our arguments have for practice? One common debate within counselling has been around the wisdom and acceptability of the counsellor demonstrating their emotion. Such demonstration may be seen as a form of self-disclosure which is powerful in effect, and the key question must be, as ever, what effect will it have on the client?

The answer, of course, is that we do not necessarily know. Several years ago, one of us counselled a woman who had been raped. She disclosed that one of the responses which she had found most difficult to handle had come from a previous counsellor who had demonstrated her own distress at the client's story. 'I felt', this client said, 'like this was much worse

'You think your sore head is bad, I'm raging'

48

than any other client's experience, and that my telling her was too upsetting for her to handle'. This was not conducive to further disclosure or to the formation of a useful therapeutic alliance. More recently, a supervisee recounted her experience of a client who had undergone severe physical and emotional trauma which they were now disclosing for the first time in many years. The counsellor quite deliberately allowed their own tears as a device to facilitate the client, and indeed this was effective in catharting the client to usefully express pent up emotion. The counsellor involved was well able to shelve their own emotion in the interests of the client's work, and a helpful outcome was reached.

The difference between the two events is not about whether self-disclosure of emotion is wrong or right. Rather, we are back again to the issue of intent, and the context of skill and experience. In the first of these two examples, the counsellor became caught up in her own responses within an interpersonal situation, and neglected to observe the effect of her revelation on her client. For her, self-disclosure of itself had value. In the second instance, although the emotion of the counsellor was genuine, the decision to reveal it was considered, and the focus of the counsellor was ultimately with the client. The counsellor was ready to 'catch' empathically the client's response, and would not have continued her self-revelation if it did not seem helpful. This is an important principle within interpersonal dynamics within counselling:

Principle: The client's well-being must be the central focus of the counsellor

This is quite different from having free licence to reveal aspects of the counsellor's feeling because it seems an intimate thing to do.

You see as much of me as I do of you

When intimacy is spuriously valued per se, it is possible to make some universal and some misleading claims about the nature of self-disclosure. Some counsellors claim that to be 'present with self', or to be 'genuine', or to share the detail of their domestic surroundings, or their personal taste through choice of furniture or clothes, constitutes a mutuality to self-disclosure in the therapeutic relationship.[6] We would advocate some caution to this view. It is not that there is anything wrong with wanting to offer an openness, a window into our own beings, or a glimpse of our preferences and histories. It is just that we can, if not careful, construct a false view of mutuality which can miss the integrity of the one way self-disclosure which occurs in counselling.

'So you've told me all about your childhood, and the sexual abuse, and you've seen my nice new curtains so we're even'

'That seems fair'

Two distinct areas of self-disclosure may be identified. One is the content of what is disclosed: do counsellors actually reveal of themselves and their emotions as the client does? This would depend on the definition of self-disclosure as being the traditionally accepted version, i.e. a communication process in which one person verbally provides personal information about his or her thoughts, needs, or feelings to another person.[7]

However, this view, dependant on research which has 'rated' the content of statements, may be seen as narrow. Talk may be the medium which most obviously defines relationships, yet we know that a high percentage of communication revolves around the non-verbal and the paralinguistical which construct more subtle and indirect signs of disclosure, intimacy or distance.[8] A second perspective to self-disclosure then is that which delineates it as the revelation of self through manner and surroundings.

It is possible however to distinguish differences between the counsellor and the client's levels of self-disclosure. A counsellor who works from home will know that whatever picture s/he puts on the wall is open to public gaze, that his/her choice of clothes and hairstyle will present some aspect of self to others for their evaluation. Their manner will reflect their motivation, their personality, and their training in communication and social skills, all of which will be deliberately presented in a learned sequence. The counsellor will be disclosing in a way which is both appropriate and purposeful to their role, and will not be seeking a particular response in terms of their own self-esteem. This is quite unlike the rules of other developing relationships where reciprocity is part of the normal sequence of events.[9] Self may be disclosed, but certainly initially, this is a controlled disclosure which does not entail high degrees of emotion, risk or trust, which have been identified as constituents of intimacy. Any client may come and see the pictures on the walls, all will be offered warmth and genuineness as these are part of the ethos, principles and skills of counselling, requiring no negotiation dependent on patterns of response usually required for developing relationships. The uniqueness necessary to an intimate disclosure is missing from the counsellor's perspective, whilst for the client, this may be a very unique experience indeed. It is common for clients to disclose events or aspects of self which they have never previously voiced: it is crucial that this is respected for the activity which it is, and that we do not pretend a mutuality which does not exist. The risk involved in the *unique* revelation, the trust, is not to be underestimated or camouflaged. From the counselling seat, the risks are of a quite different nature.

This is not to say that self-presentation cannot change to become more intimate self-disclosure. There might also be some facets of the therapeutic relationship which might not be challenging to the self of the counsellor. This is certainly suggested within some schools of therapy.[10] However, there are two apparently obvious principles attached to the use of counsellor self-disclosure:

Principle: Counsellor self-disclosure demands no therapeutic response from the client; therefore it entails a certain degree of 'having dealt with'.

Principle: Counsellor self-disclosure is offered tentatively, and specifically to aid therapeutic movement.

If these principles are adhered to, then it can be seen that counsellor and client self-disclosure cannot be equated; they are of different natures and they demand different levels of intentionality and response.

Sexuality: a powerful part of the human condition

What about the interpersonal issues pertaining to sexuality within counselling? There are many ways in which the development of psychology and sexuality are intrinsically linked in terms of theoretical development, from Freudian theories to the advent of sex therapy. The construction of sexuality is complex, and deserves brief mention before proceeding.

Our position here, is that sexuality is itself a social construct which is a part of how we construct our identity.[11] It is clearly too simplistic to reduce sexuality to the physiological or essentialist view of sex; in other words, it is about much more than just a physiological urge to procreate, inherently given and acted upon. It is about a more complex set of social and interpersonal relations, to do with physiological drives *and* to do with issues of identity. Thus we describe ourselves as gay, straight, bi-sexual, monogamous, polygamous. Our understanding of sexuality is culture bound, and differs between individuals, depending on their experience and view of the world.

Sexuality itself is also culture bound. Through various means of social discourse, e.g. family, school, religious institutions, the legal system, peer groups and mass media such as TV, magazines, we are given strong messages about the shape our sexuality should take, indeed even what shape our bodies should be to be sexy. We are even provided with 'legitimate' or 'illegitimate' representations of sexuality. Thus while media can present images of women in any state of sexual exposure or arousal, the erect penis is effectively outlawed - what a curious state of affairs! This makes for a social construction of sexuality which is under constant review and challenge, as to what is 'normal', what is permissible.

'Where I come from, we all cross-dress'

The narrowness of the western norm, and confirmation that it is socially rather than naturally constructed, is evidenced by acknowledging the varying practices of other cultures. For example:

- The Kerabi bachelors of New Guinea practise homosexual anal intercourse as a part of puberty rites.
- The Toda of India permit women to have several lovers and husbands.
- Hopi Indians keep boys and girls apart between the ages of 10 and 20.
- Polynesians see love as the 'life force'. There are no words in their language for sexually obscene, indecent or impure, nor are there words for illegitimate, adultery, bigamy or divorce.

It is clear, then, that sexuality is a complex construct, which intrinsically has no norms to adhere to. On the other hand, it must also be recognised that we operate within a specific Western culture; so that it would be reasonable and ethically desirable to acknowledge the norms of that culture. We say this with caution, given the appalling narrowness and bigotry that has been associated with various schools of psychology.[12] By norms, then, we mean norms of *conduct* on an interpersonal level. Thus we might accept that any behaviours which involve either primary or secondary sexual characteristics is likely to be experienced as sexual. All behaviour which is motivated by the sexual urge or gratification of either party in an interpersonal relationship will also be experienced as sexual: and any behaviour which stimulates the client into any kind of eroticized response must be acknowledged as sexual.

What then are the interpersonal issues of sexuality which affect the counsellor and their client? Broadly speaking, we have found that blank minds and sticky moments may be banded into four categories, as follows:

Wow – my client is a sex God/Goddess

Sometimes, there may be a physiological attraction to the client by the counsellor. We are, as we must repeat, merely humble human beings, not, after all, Mega beings. Therefore it is reasonable to expect that at some point in our counselling careers, we might encounter a client who we find very sexually attractive. This may be manifested in their looks, their manner, their dress, or some other source of stimulation which appeals to our taste.

There is nothing wrong with such attraction - how can we possibly say that attraction can be graded as 'right or wrong'? What is inappropriate, however, is for the counsellor then to act on that attraction, or to become preoccupied with it in such a way that it contaminates the counselling.

For example, one counsellor we know, a heterosexual male, had a female client who was classically beautiful, in his terms. He felt low level sexual arousal almost instantly. He had several choices to make:

- Leap across the room and embrace her with declarations of lust.
- Pretend nothing was happening.
- Disclose the attraction in the first five minutes, with reas-

surances that he would not act on it.

- Disclose the attraction with no reassurances. Suggest continuing the counselling over dinner.
- Acknowledge the attraction to himself, and take this issue to supervision.

There are many more possibilities of course, and it is clear that some are more appropriate than others. In the event, the counsellor acknowledged the attraction to himself in the first instant, and then disciplined himself to focus his attention on the whole client, not merely her sexual persona. He then discussed his responses in supervision. He felt less threatened about the sexual element, and was then able to manage it appropriately. At some stage in the process, when a strong working partnership was established, he was immediate about how attractive he found her, at a point when she was talking about her self-image. Thus it was relevant and purposeful information for her to incorporate into reflections. He was also able to refer to his initial contract which had discussed the parameters of the counselling relationship in some depth, including the recognition that this was not to be a social relationship, a move which had helped to set the context for both parties. Thus the client was able to experience her sexuality as a positive attribute which was not an overpowering force to other people, rather just one part of her whole being. Such a perspective can be crucial where clients have experienced abuse and exploitation, and consider themselves at fault.

We are aware that this is a contentious area, and that sexual attraction can be a very subtle process - it is not always a case of 'Phwoar, isn't he gorgeous!'. Nevertheless, we believe that self-monitoring is crucial to safe practice. Just as it is difficult to legislate for sexual licence or rules in life generally, so it is within counselling. The extreme arguments are that sex with a client is fine - after all, everybody's adult aren't they, through to sex must *never ever* be allowed between two people who have had a counselling relationship. This begs questions of equality and autonomy, which are too detailed to go into here.

However, we do know that manipulation of a counselling relationship to satisfy the sexual gratification of the counsellor is detrimental to the client.[13] Therefore, we feel quite safe to say that the counselling relationship should not be a sexual one. It is therefore incumbent on the counsellor to self-challenge and seek support and supervision if they find themselves attracted to the thought of ending the counselling in order to free the boundaries of the relationship, just as they would if they felt they would like a friendship with this client - and how many people would do that?? We do not believe that sexual attraction is an uncontrollable desire - flames must be fanned to make fire. However compelling a sexual urge may be, we will not explode if it is not instantly gratified!

My counsellor turns me on

Sexual attraction to the counsellor has been well documented in all the therapeutic traditions, particularly those of Freudian origin. Whatever paradigms we operate in, it seems clear to us that we do well to remember we are in a very particular and specific role to the client, which carries with it some expected norms and some responsibilities. While it may be flattering or frightening, then, to be the object of someone's sexual attraction, it is imperative that we understand that all our activities and responses remain intentional to the client's welfare, and to exercise self-discipline.

'He's so caring, so non-judgemental, he's obviously got the hots for me too. If only he wasn't so professional. My problem now is – I just want him so much . . . !'

Where we are tempted to respond to a flattering invitation to sex from a client, it is perhaps time to evaluate our own lives, in terms of our own relationships and fulfilment. This is not to say that sexual misconduct is always the product of *sexual* dissatisfaction. This could be a dangerous view which claims 'mitigating circumstances' for unacceptable conduct. However, if the counsellor is playing games with the client, if his/her counselling practice is so much the whole of life that it has to provide his/her titillation and erotic gratification, then we would suggest that something might be out of balance, and some fulfilment may be missing - time to get a life!

'She'll be coming soon. Is it my imagination or does she want to fuck my brains out?'

We need also to consider the *role* aspect of being a counsellor very carefully. Clients who invite their counsellors to a sexual relationship may be simply repeating patterns of behaviour which are well entrenched, and which have little to do with the counsellor's individuality. In other words, they might be attracted to people who are in positions of perceived authority. They may confuse the pleasure of being carefully listened to with love. They may have never had a close relationship which did not include sex. In such a circumstance, to accept the invitation is to deny the client the opportunity to develop insight into his/her behaviours, and to preclude the possibility of change. In our view, then, it is highly unethical and ill-advised to collude with such behaviour.

Tell me more about where she touched you . . .

It is possible to become aroused by the content of what the client is telling you. One of us once had the experience of hearing a client recount in some detail an episode which she had experienced as abusive. On hearing the interview played through on tape, the counsellor was mortified to find themself feeling sexually aroused. The *real event* which the client had described matched a private sexual *fantasy* which the counsellor had created. An instant response of self-aberration was helped enormously by acknowledging what was happening, and the counsellor was supported by being able to discuss the occurrence without fear of judgement or recrimination.

As ever, there are no hard and fast rules about what should be done in such a situation. Each person needs to use their own resources and strategies to separate out their own responses and feelings so that they can focus on the client's world . What must *not* happen is that the counsellor direct the client to tell them more about this event which they have found so arousing. Such action would be abusive and for the gratification of the counsellor, not to serve the interests of the client. We need to take away some of the power of feeling sexually aroused by remembering that it can be just another form of identification. After all, we don't hang someone because they have felt sad at an account of bereavement, we simply recognise that our own feelings need to be managed and channelled so that they are not contaminating the counselling. Sexual fantasy is no different in principle from this.

He did what – urgh, how revolting

Conversely, we may feel disgusted by what the client is telling us, particularly around episodes of sexual abuse. It is not uncommon to initially feel revulsion or anger when we are told of such events. Or we might feel uncomfortable with some of the practices between consenting adults which clients describe.

Either of these possibilities carry the danger that the counsellor might be offering a judgement on the client's experience or behaviour which leads them to direct the content away from disclosure. People are not stupid; when we divulge risqué material, we can tell from physiological indicators whether our revelations have caused disgust or alarm. So in a counselling relationship, the counsellor who is repelled but who tries not to be may well have the effect of suppressing any more disclosure. Equally, the counsellor who tries to steer or direct the client towards some ethic of 'normal' behaviour will be acting oppressively.

These are difficult areas with no easy answers. Three approaches strike us a having realistic and helpful outcomes. One is to be self-educative in the arena of human sexuality. If we conceive of sex as a heterosexual procreative activity which takes place in bed with the light off, man on top and not too much noise, commonly offered as the best forty seconds of a woman's life, then our shock threshold is likely to be low. If however we have an awareness that sex can constitute a whole range of pleasure focused activities, then shock is not so likely. Secondly, we need also to distinguish honestly between where we are ignorant and where we are prejudiced, and to challenge both. And thirdly, we would say to have confidence in the use of immediacy if we do feel taken aback. An honest admission of shock, if accompanied by a genuine desire to understand, is rarely offensive, and is a constructive way forwards - much more respectful than pretending we know every-

'He did that and you let him! But why?'

'Well, he said it was OK because we were in a stable relationship!'

thing, or pretending that we have no response at all.

In summary, then, while acknowledging the difficulties inherent in this subject, it is possible to elicit some guidelines as to what is *appropriate* sexual behaviour in the therapeutic situation. This will be behaviour where the counsellor:

- is able to facilitate the client's exploration of sexuality when this is intentional to the client's goal
- takes responsibility for setting and maintaining clear boundaries
- does not exploit the client either covertly or overtly for his or her own gratification
- sees the client's psychological needs as being paramount in the relationship
- has an awareness and an understanding of the intentionality of their own actions and is able to communicate that intention to the client.

There is not an easy how to do it, but we believe that if these *principles* are adhered to, in sexual matters as in others, then counselling will remain productive.

Friendship

Just recently, it has been acknowledged within the literature that some counsellors, even *eminent* counsellors, do counselling with their friends from time to time.[14] This is of great interest, for it is *contra* the received wisdom of counselling culture. It is, however, directly in sync with our own experience where we have on occasion either given or received counselling from both colleagues and friends. For demonstration purposes in groups, we have also counselled each other, and on occasion, have given each other some 'time' in which we have clearly designated roles in line with counselling ethos. We would both practically and ethically defend such practice.

We also know that sometimes, students on counselling courses become so enthusias-

'Sorry Margery, I can't! I know you're suicidal but I can't help you . . . you're one of my closest friends.'

tic about their skills and newly found direction that they provoke hostile responses from friends, loved ones and colleagues, along the line of 'if you check out what I'm feeling just once more, I shall have to slap you'. People get sick of 'being counselled' when all they want from their mates is a sympathetic ear, or a little guidance or advice, or some dependency. What then differentiates one set of activities from another, and how do we decide what is okay? And what are the rationales, the arguments, the beliefs and the myths which the practice of counselling friends evokes? And why could it be different to counsel friends than to make friends through counselling? Let us first look at the myths which surround counselling friends, and then look at the principles which can make such activity feasible.

Putting you before me: trick or treat?

One of the common (mis)understandings of counselling is that the anonymity of the counsellor and, indeed initially, the client, is of paramount importance because it can provide a certain form of *'objectivity'*, and the counsellor can act as an uncontaminated mirror for the client, in which they suspend their own agendas and interests. There are two relevant arguments to consider here. First, the nature of objectivity. Objectivity implies that the counsellor has no prejudices, no invested interests in the client's welfare, no preference as to the client's choice of action, no concerns, and no identification. It is highly doubtful that such a state is possible. Many counsellors, when asked what they bring to counselling, will answer a part of such a question with 'myself'. The uniqueness of each counsellor is unquestionable; the desire to be 'for' the client is often paramount; the objectivity therefore is highly questionable.

In order to minimise contamination, therefore, counsellors are in a constant state of monitoring themselves to check whether they are following the client. At best, then, they are able to work in a manner which suspends their subjectivity, or produces a critical subjectivity - i.e. they reflect on how their presence in the relationship affects that relationship, and use this informed stance to best advantage. The second key argument then to debunking the myth that anonymity is necessary to 'objectivity', or rather to this state of 'critical subjectivity', is that if a counsellor can perform such activity with strangers, who may provoke all kinds of feelings within them, then they can produce it with friends. The suspension of personal agenda is a technique, a deliberate enterprise, which can be managed if motivation, self awareness and skill level is present.

This is why counsellors go on courses, and, indeed, why they read books. Being 'client - centred', suspending self-interest, this is not some trick which occurs because 'we don't know each other'; it is a deliberate strategy which can produce a helpful intercourse which focuses on the 'content' of one person, and as such may be seen as something of a treat available to all.

No safety in knowing you . . .

One of the myths of the anonymity of the counsellor is that it is essential to providing a safety for clients. Sometimes safety is provoked by the knowledge that they might choose not to return to the counsellor at any stage; and perhaps by knowing that they do not have to face someone who knows certain intimate areas of their life at , say, a social gathering. Now, if a goal of counselling is that the client feels safe, then anonymity is certainly one way of achieving this end. It is not, however, the only way. It is perfectly possible to achieve safety, control over 'material', and trust within counselling, with someone who you know.

How can this be? Because all of these qualities, or states of relationship, are actively worked at within counselling, deliberately pursued and produced. It is perfectly possible, through contracting and self-discipline, to create safety without anonymity. For example, whenever we work together on counselling courses, it is probable that we use each other as models for students to observe skill. In the interest of authenticity, we always use real material. Invariably, because we also live together, it will be about us, our relationship, or some intimate part of our daily lives. This could be dicey, or at the very least uncomfortable, However, it isn't, because we contract very clearly to leave the modelled material in the classroom. It is only ever opened up again when both of us agree and we recontract to do so in the appropriate place.

Key to this possibility is of course the establishment of trust. We have to know that it works, that statements made in a counselling contract are not 'used against us'. Once such trust is established, however, and we have both established such trust in various relationships where we know people as friends, then the *real* safety, the intrinsic worth of an honoured confidentiality, can be experienced. It is even possible to argue that making anonymity essential is rather devaluing, going for the 'quick and dirty' rather than the more robust route. Rather than invoke this polarity, however, our key point is that anonymity is not essential to the counselling relationship; confidentiality, however, is.

Only strangers leave their black caps at home...

A third myth which leads people to rail against the thought of friends counselling friends is that knowing someone automatically means that you will have some judgement about their course of action, their perspective, their feelings. Again, we would argue that should this occur, then the counsellor has the same task as when they experience judgement with any other client - this is a conscious activity.

Moreover, we might also take a perspective wherein part of the essence of friendships is that we are accepting of each other, that we do suspend judgement.   Friendship is commonly held to embody expectations of honesty, openness, and the sharing and keeping of confidences. Respect is another common feature of friendship. Sound familiar? There is, then, no reason for counselling not to be feasible with friends. Such feasibility, however, hinges on four basic principles:

- ■ Counselling and communication skills are the property of the human race. They have developed from human interaction and can be applied to any human interaction.
- ■ The contract is the key issue to being able to counsel friends; informed consent by both parties enables counselling with friends to work.
- ■ To share the art of counselling with friends is different from procuring friendships via counselling.
- ■ Counselling is a strategic activity: it embraces an ethos and a repertoire of skilled approaches which can be applied to anybody.

Culture

We operate always within a cultural framework. We use this term broadly, to encompass a myriad of forms of differentiation: societal culture, race, class, gender, levels of education, political leanings, mental state, physical state, religious beliefs and background, organisational cultures. Our cultural perspective influences all our interactions through the value systems which they imply, and the behavioural manifestations of communication.

There is currently an increasing debate on whether or not counselling can ever be totally value free. There is also debate regarding the significance of how cultural difference or similarity affects the effectiveness of counselling. Such debates are huge, and deserve to be the subject of great consideration. Within the scope of this work, however, it strikes us that there are at least four ways in which values enter the counselling relationship with specific regard to culture;

- moral values
- helping paradigms - the intrinsic value of counselling
- clinical judgement - evaluation
- communication patterns

In this section, then, we will take all in turn and discuss briefly some key salient points.

You don't want to be doing it like that, you want to be doing it like this . . .

Moral values are the underpinning of behavioural norms, and present a great challenge to the counsellor. In pure theoretical terms, it is seen as antithetical to counselling to adopt a moral position on the culture or the behaviour of other people. We are taught to suspend judgement, to be acceptant and to offer unconditional positive regard. It is not considered acceptable to perceive one race of people as of higher value than another, or to behave in a prejudiced way against groups who exhort one sexual preference over another. In terms of culture, moral values may lead to prejudice and oppressive practice. If we believe that all Irishmen are thick, or all Middle Eastern men are shifty, or all white middle class people are arrogant sods, then the values which we attach to your culture will prejudice the counselling. We are urged to self-challenge such values in pursuit of unconditional positive regard; this concept is discussed in some detail in Chapter Nine.

Ultimately, we never achieve unconditional positive regard, because we give ourselves let out clauses in the guise of limits of confidentiality. We may also argue that such a position is desirable, if we are not to perceive the individual in a societal vacuum. Thus if you are a client and tell us that you want to become a more effective rapist, then not only would we not counsel you, but we might break confidentiality in the name of precluding exploitation. This stance can be justified under the heading of moral values, because as members of a society we have a moral duty to pursue shared values such as equality or fairness. Thus to condone racism, or sexual harassment, is as unacceptable as to practice it oneself.

In practice, then, we are not bound by the promise of unconditional positive regard no matter what. However, we *can* aspire to
suspending judgement for the greatest part of our counselling negotiations, and to offering respect to the client, and again, this
position is debated in greater detail in Chapter Nine. In regard to
culture, however, it is clearly not acceptable to take a moral stance
on someone's behaviour on cultural grounds, or through ignorance
of cultural norms. At its worst, such ignorance and prejudice has
resulted in people being confined to psychiatric units on the basis
of cultural and racial difference.[15] We would suggest then that
while we need to acknowledge the reality that counselling as a social practice is not devoid of moral values, it is incumbent on the
profession not to offer valuation on the basis of culture or race.

Counselling ten, witchcraft nil points . . .

Secondly, the very social practice of counselling is thoroughly value
laden, as we imply throughout this book. It presupposes a particular model of the self in society, a self which is open, honest,
self-determining and authentic - in dominant Western terms. While
this point is made in Chapter Three, and contextualised in Chapters Seven and Eight, one or two points deserve mention here in
direct relation to culture.

Firstly, it is well to remember that the development of counselling in Britain has been closely linked to the Christian church as
the traditional religion. There are of course also strong links between the philosophies and practices of counselling to Judaism.
Such is the relationship between Western tradition and the Church
that the notion of selfhood propagated through counselling, with
the concept of free will as central, is compatible with that of the
Church. This is not the case with all other religions. It is recognised that counselling is being increasingly experimented with in
Muslim cultures, and our own involvement in the initiative taken
by the Kuwait government was educational. Implications of the
mix of the very different philosophical tenets of Islam with those
which advocate self-determination are as yet unclear. It has been
argued that Western and Islamic paradigms are irreconcilable, and
that Muslim human development theorists should heed this stance
as they develop their conceptual frameworks.[16] The main point is
that for counselling to be adopted, cultural norms would have to be
severely challenged.

Further, and related, there is a real cultural value given to the
internal life in counselling, with not much room for the unknown,

or for magic which we do not understand. The counselling venture is very much a part of humankind s attempt to be able to understand, predict and influence human behaviour, a part of the rationality of the twentieth century. There are attempts to reconcile counselling with cultures where internal misery is conceptualised as being bewitched , the argument being that the structures of therapy are less important than the discovery and reinterpretation of shared meaning.[17]

There is undoubtedly a process of negotiation and change to be encountered between the cultural norms of counselling discourse and those of whole societies or sections of societies. Our guess is that such a process could be enormously enriching and very exciting if some sort of real integration and shared learning takes place. However, there is also scope for the imposition of one version of self, written through the symbols and icons of western psychology, onto others. It is important to remember then the value laden nature of the counselling movement.

Tell me what you want, what you really really want

The third kind of values which might operate are to do with clinical judgement, again, an e-valuative process. In a first interview, the counsellor will be, hopefully with the client's involvement, assessing whether they can offer help which is appropriate to the needs of the client. A number of factors will influence this process; expressed wants of the client, level of articulation, orientation of the counsellor, the nature of the issue or problem, whether the client is on medication and if so what effects that might have, expectations of responsibilities, whether ethical codes are acceptable, and so on.

Later in the process the counsellor will constantly be making judgement calls . Acting on the data they receive from the client, they will be choosing an intentional response. This may be on the micro level: I will empathise here, whereas here I will offer a challenge to perspective, and so on. There may also come times when the counsellor wants to challenge the motivation of the client, or indeed may want to break confidentiality for ethical reasons. These are all forms of evaluation of what is going on and what will be useful next.

Culture may be one of the variables which influences clinical judgement. The client might want a counsellor who is the same race, the same religion, the same gender, experiencing a similar physical impairment, and so on. This must be a matter of choice for the client. Where the counsellor needs to be careful is that they are working in a way which is open to a cultural awareness - in other words, they must accept different norms of expressive behaviour, without letting this cloud clinical judgement. So the impassioned revelations of a person from one culture might contrast with the apparent passivity and lack of eye contact from a person from a different culture. On its own, however, such difference should not be an influence to clinical judgement. This leads on to patterns of communication, which are key to transcultural work.

It could be like being like me, to be like you, or it could be very different - what shall we go for?

Values always underpin how we communicate. All communication is produced and modified through cultural filters. In mainstream counselling culture, it is regarded as *valuable,* as a sign of respect, even of authenticity, to make 'good eye contact', whatever that may mean. It is regarded within Western counselling culture as jolly good form to vent the emotions. It is not considered particularly nice to say fuck or shit. Our language is a powerful mediator in cultural prejudice.

What can we say about this subject in an unspecialised work, so great is its potential. We have views, which perhaps are useful. We have worked within multicultural settings and on a transcultural basis. Many of the books on the subject urge us to find out as much as possible about the other culture before working. Our attitude, however, has been to see the challenge of how we communicate in the here and now as the most fruitful way forwards. So we have gone into situations culture blind , and learned from them. We follow a belief that effective communication relies on sharp observation, and the production of negotiated meaning, with a lot of checking out. We are not embarrassed to ask, or to get things wrong.

We can also say that learning about and experiencing other cultures has value, in terms of making such communication less cumbersome. So we would urge the counsellor to do whatever they have to do, or want to do; to facilitate inter-cultural communication. This may involve much self-challenge and questioning, and certainly an open mind. It is also true to say that it hinges on a belief that goodwill is available and recognised in all cultures, and can be conveyed in a thousand ways. Ultimately, we need both cultural and individual sensitivity.

This is not to say that taking active steps to educate ourselves, to be pro-actively anti-discriminatory, is not valuable, indeed essential. We would also like to see far less control of the production of counselling discourse in the hands of society's dominant group, i.e. the middle class white man. By this, we mean the owners of developmental notions of self and models of counselling, key editorial figures, and so on.

But perhaps our worst fear is that reading about it, and trying to do all the right things, can produce a rather stereotyped version of the culture in question. Cultural groups are not homogenous, not all the same in how they do things and what they want. We dread becoming Dolly the counsellor, who has learned how to bleat self-consciously toward the appeasement of cultural difference.[18]

Concluding remarks

In sum, then, it has been suggested that although interpersonal relationships cannot be defined and legislated for, their nature can be clarified, and they can be conceptualised as purposeful. The difficulties which lack of pure definition invokes do not make counselling impossible to define. Other professions whose success hinges on the formation of rapport and the offering of personal qualities still manage to define themselves, and so can counselling.

We have acknowledged that there are some themes regarding interpersonal relationships which cause speculation and difficulties. We have questioned whether intimacy is a necessary part of counselling, and challenged some understandings of this concept, particularly in relation to the myth of mutual self-disclosure. We suggest that issues of sexuality, boundaries of friendship, and issues of culture are all negotiable in a spirit of good heart and integrity.

It is not possible to be value free within counselling, and neither is it necessarily desirable. While moral judgement is not useful to counselling, we suggest that clinical judgement is necessary to safe and effective practice. In terms of intercultural work, negotiation is the best we can do. Finally, we have suggested that the practice of counselling itself is a value laden venture; the challenge is retaining flexibility and *negotiating* its values among different cultures.

Endnotes

1. For Carl Rogers (1951, 1961), the nature of the relationship within counselling is of paramount importance, and is the substance of much of his writing.
   Elements of relationship were also of course paramount throughout Freudian theory and its derivatives. Extreme lassitude in boundaries within Freudian theory can be found in the practices of Sandor Ferenczi, who was very
   much of the 'let's take the client on holiday with us' school, the rationale
   being that the unboundaried relationship was the therapy.

2. See for example Berne, (1964); Rogers, (1951); Ehrenberg, (1992); Lerner,
   (1989); Dryden, (1989), Rowe, (1991). Dorothy Rowe, for example, states that
   'intimacy with other people (is) the greatest pleasure we can know' (,1991:244),
   while Eric Berne suggests it is the 'most perfect form of human living'
   (1964:55). High praise indeed!

3. One piece of research into counsellor's 'successes' offers the observation that:-

   > (A) common feature of these descriptions was the degree of intimacy
   > between client and counsellor. Indeed some of the descriptions
   > seemed to equate success and intimacy; as one counsellor reflected:
   > 'Such caring, such willingness simply to be fully in each other's pres-
   > ence, always led to creative movement in the end' Mearns, in Mearns
   > & Dryden, (1991: 195).

   We would see this as a representation of what might happen, rather than
   what must happen for counselling to be fruitful.

4. Paul Nicholson in She magazine, November 1995.

5. See Russell, (1993, 1996), and Rutter, (1990) for discussion regarding inappropriate sexual intimacy. Little work is yet available on inappropriate intimacy in wider contexts, although this is becoming an increasingly important
   theme.

6. See for example Goffman (1959:33-40), and Argyle, (1987:44) for discussion
   on presentation of self. Ingram (1991: 408) discusses the intentional nature
   of the therapeutic relationship, and therefore the improbability of self-disclosure as being mutual.

7. See Falk & Wagner, (1985: 558) for further discussion on this point.

8. Duck & Pond, (1989: 26-27)

9. See Duck (1988:44).

10. See for example Ingram (1991) and Ehrenberg (1992) who both elucidate on
    the uniqueness of each relationship while focusing on the particulars of
    situational and role oriented disclosures.

11. For excellent discussions of sexuality as discourse and as construct, see
    Foucault's (1981,1987) work on The History of Sexuality, or Jeffrey Weeks
    (1986), Sexuality.

12. Psychology has been instrumental in providing theories of human develop
    ment which have actively outlawed homosexuality and masturbation as un
    natural practices. Of course, as trends change, so do the psychological norms;
    nowadays it might be seen as 'abnormal' not to masturbate!

13. See Russell, (1993) Out of Bounds for a client centred discussion of these issues.

14. cf Colin Feltham, (1995).

15. The pioneering work of Lipsedge and Littlewood on this issue makes classic reading, and illustrates perfectly the dangers of moralising from an oppressive position.

16. See for example Rashid, (1992), who argues for such articulation in language of the Qur'an.

17. See for example Ross & Lwanga (1991) for a detailed account of such transcultural experiments.

18. This point is made eloquently by the main character in the book Primary Colours, Anonymous (1996:27).

> Most white people do this patronizing number: they never disagree with you, even when you're talking the worst sort of garbage. It is near impossible to have a decent, human conversation with them. They are all so busy trying not to say anything offensive - so busy trying to prove they aren't prejudiced - that they freeze up, get all constricted, formal. They never just talk.

Chapter Four. Challenging : do I really have to sit here and listen to *anything*, even when I think it's drivel?

Introduction

The art of challenging seems to be one of the most difficult areas for counsellors to grasp. Counsellors can become really good at empathising, clarifying, finding out more and more story. Yet it seems as if the word challenge provokes images of throwing the gauntlet down, or some obligation to challenge the validity of what the client is saying. We use the word challenge advisedly - it refers to interventions and styles which invite the client to find a new perspective on their situation, feelings, thoughts, behaviours or wants. Just because the client has got stuck in the bunker doesn't mean that the counsellor has got to climb in there with them. And yet many counsellors lack the assertiveness to challenge, as well as the skill. Thus counselling can become known as a somewhat hand holding exercise rather than a dynamic process of negotiation with opportunities for change.

'Just 'cos you're stuck in the bunker, don't think I'm coming in too!'

Any self respecting counsellor trainer will tell you the answer to the title question is 'Yes'; the more honest and adventurous trainer might say 'Maybe'; and we say 'Probably Not'! However, this should not imply any disrespect for the client, neither should it imply that we do not try to follow the principles of self determination and non judgementalness.[1] We do however feel that a lot of time, yours and the client's time, can be wasted listening to comparatively trivial substance trotted out by the client because both parties believe that this is what is expected! The client thinks it is necessary to describe every bit of his/her life minute by minute, and the counsellor has been trained that it is disrespectful to stop them. Good contracting is one antidote to this scenario and effective challenge is the other; the latter is the concern of this chapter.

Moreover, clients often come for counselling because working with their own resources at that particular time has resulted in them getting as far as they can; they keep on reaching the same old stumbling block, they have a fixed solution in mind which really they dread, they know the kind of changes they want but have become frozen in fear, or have hit some other sticky moment in their lives which they just cannot move out of on their own - yet.

Working with clients can be extremely frustrating or extremely rewarding. We would like to think that the better you become at counselling the more it stays at the rewarding end. By better we mean when the counsellor has acquired greater skill, increased their range of techniques, has more confidence and assertiveness, and is generally more at ease and at home with the process. At this point it may be necessary to draw a distinction between work and play. Counselling is always work, but work that is rewarding can be enjoyable. However, no matter how enjoyable it becomes, it should never become play!

For example, the counsellor who is able and skilful may find a

'It might be fun, but I'm getting dizzy and more confused.'

particular client tough to get through to; the client may be unclear, reluctant to disclose to themselves, or go round and round in circles. The feeling of connecting to this client, helping them clarify their thoughts and get on to a point where they can make changes for the better in their life is extremely rewarding. Alternatively if the same client continues to go 'round and round the Mulberry bush', remains superficial, confused, and makes no changes in their life, then the counsellor may become frustrated. However, no matter how frustrating this client is, there is no excuse to reduce the counselling to play. Some counsellors, faced with such a situation, may be tempted to liven up the sessions with techniques that they are largely using for their own training or entertainment purposes. The situation we mean goes a bit like:- 'I'm getting nowhere with John, and I've just learned about "the empty chair technique" in Gestalt Therapy, so I'll try that this week with him'. In principle we suggest that no matter how frustrating the counselling sessions become *the counsellor must remain ethical!* This is not to say that innovative techniques might not be used if they are thought to be purposeful to the client's work.

This chapter sets out to describe the principles of remaining ethical while moving clients on. It explores the question of what to challenge, and what not to challenge. It discusses when to challenge, and when not to. And it looks at some classic skills of challenging, portraying some of the techniques that could be used to enable greater connections, and to encourage the client to make self determined change in their lives. It is not exhaustive, but we hope that it is thorough enough to remind the counsellor of those things they already know, and perhaps hone up on those things they know less.

What to challenge

Ownership

Many clients will bring problems and goals that are not owned, that are 'other' stated. It is very easy to portray oneself as a victim of other people's circumstances, for example to present with *unowned problems* such as;

■ My wife's an alcoholic.
■ I'd like to be more assertive, but they won't let me - they're out to get me.

This is not to say that we do not accept that the client is encountering problems because of his wife's drinking habits, or feeling unable to change behaviour at work. It is simply that currently, the problem is not stated in terms of 'me'; it is described in terms of a situation which cannot be changed. Similarly with goals; clients (and for clients read people) are brilliant at stating *unowned* goals:

- I want my children to be happy.
- I want my children to be treated fairly at school.
- I want my mother to realise what she did wrong.
- I want my partner to love me more, to bring me surprises like s/he used to.

We may want these things as much as we like, and could spend a lifetime ruing the fact that we cannot/did not attain them. So, out of respect for the client, each of these stated issues needs to be challenged in order to enable the client to see how they themselves are involved in the statement.

Without the problems and goals being owned it is impossible to help the client to see strategies or develop insights that will work for them. We all know, albeit reluctantly at times!, that we cannot control other people. Sometimes in problem situations the client is not clear on this, and indeed we have known counsellors to collude with passivity. The key question, then, is 'how can the counsellor convey the importance of owning the problem to the client?' Counsellors can become blank or stuck when they try to remain in counselling mode and to refrain from teaching. For example, we have both manipulated clients with what we now consider to be 'pseudo-*counselling*' manoeuvres such as the following:-

- 'Everything you try leaves you feeling frustrated, and you're slowly beginning to realise that the only real control you have is over your own feelings.'

- **OR** - 'So when you say you want your children to be happy, you know that's not completely under your control, so I'd guess you really want to feel you're doing your best for them - that way you'd find some peace of mind'

Either of these does of course get the client headed towards an owned state, but they do involve trickery, not just empathy, *unless* they are data based rather than mystical. It sounds counselly but it has lost non directiveness, added some counsellor expertise and short circuited the long painful wait for the client to realise for themselves what they can and can't control.

The easiest, crudest and most neglected challenge to an unowned problem is simply :-

- **'And what about you?'**

This is a direct invitation to the client to take some ownership of what is going on, and of what they might want; 'so you're wife's an alcoholic - where does that leave *you* then?'. The client may well respond with a vague answer and return to the *fact* that his wife is an alcoholic. The counsellor, then, needs to be able to gently persist in the intervention; you may pick up empathically how the client has responded - 'so you sound as if you feel quite helpless'. Already, this begins to identify what the problem is for the *client,* not for their wife.

Slightly more sophisticated is the information giving challenge:-

- ■ 'I could just let you tell me more and more about your wife's behaviour, but it's my experience that you can only change the things which are under your control'.

For the unowned goal, the simplest challenge is:

- ■ 'And what will *you* get out of that?', or 'What would that achieve for *you?'*

So, for the client who wants their children to be happy, the response could be something like: 'You also said that you want your children to be happy, but what would it achieve for *you* if your children were happier at school?'

Although this does have a 'teachy' type component to it, it remains acceptable because it makes clear what is the counsellor's view/knowledge and then uses the client's material to return immediately to the clients chosen disclosure. It is of course directive, yet follows the principle: *control the process not the content.*

The challenge to ownership is a very strong one. We are at pains to say here that it is not a challenge which ignores the situation the client is in; all problems occur in a context. However, if a problem is suitable for counselling, then it must be stated in terms which the client has some hope of changing. This means that we would suggest that some situations do not justify counselling *of themselves,* such as acute/immediate stages of bereavement, or homelessness, although individuals facing such situations may benefit from *support,* which will often entail the use of counselling skills. To designate them as issues for counselling, however, is both unrealistic and ethically questionable. Problem ownership is essential for effective counselling; to personalise social problems to this end is questionable.

Strengths

One of our first clients told a horrid tale of woe. This fifty year old woman had two children in a loveless marriage. She had promised herself that when they were both independent she would have her life back. Being a person who believed in her promises to God in regard to her marriage, imagine the feelings of suffocation she suffered when her husband became seriously disabled shortly after her second child left home. She felt trapped, desperate, alone and futureless; we reflected this back to her in true Rogerian fashion. At the end of this first session it was clear that the client had been given every opportunity to ventilate her terrible situation, explore every negative emotion, and inspect every facet of her problem scenario. Perhaps it should not then have been such a surprise, nay shock, to hear her response to the question 'has that been helpful'. She simply and sadly said 'Yes. When I came I realised it was bad, now I understand just how hopeless it really is!'

Further experience has shown us how typical such counselling situations may be when the counsellor demonstrates lack of experience or ineptness in the important area of feeding back strengths. We are trained to empathise with emotions and to listen carefully to the client's story, and this was done impeccably with the client in the vignette above. However, what was sadly missing was reflection of the FULL story and empathy with ALL the emotions. It is so easy to listen only to the problem, only to the negative emotions, and then only to empathise with the misery. Thank goodness I don't make mistakes like that one you're probably thinking to yourself! Well if you were, and even if you weren't - take a moment, before reading on too far, to answer these questions in regard to the client's story above.

- What were the strengths in the clients story?
- What would you have reflected back to her if you'd been her counsellor?
- What were the positive emotions revealed in her story?
- What could the counsellor do in these circumstances to enable the client to have some hope, without compromising the fundamental principles of counselling? - (i.e. without reassuring, comforting, guiding, or advising).

It would appear to us that there are many strengths and qualities that need reflecting back to our client:

■ She is seeking help, she has insight into her dilemma. She has a clear commitment to her faith, despite this presenting a problem to her currently, and she is a person who has integrity.

The counsellor had opportunities to reflect back to her the strength that she demonstrated in waiting so many years, how steadfast she had been to her promise and how much integrity she had demonstrated in her resolve to ensure the children could grow to independence.

The positive emotions revealed but not reflected were numerous:

■ The love for her children, the concern for their independence. The concern for herself in her promise to have her own life. The joy of anticipating a different life. The patience she has had in waiting.

Finally, without jeopardising the principles of counselling, the client could have been challenged to look more closely at what she wanted for her future that could still be possible. The classic challenge of "what would it look like if it was just 'a little bit better'" might have been immensely liberating.

It has been our experience that many of the potential challenges for clients to look at the positives in themselves is lost in the intensity of negative reflection and in going with the superficial 'mood' of the client. Our view is that the client is served better when all aspects of themselves are reflected back to them, not only the selected negatives.

Discrepancies

Opportunities sometimes arise for counsellors to challenge discrepancies, games and smoke-screens that are presented in client disclosures. These fall largely into the following categories:-

i.   What clients say they do / what they actually do.
ii. What they say they want / what they actually want.
iii. What others think about them / what they imagine others think of them.
iv. What they believe happened / what actually happened.
v.   The relationship between cause and effect. i.e. He started to cry - I made him cry.
vi. What was observed / what was interpreted.

vii. Over estimating their impact / under estimating their impact.

viii. What is said/how it is said.

Each of these and possibly many more are simply opportunities for the counsellor to challenge. One of the most powerful of all challenges is accurate empathy; another is simply to paraphrase discrepant statements together and invite reflection. To illustrate what we mean, examine our examples. Using the categories from the list above, we give firstly an illustration of how accurate empathy could be used as a challenge (AE) and then illustrate how paraphrasing discrepant statements (PDS) together would create challenge:

i. You feel really **proud** when you support your wife, and **irritated** by her when she's moaning. (AE) You say you always support your wife, and yet you tell me that on occasions you refuse to listen to her 'moaning on' (PDS) .

ii. You feel **insecure** when they manage without you, but really **pressured** when you're left to do everything. (AE) You have said you want more relaxation yet you say you need to feel indispensable. (PDS).

iii. You feel **inferior** to the other workers and **surprised** that anyone seeks your advice. (AE) You imagine that people think you a fool, and yet you tell me that your advice is sought after quite a lot by your managers. (PDS)

iv. You feel **responsible,** in some way to blame, and yet you are **certain** that you were clear about saying 'no'. (AE) You say you must have led him on, seduced him, but when you said 'no' he ignored you. (PDS)

v. You seem absolutely **certain** that when he cried you were the cause. (AE) After you told him you were leaving, he became tearful. (PDS)

vi. You **worry** about his drinking and have **no doubt** that it's connected to the loss of his parents. (AE) You notice that he drinks heavily at Christmas, and assume this is because his parents died around that time of year. (PDS)

vii. A lot of the time you feel **ignored.** (AE) No-one listens to you, but they all seem to know how troubled you are. You are **fearful** of being deserted so you don't criticise them. (AE) The merest hint of criticism from you and they'd leave home, but they've stayed on despite the row you had with them last week. (PDS) viii You *tell* me that you feel **afraid,** and yet you *look* very **excited** (AE). You are fearful of making these changes, yet have already begun by saying no to your boss (PDS).

The discerning reader will be able to spot that some of the so called accurate empathy may have a paradoxical effect. Clients receiving their intense emotions accurately reflected and attrib- uted so tightly can quickly sense any implied message from the reflections absoluteness i.e.- 'should this be so, is it really that simple, or am I right to be so sure'. The experienced and confident practitioner will also know that to inflect some sarcastic tone to an accurate empathic response, or to issue it with a questioning tone, automatically changes it to a challenge.

Thoughts

Thoughts, as expressed in language, offer some potential areas for simple and yet effective challenge. The technique here is calcu- lated, not for the counsellor to elaborate their views or opinions about the client's thoughts, but to throw down an invitation for the client to reflect upon more precisely what it is they mean. Most of the groundwork and thus credit for this approach must be given to the cognitive therapists.[2]

Often clients will say words such as **'must', 'should', 'ought',** which are almost instantly available for the counsellor to simply echo in a questioning tone. For the less speedy client this chal- lenge can be elaborated to 'when you say 'must' does that indicate some sort of pressure to do that, as op- posed to simply wanting to? The more confident and experienced counsel- lor may try something like 'You say you must, I won- der if you could tell me what it is you would freely choose to do instead'? This approach has the effect of gently challeng- ing and also inviting the client to briefly visit their goals.

'Everybody tells me I'm no good and I have to do everything.'

Equally powerful are words spoken by the client which indicate their thoughts are somewhat concrete or absolute. Words such as **'always'** and **'never'** are in this vein; they are almost **always** challengeable and should **never** be missed! Once again the same parroted word in a questioning tone is usually enough to invite the client to reflect. Challenging conceptual thinking is one of the most powerful interventions that can be made, so powerful that they must be considered carefully before hurling them at the client impulsively! An illustration may serve to make this point more forcefully. A student on a cognitive approaches type course was the subject of a demonstration. His problem elaborated out to his neighbour's rude and aggressive behaviour in regard to this student's dog. No empathic reflecting nor gentle invitation to consider the neighbour's view was successful in challenging the student's position. At this point the student was asked to say what he preferred about dogs as opposed to any other animal. His list of preferences included such concepts as loyalty, friendliness, trust, warmth, acceptance and peacefulness. When subsequently asked to say what the opposite of these concepts were his list included betrayal, unreliability, uncaring, cold and standoffishness. Without much need for probing, but by simply asking if any of this related to his stated problem, it was revealed that his list of opposites almost directly applied to his neighbour. To challenge the student's thinking it was simply a matter of asking him to examine what the disadvantage of his preferred list were and the advantages of his list of opposites. Although at first this was difficult for him, it eventually led to some rather different conclusions about what he had recently quite firmly believed to be obviously correct. Eventually the student disclosed that he could see that barking in the night, the occasional smell of faeces, the trampling of plants and being jumped on with dirty paws might be unpleasant for other people.

This approach uses both laddering and pyramiding which are based on Kelly's Personal Construct Theory. Taking time with this approach is important because in the process of asking about preferences some underpinning values are often disclosed. In this case the student's concepts such as loyalty, trust and warmth were very important to him; asking him to explore possible disadvantages to them can not only be uncomfortable but alarming. Care should be taken in this regard, as the client's value orientation is exposed and potentially vulnerable.

Behaviours and proposed behaviour

Perhaps one of the most obvious opportunities for challenge will present itself through the client's behaviour. At first, this may seem paradoxical - counsellors are trained to be 'non judgemental' so how can they challenge behaviour? Yet all behaviour is linked to a goal. In simpler terms behaviour is the result of a person trying to achieve something! The challenge then is not directed towards whether the client should or should not act that way, it is just to check out *what* that behaviour is achieving for them.

One acquaintance of ours spent some time in prison several years ago, and was incensed at being kept in cells at the police station in poor conditions. He steamed himself up and threatened the police that if they didn't treat him better, he would urinate in his cell. They didn't, and he did. Now he was left in his cell for a long period with the smell of urine. Thirty seconds satisfaction for several hours of discomfort might not have been what he really wanted to achieve.

It is our experience that people often act without thinking about where they want to get to - give a person a problem, and ninety-five per cent of the time they will move immediately into what they're going to *do* about it. Thus all behaviours presented to the counsellor can be challenged by asking - 'when you do that, what exactly do you expect to achieve by it?' This rather crude challenge holds good in a whole variety of situations. For example:

■ A self harming client - 'So when you set about cutting your wrists what do you imagine it will achieve?'

■ A sulking child - 'What exactly do you get out of refusing to talk, going to your room?'
Or - 'What would you prefer instead, and what would you have to do to get that?'

This approach to challenging behaviour need not be reserved for challenging present behaviour; when clients make impulsive decisions about what they are going to do, the same challenging approach is useful.

■ The suicidal client - 'So if you were successful in killing yourself, what would you have achieved?' After the answer this is followed up with 'Can you think of any other ways of achieving that without killing yourself?'

■ The desperate client - 'If you walk out right now, with nowhere to go, what exactly will you realize for yourself.'

■ The violent client - 'If you poison him, what do you gain for yourself, and what are the likely consequences for you?'

Essentially this simple technique halts the impulsive client in their tracks and enables them to reflect carefully upon their behaviour and what it intentionally and unintentionally achieves for them. This does not require the counsellor to be judgemental, simply alert and questioning to previous or future behaviours which are as yet unconnected to goals. To miss such opportunities may mean that the counsellor colludes with unhelpful behaviour for the client.

For example, one of us had occasion to counsel a young woman who had recovered memories of sexual abuse and had immediately confronted both her parents. She wanted them to feel punished, and her to feel better. She subsequently regretted this action, as it had totally unforeseen consequences. Had she been helped at the time to consider her goals more clearly, she might have realised that they were both unclear and unrealistic. A lot of pain and waste of energy could have been avoided.

Prejudice and stereotyping

We are taught to be non-judgemental. However, this can leave us vulnerable to allowing our client's prejudices to pass unchallenged. Doubtless, we all to some extent hold some prejudice, whether this arises from a form of preference - i.e. 'I prefer to chat to someone who is extroverted rather than introverted' -or whether it is oppressive and offensive - 'I would never give a job to someone black'. Both hold some prejudice and discriminate behaviourally against the disliked person. However, one issue that separates the two examples is the oppressive nature of the prejudice, and the power base for its exercise. It is not sufficient to argue that 'I don't have prejudice, I simply exert a preference', when this translates into an oppressive practice. Hence, by degree, it could be seen that to ignore all extroverts would be oppressive practice, while to avoid excessive social contact with a particular extrovert might be eminently sensible!

In considering whether to challenge prejudice in client disclosure, the counsellor has to contemplate whether the prejudice constitutes a serious threat to a greater social justice. They have to also consider whether it is useful for the client to be challenged, in relation to the contract. Further, they might simply be compelled by their own response to use immediacy in terms of how offended they might feel.

The issue is complex, but the reality which each counsellor has to face is that they will feel the periodic need to challenge client prejudice. There may be tension between this need and the drive to a non-judgemental, warm and genuine relationship. However, to be genuine means treating both yourself and the client equally, and therefore being able to challenge prejudice from within your own value system. We offer some ideas here based on our experience, in an honest attempt to be realistic and practical, rather than give some half arsed theoretical answer that leaves the reader no clearer as to what to do! We will use the example of a man who is derisory to his gay single parent neighbour, who has not kept her part of the garden tidy. This seems to be a trigger for the client to run down all women, to want to outlaw lesbianism, and to slate single parents. Some options we would consider are:

A.   Challenge the client's qualities, strengths and values. Use these to expose any discrepancies between the client's potential positives and their disclosed negative attitudes. e.g.

'You give the impression of being a very caring person, and yet you seem to think so badly of your neighbour who you don't yet know very well?'

B. Use a little self-disclosure of your emotion and challenge the prejudice from their frame of reference. e.g.

'I suppose I am a bit surprised (disappointed, frustrated, irritated) to hear you say that, especially when you yourself have been a target of prejudice for being unemployed?'

C.   A straight forward empathic response with a questioning tone accented on the paraphrased prejudicial thinking. e.g.

'You sound absolutely certain that your neighbour is lazy, and you seem to think that that is because(?) she is female, gay and a single parent?'

D.   A combination of empathy, self disclosure, and challenge of the prejudice. e.g.

'You seem resentful towards your neighbour because you think she is lazy, but I suppose I m a bit confused, are you also saying that ALL gay women that are single parents are lazy too?'

E. Immediacy

'I feel really uncomfortable with you asserting that all gay single parents are lazy wastes of space. Is that an effect that you hope to achieve with people?'

We don't propose these as ideal, and proposing such ideas without stereotyping examples is quite difficult. Our main point, however, is that while suspending judgement of the person, we cannot help but have some responses to prejudices. It seems to us that there is a complex relationship here between disclosure of prejudice and goals of counselling. If we work with an extremely sexist man, for example, who wants to better his relationship with women, then the declaration of prejudice is an integral part of the work, and can be challenged easily in relation to goals, and worked with to develop insight and change. If however our client tells us that he really cannot stand anyone in a wheelchair, and wants to gather strength to form a campaign to have all known spinally defective foetuses aborted, then the counsellor might not only challenge such prejudice, but refuse to be involved in the work. There is a sense, then, in which we are never fully non-judgemental - we make constant clinical judgements as to what we can work with, and constant value laden interactive and personal judgements about what we want to be involved with. Ultimately, some of our challenges around prejudice are from a position of our integrity rather than necessarily in the interests of the client as defined by them.

'My burden is awful, terrible, completely overwhelming . . .'

Unrealistic Expectations of Self, Others and Life; Disputing Awfulising and Catastrophyzing

We believe it is one of the counsellor's responsibilities to enable the client to see themselves as clearly as possible. This from time to time requires the counsellor to challenge the clients objectivity in regard to the social, cultural and behavioural norms in which they are confined. Take Raymond for example:

Raymond complains in the sessions that his partner doesn't love him enough, that he knows that it is wrong to gossip about others, but he finds it too great a temptation on occasion, to resist. He has stated that life is dull for him, he has no excitement any more and his job is boring. He says that if his partner found out he was gossiping the scene would be awful, he would not be able to cope. He describes his worst fear as his partner admitting they didn't love him any more, this he says would be disastrous.

This is the sort of client that on some occasions you want to take hold of and shake, or to offer some SLAP[3] therapy However, this is not fair or useful; no client means to be irritating,   and everyone's problems are important to them. Sometimes, though, even though you want to be helpful some clients may represent a stark contrast to other clients. This may especially be the case if your other clients comprise victims of sexual abuse, grieving mothers, homeless single parents and young adults with   inoperable cancers. In these circumstances Raymond's issues are in danger of paling into insignificance, even though to him they may be awesome. Some useful challenges for Raymond at this point are suggested from the rational emotive school of therapeutics, for example:

- 'Raymond, can you tell me exactly what would happen if your partner discovered you'd been guilty of gossiping? - *'It would be awful!'*
- 'What feelings would be associated with this awful situation? - *'I'd be embarrassed, and uncomfortable, I'd feel really silly.'*
- 'So what you really mean is you wouldn't like it to happen, but if it did you'd survive it?' - *'Yes, I suppose so - now I've said exactly what I'd feel, it doesn't seem so awful.'*
- 'Raymond, you say that if your partner admitted he didn't love you any more it would be disastrous; when you say disastrous can you be more specific, I mean say exactly what would be the result for you?' - *'Well, I'd have to leave, wouldn't I, It would mean I was no good, useless, and everything would be over forever.'*

  'Well I can see the prospect distresses you, but let's just see how accurate all of that really is. . .you'd **have to** leave, it would be a certain indication that you were **no good, useless** and **everything** would be over **forever** would it?'

  (Questioning accented hesitation on all words in bold)
- 'Raymond, when you say life is dull and your job is boring, I notice that you seem very resentful; without wishing to

be at all critical of you, I wonder if I could ask you what influence you think you have over the dullness and boredom you perceive?'

or shorter - 'You seem resentful about your dull life and boring job, and **helpless** because you have no influence over those emotions?' (helpless accented with irony).

■ You feel unhappy because your partner doesn't love you enough, I wonder if perhaps you could take some time to think about the exact amount of love he **should** offer you?'

The point about such challenges is that they help to reality test. We are a culture who tend to dramatise verbally. Much critical and popular theory of the last twenty years talks about life in terms of 'surviving' divorce, 'surviving' redundancy, 'surviving' cellulite. People talk about being 'devastated' by their boss's attitude, the failure to reach an expected promotion. If we use such language frequently enough, then we exaggerate our feelings and reduce our coping mechanisms. Survival and devastation used in the context of the former Yugoslavia, or Rwanda, have a very different meaning. It can be helpful to check out exactly what we mean, not to deny problems, but to exercise some responsibility and choice about the reality of our emotional and cognitive world.

Unrealistic Goals

I want to train to be a ballet dancer, said the eighty-three year old woman with arthritis. I want my dead husband back, said the bereft young widow. I want to win the lottery said just about everyone! Fortunately for us, unrealistic goals are nearly always phrased as  strategies rather than true goals. What the person asks for is usually an action, experience or something to happen, rather than an emotion or state (true or absolute goal). Thus the automatic challenge, which is almost always effective, is the one which helps the client discover what it is that they will achieve through the action, experience or happening. For example:

■ 'So if you could actually become a ballet dancer what does that feel like? ' - *'Oh a sense of freedom, feeling the audi-ence appreciate me, feeling proud, a sense of achievement'* 'How many other things can you think of , perhaps easier to achieve, that might result in those feelings of freedom, pride, being appreciated and that sense of achievement?'

- 'I know that you realise that to have your husband back is impossible, but perhaps you could tell me what you miss about him most?' - *'Oh him just being there, to hold me, to be able to share things with him, to be part of someone. To feel loved.'*
'So if he was here with you now holding you, what would you feel?' *'Secure, loved, belonged to.'*
'So you might hope that at some time in the future, when the sadness and loneliness you feel now is less acute, you may be able to find ways of feeling loved, secure and be-longed to - again?'

- 'I guess lots of people want to win the lottery - but if you did- what exactly would you want for you?' - *'Lots of things - new car, house, boat, to live in the country, give up work, have a holiday, oh all sorts of things.'*
'Okay, so say you've got all those things, what do they all achieve for you personally, for example what do you get from a holiday, giving up work, living in the country?' - *'Freedom, space, to be able to choose what I want to do for a change.'*
'So the lottery is just one way of getting those things, I'll bet you could get some of those things without having to win the lottery though couldn't you?'
It is important to remember that the challenge is issued to the client for them to determine what is realistic and unre-alistic, even when it is tempting for the counsellor to as-sert their own view, or choose what they believe is a realis-tic goal.

Goal Hierarchy or Ladder

It seems to us that there is a lot of confusion about what consti-tutes a goal, and how it differs from a strategy. This is evidenced by how few people seem to be clued in to their own personal or profes-sional goals.

This assertion is justified and exemplified when you explore what you say to yourself when in a crisis or stuck. The burning question is often 'What *shall / can / should / ought* I to do?' If this rings a bell for you, then the point is made. Good facilitators, communicators, and consultants help people ask the more appropriate question . . . What do I want instead? Helpful prompts which help people get in touch with their futures are the Willy-wobblers:-

What Would It Look Like If It Were A Little Bit Better?
What Would It Look Like If It Were A Lot Better?
What Would It Look Like If It Were Perfect?

All these are ways of asking What do I **want?** The question may be qualified by the use of suffixes such as 'professionally', 'personally', or 'organisationally', but it is always specified as a future wish, desire or want, not in terms of an action. That comes after you know what you want!

Principle: Knowing what you want and examining the ethical, moral or consequential issues surrounding it must logically come before 'ways of achievement' strategies are generated.

Goals are closely associated or synonymous with values, and ultimate goals are always consonant with a person's value orientation. Ultimate or pure goals are always specified in terms of emotions or states of being, e.g. At peace, stimulation, challenge, freedom, free to choose, independent, relaxed, fulfilled, satisfied etcetera. It is important to notice that it would be highly unlikely for an individual to have only one ultimate goal, especially when goals often compete for fulfilment. For example one may want peace, but to have nothing but peace might produce a state of boredom. Therefore the goal of peace would occasionally be in competition with other goals such as excitement and challenge. This leads to the insight that a way of helping people express their ultimate goals more practically is to insert the word **'more'** in front of them. Thus, once someone's goal to achieve 'peace of mind' is uncovered, it can be quickly converted to 'more peace of mind' in order to immediately assign it greater realistic possibility.   When this has been done they have been converted to what can now be termed **1st level** goals.

At the next level of the hierarchy are **'Second level'** abstract type goals. These are often expressed with some behavioural component attached, but are not yet behavioural goals.   For example people may say that they would like to be able to be successful, have greater self esteem, to be more socially skilled, assertive, more loveable, and so on. These are not the highest level of pure goals or even 1st level goals because they can have the question 'What will that achieve for you' addressed to them, and an answer can be given.

The next level can be termed **behavioural goals,** as they are specified in terms of what will be happening if the ultimate goal was achieved. Note this is still expressed in the future tense i.e. **I will be able to** - say .... do .... go .... see.... think...... feel...... It is vital to note that this is different to expressing what **has to be done** in order to achieve the goal! Although this is very subtle it is extremely important to differentiate a goal from a strategy. Behavioural goals are generally useful to clients because they can be tested for criteria that ensure they are realistic. You can ask of them:

Is that under your control?	(Ownership)
Is it within your resources?	(Ownership)
Is it worthwhile?	(Substantive)
Does it seem right?	(Appropriate)
Will it really be so different?	(Substantive)
Will you know that you've achieved it?	(Measurable)
Will you feel OK with that if you achieved it?	(Values)
What will be the consequences of achieving that goal?	
	(Commitment)
What would be the consequence of not achieving that goal?	
	(Commitment)

Remember at this point to help clients develop positive goals not negative goals. For example, saying 'I won't be anxious any more', 'there'll be less hassle , 'people won't belittle me', 'I won't feel disappointed' is simply respecifying the problem, not saying what they want instead. When meeting these negative goals simply say:- 'So what would you feel instead of anxiety?' 'So what would you like to replace hassle with?' 'So what would people be doing instead of belittling you?', 'So what will disappointment be replaced with?'

Any subsequent work on goals after this level will probably be approaching strategies. Bear in mind that some grand strategies look very much like goals. For example 'to win the lottery' looks like a goal; it is of course simply a means to the goal, or something that has to be done (or appears to) first before the goal can be reached.

To explore up and down the ladder between goals and strategies two very simple questions are used.

To go up:

In response to any client utterance which involves an action ask **'and what is it that you think that will achieve for you?'**

To go down towards strategies:

In response to any abstract or vague description ask **'and what exactly would that look like in practice?'**

Variations on this may be any of the following specific questions:-

What would you be saying, thinking, doing? What would other people be saying, thinking or doing? In this better future vision what would an average day look like?

An example of a 'goal to strategy ladder might look like this:-

'Goal to Strategy' Ladder

Ultimate or Pure Goal	Security
1st level goal	'More' Secure
2nd level goal	Able to cope with stress, be successful, more assertive.
Behavioural goal	I will be saying what I mean. My heart rate will stay down. I will be able to make decisions easier. I will communicate openly with my partner. I will work more efficiently.
Grand Strategies	Get demoted. Win the lottery and retire. Find another job.
General Strategies	Work on my assertiveness. Take up a re laxing hobby. Do a course on decision making.
Possible Strategies	Talk to my children. Say 'no' more often. Learn to prioritise.
Micro strategy	Buy a cinema season ticket. Take the earlier bus to work. Do feelgood session when I come in. Try not to look out of win dow at 11.30 for Diet Coke man.

For us, this work with possible futures is key to change work. So often people make a change with no real consideration of what they would like instead, rather than what they want to be doing.

Finally in this section, a little story which illustrates how strategies and goals are connected, and how, ultimately, fate often has a hand. Have you ever heard of Lupe Velez? Lupe Velez was a movie star in the thirties, who went downhill and hit skid row. Lupe's ambition, her goal in life, was to achieve immortality and notoriety. Since she hadn't been able to do this through her acting, she decided to make one final act to achieve her ambition, i.e that she *would* be remembered, by becoming notorious for the way that she died. She planned, then, a lavish suicide. Picture the scene; a beautiful hotel bedroom decked with flowers and candles, favourite music playing, sheets made of satin, and Lupe's gown made of silk. Lupe takes her tablets and lies down, imagining how beautiful she will look on the front pages of tomorrow's newspapers.

What Lupe hasn't reckoned with, however, is the chemical reaction between the tablets she has taken and her last chosen meal, lobster thermidor and fresh strawberries. Feeling distressed and nauseous, Lupe stumbles to the bathroom, trips on the marble steps and falls headlong into the toilet. There she stays until she is found the next morning. Her unusual death hits the headlines. So, even though things might not happen the way we planned, if we know where we want to get to, they have a habit of working out anyway.

Summary

This has been quite a lengthy exposition, then, suggesting what sort of things we might challenge within counselling. These have been suggested as the following:

- Ownership - of problems and of goals
- Strengths, qualities and 'positive' emotions
- Discrepancies in behaviour, wants, others' evaluations, perceptions, cause and effect, fact and interpretation
- Thinking patterns ; absolutes, behaviours and proposed behaviours, prejudice and stereotyping
- Unrealistic expectations of self, others and life
- Unrealistic goals.

It is perhaps equally important to have some idea of what not to challenge, and the next section addresses this question.

What not to challenge

Values and Beliefs

Generally speaking, it is not appropriate for a counsellor who believes in the fundamental principle of self determination to attempt to persuade, or challenge a client's values or beliefs. This is perhaps quite easy to appreciate when the belief is, say, religious, for it then seems obvious that we would not challenge a commitment to Judaism, or Buddhism - doesn't it? In 'good' counselling practice, no-one would challenge such self defining issues such as these. However, with a little more thought, it can be easily seen how this might get complicated.

For example, what if the religious fundamentalist wanted to join the very same abort 'imperfect' foetus group as the client outlined above, that in fact their value system resulted in out and out prejudice which was detrimental to others? What if the client had some obvious 'delusion' (a false belief that cannot be shaken by reason or argument and is not in keeping with the person's cultural context) such as a belief that they *are* God? What if their religion is a Satanic cult which makes live sacrifices? Here the counsellor would have to make decisions on the basis of their contract with the client, their personal and professional ethics, and their experience and judgement.

Generally, however, it is not the place of the counsellor to challenge values which are simply different from ours. For example, we might see the nuclear family unit as a very negative structure in society, whereas it may be the belief in this very structure which prevents one client from leaving home. People who have a strong belief in the sanctity of heterosexual Church blessed marriage will need to consider this as an important value if they are unhappy in their marriage. Such intrusions into the spiritual areas of a clients values and beliefs should generally speaking be avoided, unless they are detrimental to others. A veritable minefield!

Of course, values and beliefs will be affected during the counselling process. It could be argued that this is a part of the efficacy of counselling, and we believe that it would be impossible to interact in some deep and meaningful way without engaging with the client's (and in a certain sense, the counsellor's) values and beliefs. However, it is not generally the counsellors job to challenge, change or interfere with clients values and beliefs from our perspective, but simply to invite exploration of those that exist in the client's selfhood for them to consider if change is required.

Both of us have come across clients that have alien, and sometimes repulsive value systems. Working with sexual abusers, for example, has required courage to invite them to explore their values and beliefs; without such exploration, no change is possible for them. Where we consider that there is possible motivation for change, it has been both reasonable and possible to suspend judgement in order to facilitate exploration. On the other hand it has been mostly quite obvious with careful attention when the client has no intention of exploring their values, with a view to changing their behaviour towards a more social end. For these individuals, the most charitable interpretation is that they are not ready for challenge, and the most forsaking conclusion is that they are beyond the pale. Whichever of the latter conclusions is drawn, the counsellor is faced with a client who is currently choosing to stay as they are; it is not within the remit of the counsellor to continue working with this person. Sometimes society says that this person requires treatment in order to *compulsorily* effect change. We do not believe that this is possible with a counselling approach.

Values and beliefs are a complex area, inviting many paradoxes to operate within counselling:

- Respect values and beliefs, acknowledge they might need to be explored, possibly changed;
- Don't operate your own values and beliefs: believe in the value of counselling;
- Don't challenge your client's beliefs - unless they're prejudicial or oppressive (and guess who gets to evaluate?);
- Suspend your values, unless you make an ethical or clinical judgement not to work with this client.

Ultimately, we do the best we can with an awareness of these paradoxes. The best check we can think of for ourselves in unclear situations is what challenge will achieve for us personally, for us professionally, for the client and for the agency - what purpose will it serve? We can only make our best judgement based on skill and experience.

Past Behaviour

Challenging past behaviour is largely a waste of time. The past has gone, the present and the future is of the paramount concern to the counselling practitioner. This does not mean that past behaviour is not sometimes useful to reflect upon in order to explore the rationale for its manifestation. Neither does it mean that lessons cannot be learned from the examination of past behaviour. On occasions it may be helpful to cite examples of past behaviour in an attempt to enable the client to see what it achieved. This may be an example of a challenge, but its *purpose* is to challenge the present behaviour or proposed behaviour; it is not in itself a challenge to the behaviour of the past.

When to challenge
When confusion exists

Confusion is a sure sign that some sort of challenge is required. Mostly this simply means that the client needs to be challenged to slow down, to sort out exactly what is going on, and to carefully attribute the emotions experienced to the situation or events they derived from. Sometimes confusion indicates that some of the client's thinking or conceptualisation about something has been shaken, or that values that previously served the client well are now under review. Things that were taken as read by the client previously may now be doubted. The counsellor's task in these situations is to enable thorough exploration of the confused ideas and to look at them carefully without panic.

When the relationship is solid

Strong challenges are like strong medicine; they are very powerful and therefore need to be used in small doses. One thing that we are both sure about is that strong challenges will not be heard unless the relationship between the client and counsellor is sound. Any lack of trust, or insecurity within the relationship is a precluder of strong challenge. The relationship needs to be one that leaves the client in no doubt that the counsellor is for them , on their side , and definitely not critical of them, and counsellors need to be very honest with themselves about this. Without this certainty within the relationship, or of the *intention* of the counsellor, any challenge may be perceived as an attack, and therefore potentially damaging to the therapeutics, or at the very least, largely a waste of time. This is not to say that gentle challenge is not sometimes appropriate when there seems to be difficulty in the relationship. If there is a perceived lack of trust, or reluctance from the client, then the counsellor might want to be immediate about this - 'I notice that you look uncomfortable with me today, and wonder whether you have difficulty with trusting me with this material'. This can be part of the formation of the relationship, in that slight risk might up the trust levels.

When the purpose is clear

The counsellor should know why they are challenging. Many of the tapes and discussions with students indicate to us that challenging skills are the most difficult skills to acquire. This is partly due to the fact that challenge requires a significant amount of confidence from the counsellor, and also because effective challenges are so difficult to teach. The basic skills of counselling can be simulated into practice groups using real material, and students gain confidence in using them. Unfortunately simulating situations where challenge is appropriate is much more difficult, and so fewer opportunities arise. Given this lack of opportunity to practice, it is not surprising that knowing exactly when and how to challenge in the real sessions with clients becomes difficult. This may mean that our preference to have a clear purpose before you challenge might be a little obscure. However, there are some guidelines in regard to purpose which we can offer.

Challenge is purposeful to the following ends:

- ■ To help the client avoid making *assumptions* about themselves, their world, and their relationships;

- ■ To enable the client to look at their story from all angles, to consider a wider view, and to see their story more 'objectively';

- ■ To see the positives of their account not just the negatives;

- ■ To be able to see themselves and their behaviour as others see them and it;

- ■ To help clients take care about decisions; to consider cost and consequences of actions; and to weigh carefully all of their options and choices.

When you know what you're doing

To practice challenging is necessary at some point in order to change from novice helper to a more effective and accomplished counsellor. So it is obvious that at some point the trainee counsellor will have to practice before they know what they are doing. However, it behoves the trainee or inexperienced counsellor to plan appropriate challenges and discuss these with their tutors and supervisors rather than plunging in impulsively and damaging the relationship which took such hard work to build.

When the data is accurately perceived

Be aware that challenging should be based around *accurate data* acquired from the client. Wild guesses or stabs in the dark are not an appropriate starting point for a challenge. Imagine a client discloses his story which is about his divorce. Although the story is related calmly the counsellor responds with:-

'You felt upset when your marriage broke up and although you sound very calm, I sense that underneath you are very tense.' - *'What on earth makes you say that, I didn't feel at all tense until you said that'.*

The counsellor who was guessing or making wild stabs in the dark can do nothing but apologise in situations such as this. However the counsellor who based the guess on accurately perceived data can recover:-

'Well, I can see that you re upset by my remark, but it was simply that I noticed when you talked about you wife leaving your hands were clenched and your knuckles looked white, however, I m sorry if I got that wrong. *'No you didn't really get it wrong...its just that I am angry and I suppose it irritates me to be so transparent'.*

Then I was slightly wrong, its anger rather than tension. And it irritates you when that shows despite yourself?'

There is no substitute for accurate observation, and it is these observations that are the precursor to good data based challenges.

When not to challenge

Too Early, Impulsively, or Constantly

Perhaps the title of this section makes the point without very much extra to be said, but for those that need reminding:

- The relationship must be one of negotiated understanding before challenges can be made effectively.

- Because something is alien to your values or seems strange or foreign does not mean you have to impulsively challenge it. Think before you leap; you may be interfering with the integrity of the clients values and beliefs.

- Constant challenge will inevitably place a strain on the relationship between yourself and the client, warmth may be perceived as waning, and it is possible that you may signal judgementalness to the client.

When you are emotionally affected by the material

On a similar note to that of impulsive challenge, we would warn the counsellor who contemplates challenge when they are immersed in a swell of emotion generated by the client's material. On one such occasion one of us challenged a client's partner about his violent behaviour. This was done rather unskilfully, from a position of judgement, and so strongly, that although it generated a good feeling immediately afterwards, the repercussions of it are unknown to this day. This is particularly worthy of reflection because in this case the client and her partner failed to return for further sessions.

How to challenge

Invitationally

Challenge is best achieved by invitation. That is, the client feels invited to reflect upon an issue, goal, discrepancy or behaviour. The client is therefore freely contemplating the alternative possibilities and ways of addressing issues, not being dragged kicking and screaming into the counsellors cold reality or more objective frame. An effective challenge is easy to distinguish from an ineffective one. How? Watch the reaction of the client to the challenge; if the posture changes to one manifesting offence, hostility or defence, then you've probably wasted your breath. On the other hand if the client's eyes look upward, and although relaxed they look pensive, then the challenge has probably been successful, simply because it has invited more careful thought.

As well as stating the obvious, that effective challenges are delivered in a timely tactful and sensitive way, there are some useful technical skills which have been most helpful to us in our endeavours in counselling. We cannot cover them all here, but would like to set out and illustrate our own version of some of the 'classic' challenging skills.[4]

To do or to dare: the Classic Challenging Skills: Empathy Sandwich

The 'Empathy Sandwich',[5] or data-based hunch, is our version of advanced accurate empathy. What is meant by this is that at some point the counsellor may have a very strong feeling, based on some information gathered, that the client is feeling something other than what has been overtly disclosed. At this point the counsellor may start with an empathic statement, "......" offer the hunch or strongly suspected emotion that the counsellor is fairly sure of "........", and then follow up with a "here and now" empathic response. This final part acts to prevent the counsellor being too far away from the client with the hunch if it is inaccurate. It prevents the client feeling "second guessed" or that the counsellor is in some way making assumptions. Thus the final empathic response is for safety, so if s/he has got it wrong then s/he still remains with the client. Example:

A client has described an incident where they were attacked by someone they considered a friend; as well as being surprised, they are very angry. Here is an example of the empathy sandwich:

Empathic response
'You say that when you were beaten up, you were both surprised and angry, and you still seem to be very angry.'

Playing the data-based hunch
'I'm not absolutely sure, but the way you told me, makes

me wonder if perhaps you feel . . . a little bewildered by the whole incident.' (Client looks relieved yet startled)

Follow up empathic response
'You seem a bit surprised, and yet relieved, and yet this might make it a bit easier to talk about?'

The important thing to note here is that even if the hunch had been wrong the follow up empathy would have ensured that the development of the relationship and the growing understanding would not be entirely lost. Consider what might happen if the hunch was wrong:

Empathic response
'You say that when you were beaten up, you were both surprised and angry, and you still seem to be very angry'

Playing the data-based hunch
'You still feel some hatred towards your friend even though it was a long time ago' (Client looks startled and irritated)

Followed up empathic response
'You look startled and a bit irritated...I guess I got that quite wrong'

When hunches are data driven, they are not likely to be very wrong very often; however, at times they will be wrong, and it is helpful to know that by careful attending, it is not too difficult to retrieve the situation. This is important as this sort of hunching skill is absolutely invaluable in moving the client on.

Immediacy

Immediacy is a skill that a counsellor may need to use from time to time to get things moving. Sometimes clients and counsellors can get stuck, and the thing that is making them stuck is the relationship between them, or the feelings of the counsellor.

It may be, for instance, that the counsellor believes that the client is avoiding the issue, and because of this she or he is getting irritated and frustrated. It may be that previously the counsellor got something wrong and the client has lost trust with them, or even some emotional issue is arising such as love, sexual arousal, or revulsion that requires resolving before effective counselling can continue. It may also be that the counsellor is fantasising about what s/he thinks the client is thinking, when actually they themselves have some uncertainty or embarrassment. These sorts of barriers to effective counselling need to be skilfully shared with the client in order to move on. Immediacy is therefore one of the most powerful tools to prevent circular discussion. Immediacy addresses what is going on here/between us .

For example, a client of ours who had experienced considerable homophobia amongst his peers talked at length about his suspicions that straight people always had some prejudice against gay men. He had disclosed many of his sexual preferences, history and disappointments, and had developed considerable insights into what he wanted in a relationship. At this point, he had moved into bemoaning how difficult it was to get this and what hostility he was up against. The counsellor had questioned their own responses to the client, and was now imagining that the client was feeling hostile towards them.

'I am aware that recently the tone of the sessions have changed. Forgive me if I m wrong, but I'm wondering if you feel a bit uncertain of me, or a bit hostile towards me just now? I know I've just felt a bit uncomfortable, and I was just wondering what it was about'.

This disclosure from the counsellor makes it clear that any issue between them both can be addressed directly and that there is no need for game playing. Such immediacy enabled the client to declare apprehensions and also his own ambiguity in terms of totally trusting the counsellor, and yet feeling sceptical at times that 'really', they were just like everybody else. The work could then continue. To be this direct on quite sensitive issues can take considerable courage, but is absolutely essential for the effective professional relationship to be maintained.

Quite recently, one of us received a phone call from an ex- student of ours requesting some personal counselling. In crude terms our recollection was that the student had had a crush on the tutor. It would have been unhelpful simply to refuse counselling because of a hunch, yet perhaps asking for trouble to simply ignore the recollection. Using immediacy skills, the issue was raised there and then over the phone, and the suspicion was confirmed. Once this secondary agenda was out in the open and clearly and overtly clarified, the opportunity for some effective counselling and help for the ex-student was open.

Principle: Get the shadows into the light, don't let hidden agendas on either side stop good practice.

Confrontation

This skill is often misunderstood as somewhat adversarial. Confrontation really means to confront the clients strengths, to confront the clients resources, talents and skills, and place these into the framework that the client has brought. This can sometimes be used in combination with immediacy to invite the client to look at blocks or unacknowledged barriers to good interpersonal client/counsellor relationships. It may also involve confronting discrepancies in what is said, or how it is said, from a data base.

Challenging strengths such as courage to proceed, trust in the counsellor and commitment to be honest, are extremely valuable. Clients may seem to be hopeless, or helpless, and yet the counsellor may be able to help them to marshal all their resources. As previously mentioned, (see discrepancies) sometimes clients make smoke screens, and sometimes clients will play games. Confrontation is a way of enabling them to use their resources, skills and talents to prevent these disabling strategies. This is a way of helping the clients see their skills, talents and resources in a more objective and focused way.

Information Giving

Information giving is the skill of neutrally offering information which may help the client see their problem from a different point of view. This is NOT by offering advice NOT EVEN in disguise. It is often possible to present facts and information that challenge the fixed perception of the client and them to look at the problem from a different perspective. For example, bereaved clients may believe that they are going mad because they keep seeing or sensing the deceased presence . To be able to inform them that this is in fact a common phenomenon experienced by many bereaved people, is not reassurance for the sake of it, but information which invites the client to reframe the way they

have construed themselves. A client diagnosed as being HIV+ may think that this means impending death, whereas accurate information challenges this perspective, while fears are empathically acknowledged.

Self Disclosure

Self-disclosure is most appropriately used when the counsellor briefly shares an emotion or experience that was similar to the client's. This is usually done only when it appears that the client is having difficulty disclosing. The invitation to share the counsellor's world is issued in the hope that it will serve to reinforce the client's courage to discover more about their own world and disclose it more freely. For example, if the counsellor has themselves been through a particular experience which may be similar, some of the more deeply held feeling and issues may be shared if there is a hunch that these deeper hidden feelings are also being experienced by the client. An illustration may best serve this description here.

The counsellor has been through a divorce, and the client is talking about their divorce. The counsellor thinks they may be detecting some issues around a sense of failure for the client, however they are not entirely sure because they themselves had such issues and this may be simply contamination from identification. It is both tested and used therapeutically in the following way:

> Counsellor - 'When you talk about your divorce, I can see that you are both angry and shocked by what has happened.......One of the things that really got to me during my divorce was a deeper sense that in some way I'd....failed.....I sometimes get the sense that this might be true of you too, would that be right, or am I miles off beam?'

The astute counsellor will of course observe the client's response to be certain that they agree or disagree honestly, not simply to please, and thus ensure that words have not been placed in the client's mouth.

Summarising

Summarizing as a challenging skill is slightly different to summarizing as a basic skill. It is often possible to summarise a whole range of issues and resources back to the client for them to review within a more systematized and structured approach. The counsellor using summarising as a challenge would pull together any themes running through the individual's life, which in isolation may mean little, but together may well be enlightening. However, great care must be taken to ensure that negatives are seen in context to the individual's strengths and resources which are enabling rather than disabling; a good summary is a full summary, not a selective trip into the mire and the mud.

Paradoxical Challenge

One of the nicest things to happen to anyone in counselling, is to have developed something which you think is useful and then to read somewhere that it is an advanced technique which some eminent expert is recommending. Paradoxical challenge is one of these. Both of us have developed what we called skilled and sensitively timed sarcasm in our counselling practice. On occasions we have found it almost irresistible to sensitively provoke the client to respond when they seem to have lost all sense of proportion in their selflessness. The sort of style we are advocating does need to be carefully executed, and counsellors do need to understand the potential of this approach to backfire. However, consider the following example.

> Mavis White was a keen student, with a responsible job in an accounting firm, before she fell in love and married Ted. Over the last twenty nine years she has relinquished any ambitions she had in deference to her husband, her home and her two sons. Promising herself that she would have her life of independence once the children were grown up. It would be then her time and she could free herself of her loveless marriage and develop her own interests. Her husband's stroke therefore came as a crippling blow, leaving her feeling trapped, helpless and with no future.

The counsellor, having spent some frustrating time trying to confront Mavis's issue with empathy and conventional challenge, is getting nowhere. Paradoxical challenge is worth a try.

Counsellor -'So Mavis, for twenty-nine years, you have cooked, cleaned, and supported your husband and sons through all of their difficulties. You have put their needs first every time, taken a back seat in all situations, and now when you had hoped for a future of your own, once again someone else is more important than you. And you feel disappointed. Well how selfish can you be, that's all you think of isn't it? You, you, you!'

The counsellor's hope is that this will provoke the client to indeed think slightly more selfishly, and restore the balance of reality; however, care is needed because in the actual session it would not be unthinkable for Mavis to say 'Yes, I suppose I am aren't I'.

We have found this approach invaluable, however, in terms of reality testing when clients feel really stuck. In sexual abuse work, it is a very useful challenge when the client insists on feeling responsible for the abuse because of an ingrained feeling of guilt. It can be very useful to put together the data you have heard with the irrational feeling of the client:

> So you tell me that you were five years old, about three foot six in height, and weighed four stone; you were frightened for your life as you really believed that if you told anyone, you would be killed; and your abuser was about six foot tall, maybe sixteen stone, and in his forties. Yes , I can really see how his systematic assaults on you were all your fault, and how easy it would have been for you to stop them.

Of course such a challenge needs to be well timed and in a context of other challenging and supportive behaviours, but it can help the client to see how unfounded her (his) perspective is , and this can begin to challenge the strength of feeling which accompanies it.

Challenging from Time Frames

While skills fuel the process of effective challenge, there are also frames of challenge, which, when understood, will work through a variety of means. One of the most effective frames which we use for challenging is that of time. However stuck a client is, a change in time frame can be very liberating. This is why life-threatening illness can be so powerful an energiser - it reminds the individual that they are truly mortal, and that each day will never come again. Sometimes, then, it is an effective challenge to simply ask the client to imagine that they have only six months left to live - what would be truly important? This can help to get in touch with goals and priorities. Similarly, we can take the client on a little time travel, invite them to stand in a position which represents a year hence - where will they be, what will they be doing, and what might they have had to do to get there? Possibilities are endless in how we approach this frame.

Time frame can also be used to help to challenge the client in the here and now. For a client who repeatedly beats about the bush, or who might have a habit of dropping a bombshell in the last minute, a simple invitation to treat the beginning of the session *as if* it were the last five minutes of the last session, can be very challenging. What things really must have been addressed? What feelings/attitudes/behaviours must really be changing? Playing with time can be very productive.

In sum

We have tried in this chapter to outline some principles of what to challenge, when to challenge and how to challenge. Clearly, there are many more ways of challenging, and we would particularly direct the interested reader to some of the cognitive-behaviourists cited earlier in the chapter. However, our concern is not too much with exactly *how* you challenge, in terms of which precise intervention or skill you pick, but that the general principles of challenging are better understood and therefore that the work can remain fruitful.

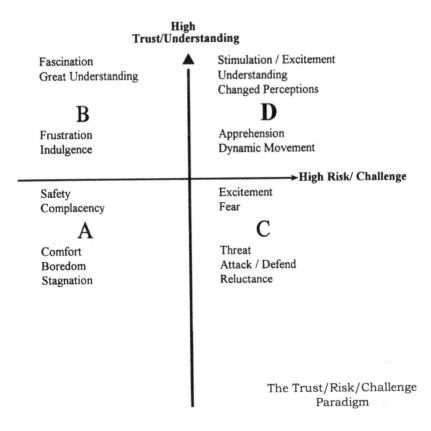

The Trust/Risk/Challenge Paradigm

We would also argue that *not* to challenge is to do the client a disservice; counselling cannot move forward without it. We use the preceding paradigm to summarise some of the principles of challenging. The idea is that with counselling, the degree of understanding will enable the degree of challenge, and vice versa. Equally, on a relationship level, the counsellor and client must take risks in order to increase the level of trust. These qualities have an incremental relationship to each other.

If a climate is engendered of low risk/trust, low understanding/ challenge, then little movement will take place. In this quadrant of the diagram, (quadrant A) the client will feel somewhat confused and anxious; nothing is happening, and there is no movement. For a short time, this might engender a level of comfort, which will quickly turn to boredom. If there is an increase in trust and understanding, but no challenge or risk, then the client and counsellor will stay in quadrant B and develop a very cosy, very gratifying in depth understanding of the client's life, which will lead to a certain level of indulgence and a high degree of safety.. If we move to quadrant C, where challenge and risk are high, but the right to challenge has not yet been earned through understanding, then the client will feel unheard, attacked, unsafe, jolted, and yet there may be something of an adrenaline rush which makes them prepared to risk that quadrant again. If the risk/challenge is incrementally increased in proportion to empathic understanding and trust, however, then we move to quadrant D and get some dynamic movement. Here change is likely to occur. Sometimes this will make for dissonance or discomfort in the process, but this is part of shifting perceptions, habits, ways of thinking, and ways of feeling. It is therefore crucial that the counsellor as well as the client can take risks, and this depends on their ability to self-challenge.

- Have I really understood? Have I even listened accurately?
- Am I really assertive enough to interrupt my client?
- What stopped me using immediacy there?
- Am I frightened that my client won't like me if I challenge? Do I want their approval?
- Am I avoiding whole areas here?
- Am I scared that I might fail?
- Am I scared of the emotions I might uncover here?
- How can I change some of this?

These are just some of the many questions which a counsellor might ask themselves in order to be really self-challenging. We are quite sure, however, that the ability and willingness to challenge effectively are *crucial* to fruitful counselling. The key is to challenge incrementally from a position of understanding and to remain empathic with the client's response to the challenge.

Endnotes:

1. We use this term in the sense of moral non-judgementalness, outlined in Chapter Three. We accept that we are making a clinical judgement when we decide to make challenges.

2. George Kelly, Aaron Beck and Albert Ellis are the pioneers in regard to cognitive therapies, the work referred to in the text borrows liberally from these three authors whose works are recommended in their own right: See Kelly, G. (1955), Ellis, A. (1962) and Beck, A. T. (1976)

3. Just to illustrate how precious the counselling world can be, let us indulge you in the story of the counselling meeting which one of us attended. Introductions were made through the usual types of exercise - chat to a partner for fifteen minutes over coffee, find out various bits of information which will enable you to introduce them to the group. It seemed so precious, that Jan declared that she did SLAP therapy - this was proposed as a severe cognitive challenging therapy for Slow Learners And Procrastinators . The partner was fascinated, and introduced Jan accordingly. Not a titter was heard in the room, as the whole group thought that this was a new kind of therapy, and asked interested questions over the day. If only we'd got the article published as well......

4. These are attributable to Egan (1994), and can be found in his 5th. edition of The Skilled Helper .

5. Our thanks go to Tony Ford for this gem of a term.

Chapter Five. Tight Lips but Heavy Hearts

Introduction

When we teach counselling and counselling skills, we are often asked the question 'what if the client isn't very articulate'? There can be a tendency to see counselling as a somewhat precious activity, only accessible for those who can articulate emotions. We would argue strongly that this is not the case. Counselling relies on the skills of communication: if the client is not an 'orthodox' communicator, then there is a challenge to the counsellor to find a way of building rapport and understanding. This may be at the level of speaking plainly. For example, we can describe a helping framework in terms of 'past issues, current issues, future scenarios, and strategic planning', and we can allude to transferences, or projections, or whatever jargonese we choose to hijack understanding. Or we can ask 'what's up, what d'you want instead, what can you do to get it?'. And we can just say if it seems that the client is putting us in a particular role, or if we feel particular vibes or energies - we don't have to explain in psychodynamic terms. It's as well to remember that any terms or language that we use constitute only a description of human behaviour, not a mystical science.

This chapter, then, offers a context for developing the use of alternatives to spoken language. Sometimes, however we speak, whatever language is used, there is still difficulty in communicating. Alternative approaches can help address the kind of stuckness you can feel if you have both run out of words, yet the client still wants to seek some change or some help. This might apply to any of us at particular stages or in particular situations, or it might apply if the client is not at all practised in talking about themselves or their feelings.

Contexts for creativity

Years ago, one of us (Janice) had occasion to develop a counselling service for young adults who were identified as having learning difficulties. This somewhat (then newly trendy) catch-all expression described a whole range of people, those for whom the school system hadn't worked, those who had a specific condition such as dyslexia, those who had emotional and behavioural difficulties, and those who had suffered some measure of brain damage. This was a group of people, then, with very diverse needs and abilities. What they had in common was a lack of practice in expressing themselves in conventional or mainstream ways. The challenge for us as helpers, then, was to find ways in which we could communicate which did not depend on words and articulation in any conventional sense.

Later experience of counselling on a University campus offered further insights. Again, the client group represented a very diverse group of people who at that period of their life were clumped together under the label of students. A curious phenomenon was observed. A certain cluster of students presented who were at the top end of the academic range, amazingly able to articulate ideas and to operate outstandingly in the academic field. They were people with tremendously well developed learning *abilities.* However, the students who are in mind found it tremendously difficult, and sometimes impossible, to identify or articulate their emotional lives, and presented with relationship difficulties and issues around low self-esteem. The challenge for the helpers was exactly that which faced us in the centre for those with learning difficulties - how to find effective channels of communication which had meaning and impact.

Both of us have also worked in the field of mental health. Many of the people we worked with were in states of being where they were mentally dysfunctional in some way. Two aspects to this experience have importance for this chapter. First, how to find means of expression where realities[1] were distorted, distractions high and concentration span low. Secondly, how to help people express themselves in way over which they had some charge, and where the expression of emotion was not go-

'It says here it can't be done, so why don't we all go for an early lunch?'

ing to exacerbate distress and dysfunction rather than relieve it. Therefore, we had to develop creative ways of counselling, where counselling was an appropriate option.

Much of conventional counselling revolves around the agreed activity of articulating emotion, or expressing feeling. Within our opportunities and challenges of working with people who find it difficult or impossible to articulate emotion in any conventional sense, we have long realised, like many of you, no doubt, that words have their limitations. They are immensely helpful; we negotiate shared meaning and understanding to the same ball park via the use of words, and we develop useful shorthand. In one sense, then, as representational symbols, words are incredibly useful.

Words are also impoverished. Have you ever experienced an occasion or event when you just could not find the word which would describe the portrait you wish to paint, or the sensation you wish to recount, or to capture the sound which you hold in your mind. Have you ever had the experience of thinking that you have described something in a way which others will understand, only to find that their inference from your words is different from their intended meaning?

And have you ever noticed how sometimes, words just rob the experience of its uniqueness, or else make real that which is only a concept. For example, the experience of a new relationship, whether with lover, close friend, child, parent, mentor, which fills us with glee and incorporates magical moments might change in expression when related to another. It may become more mundane, less special, less unique, less enchanting.[2] And a spoken thought, a doubt, a way of analysing an event, once voiced, may transform the thought to a set of activities. This is of course well known. We have expressions such as 'it loses something in the telling', or 'once I'd said it, I wished I could take the words back'. Words can be very powerful in their effect,[3] and yet limited in terms of their accuracy.

Further, the expression of emotion is far more complex both in its form and its desirability than we sometimes acknowledge. For example, it can be tempting to think that in order to express anger, the individual must conform to some standard of clenching fists, shouting, becoming red, and so on. Yet this is not necessarily so - some people's version of expressing anger is much less visible to the outsider. Further, it can be tempting to think that in order for effective counselling to occur, then the emotion of anger (or whatever emotion is appropriate) must be expressed.

Such an idea is specific to Western psychology. Our experience of teaching counselling in Kuwait led us to question the notion of selfhood which the emphasis on expressing emotion suggests. Colleagues of ours working in Hong Kong relayed that they could not teach empathy in the Western conventional sense. To empathise with an emotion was seen as intrusive upon the self. It is far more acceptable to empathise with a less personal state, for example an acknowledgement that the bus journey had been frustrating today, or something similar.

We must then be careful not to dismiss the cognitive and to place all on the emotional. There is a fine line in counselling culture between the attempt at careful understanding, and the insistence on openness to the exclusion of privacy. One of us had occasion recently to be on an interview panel for a counselling course. A series of questions had been designed by the academic institution involved to test the candidate's suitability for counselling. As you will doubtless be aware, finding a place on a counselling course depends not only on ability to master knowledge and skills, but also on demonstrating the 'appropriate' *qualities.* On the occasion in question, a candidate expressed interest, ability, and experience, and was keen to join the course. The co-interviewer asked an extremely personal question, and the candidate replied that they did not want to respond fully as they valued their privacy. This candidate was refused entry to the course on the basis that they were not 'emotionally open'.

We are suggesting two strands of thought here, then. First, we would encourage the counsellor to become imaginative in their *forms* and *modes* of communication. Second, we would encourage the counsellor to focus not only on feelings, but on thoughts and behaviours, and to resist the temptation to *diagnose* negatively those who find it easier to express cognition rather than emotion. With these postulates in mind, then, what issues arise when we work with those who do not easily communicate in 'standard' ways?

'Of course it won't talk, it's a Robin, not a Canary!'

We would like really to help the counsellor to free themselves up to explore alternative media. So while we do not want to devalue or oversimplify the skills and expertise of the trained art therapist, or the drama therapist, for example, neither do we wish to deny that we are sensory creatures. Therefore, any medium which helps tap into the human senses is useful, and we merely urge you to experiment with what seems helpful to the client. In other words, this is simply a means of enhancing communication.

As such, the introduction of 'alternative' or 'creative' techniques remains client centred. This is not a case of the counsellor thinking 'hmm, think I'll get Reg to do a bit of drawing today, that'll make it more interesting'. The type of medium introduced needs to be either responsive to the verbal cues and clues of the client, or, if these are sparse, to be introduced as an invitation to experiment. Cues and clues to a person's preferred communication system can often be picked up through language patterns.[4] For example, some people talk in terms of what perspectives they adopt, what vision they have, how they see things. Some people talk of how they feel about things, how they want to grasp the nettle, or feel their way forward. Yet others talk about whether or not they are in tune with people or policies, whether they are on the same wavelength, and whether they can hear clearly what is being said. While language alone is not an infallible 'diagnostic' as to what medium might work, it is often a powerful indicator. Equally, it becomes apparent very quickly what is not useful for clients - some people find imagery very difficult, for example, or drama therapy. So, although it may seem obvious, it is important to try to match the medium to what might work best for each client.

If there is little clue or cue, then the counsellor might take a different tack. In this case, it is important that participation in any activity is voluntary, and that the client knows that this is really an experiment. The counsellor is needs to be up front about this, for example:

> 'We've had four sessions so far, and it seems you find it really difficult to speak about what's troubling you. I was wondering whether you'd like to try some other form of work, like drawing, or perhaps playing with clay? There aren't any guarantees that this'll help, but sometimes it does, and they're often fun to do. What do you think?'

The counsellor needs to be sensitive to the client's propensity to limit themselves through constructions regarding their abilities, i.e. a common reaction is 'I can't draw', as if the client is immediately evaluating their capability in terms of technical competence, rather than expressive potential. It is important then to try to negotiate a way through this which remains sensitive to a real 'I don't *want* to', rather than an externally imposed 'can't'.

With these points in mind, then, what follows, is a summary of some alternative methods of communication. They are intended to maximise the counsellor and the client's potential of communication through all the senses.

Painting the picture

As stated earlier, words are only symbols, symbols which can be interpreted visually or aurally. And indeed for those who are hearing impaired, it is possible to understand words through the medium of touch, through their vibrations. It is possible of course to construct other visual symbols which help people to express themselves, to develop insights, and, literally, to envision a different future.

The most commonly used approach which taps the visual sense is painting or drawing.[5] This is very simple to set up and use, requiring only pens, pencils, crayons or paints, and some type of paper. There are a number of ways of using pictures which are created by the client. They can be free drawing - whatever comes into your head. They can be drawings of how you feel now. There can be self-portraits of how you see yourself now. There can be drawings of a past event, or a specific time in the past. Sometimes it is useful to draw a lifeline, starting at birth and leading up to now, with pictures of all the key things which pop into your head. And we have found pictures invaluable when helping people to envision what they would like in the future. This can be done

'What do you mean, you didn't come to counselling to learn to paint . . . I'll decide what happens here Mister!'

by asking a client to draw a picture of how they would really like it to be, or it can be done as a continuation of the lifeline - what events would you like to see on their in a year's time, two year's time, five year's time. This is tremendously useful in introducing the possibilities of change and control, in a way which is measured and manageable.

However a picture is created, it is quite crucial that to remain within the counselling remit, then counselling principles operate. Specifically:

Principle: The picture is owned by the client, to be interpreted through their schema of understanding, not the counsellor's.

In other words, stay within the client's frame of reference. Because a picture becomes concrete, this is not an excuse to start offering our own insights over and above those of the client: 'OOH, isn't that interesting, you've drawn yourself smaller than everybody else. OOH, there's a lot of red, obviously lots of anger there'.

Pictures are very powerful media. It is said that a picture paints a thousand words, and in using client created pictures, a client might very quickly develop an insight or perspective that was previously not available, and which is quite stunning. One client drew a picture of herself as having a dark line between shoulders and neck, and a steel cage with a padlock around her heart. The realisation of what this meant for her, that her heart and head were severed from each other, was immensely powerful, and somewhat distressing.

The strength of such powerful imagery, of course, is not only in the revelations it can provide about what is happening now, but also in the potential which this then holds for change. To use the iron cage as metaphor, to draw what the client would like instead, to know what would have to happen to remake connection between the heart and the head, all of these were enabled through the art work.

A client of one of us (Graham) once drew a picture of her ideal place to be; as she talked it through, it seemed rather a common place fantasy. However, as the scenario was related, a powerful and significant difference emerged;

> 'I'd be on a deserted island, the sun would be shining, and I'd be lying in the sun with a marvellous tan. The muscular slave would bring me my Bacardi and Coke whenever I snapped my fingers. He'd apply sun tan lotion delicately and some-

times vigorously wherever and whenever I wanted. He would be at my beck and call for ANYTHING I want from him! The island has got everything I want, things to do that are interesting, but what I like best about the island is that, as you can see, on each end of the beach is a machine gun turret.'

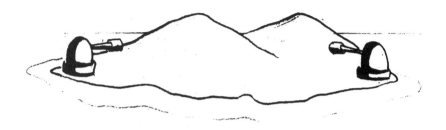

'Prepare to repel boarders and man the machine-gun turrets.'

The most important thing on this client's island was that it was safe and secure. The machine gun posts were in her words 'because no one gets on my island unless I want them to!'

Pictures are very effective when we need to create group dialogue and movement. One work team we know was involved in great dispute with their employers, and an arbitrator was called in. The arbitrator simply asked each side to produce pictures of their organisation as if it were some sort of sea vessel. This produced a number of images from one side which depicted slaves in galleys, and shark infested waters, whereas the other side genuinely believed that they were sailing some version of a cruiser! The impression that the pictures made cut through a lot of the impasse which had been reached through talking.

We have also used collage, both with individual counselling clients, training groups, and management groups who we consult to. Pictures made from cut up magazines, brochures, can all help to inspire clients, particularly in envisaging futures, or what they would like instead. The 'third person' aspect of collaging can also sometimes make it feel safer to create a depiction of a particular event, or of a state which feels uncomfortable.

Another visual medium is the camera. You may already be familiar with the practise of inviting clients to bring in photographs from particular periods in their life, of themselves or significant others, in order to help develop new insights and perspectives. When

I worked with young adults with learning difficulties, one of the media we used was the Polaroid camera along with a box full of props. Clients were invited to dress up and pose in a variety of ways: how they see themselves, how they imagine other people see them, how they think they were seen at school, at home, among friends: how they would like to see themselves; and how they would like to come across to others. This was generally experienced as fun, and generated a tremendous amount of self-awareness and energy.

As well as creating pictures on paper in some way, it is becoming increasingly easy to find visual resources in the form of cards. The tarot card has long been a consultative resource to people, although not many would perhaps use them in counselling. However, there are an increasing number of types of cards which can make for excellent visual stimulation. There are available packs of 'inner child' cards; whether or not this particular concept of the inner child is meaningful to you or your client, the cards themselves can be used as invitations to explore. Which card best illustrates how you feel now? How you felt then? How you would like to feel? What happens if you imagine yourself as the character in this card, where do you think it leads you? Again, you do not have to be an 'expert' with cards to use them as visual resources to stimulate thought and exploration.

Once you have freed up your own ability to use visual aids, then the possibilities are endless. You will be able to develop and create ways of helping your client to understand their world, and to convey what they need and want to to others. We would just say one final word on the use of visual media, and this is that they can be put away. We have found this immensely useful for two reasons in particular, although we're sure that there are many more! Firstly, the story committed to some form of paper or other material can be metaphorically closed. When emotional material is painful, this can be very useful. It can help clients to take some control over when they 'open it up' again, and can help to introduce a mental process of choice. Secondly, pictures can be compared with one another to develop some sense of progress or change, and this can be enlivening. The client who used to have a padlock on her head now draws herself as a free flowing spirit, and her earlier drawings remind her of her courage and her abilities to change, as well as her sense of identity that all of these self-images have formed who she is today. This is a powerful learning.

Feeling our way

There are those people who find it difficult to visualise or to articulate thoughts and emotions, but who find the experiences of touch and movement the easiest medium of expression. This can take many forms, which can roughly be divided into touch, as in touching with the skin, the hands, the body, or movement, where there is more a sense of the body as a whole, or perhaps as interacting with others.

The sense of touch can be stimulated through a number of different materials. One counsellor we know developed expertise with the use of clay, to offer clients the opportunity to literally mould whatever they wanted to. The finished product is of course not the only benefit; it is also the feel of the material, the texture, the consistency, the production of the finished product. The use of clay can seem quite specialised, but it is also possible to use forms of Plasticine or Play Doh for more flexible products, and more instant results.

It is also useful sometimes to play with stones, coins, or any other objects which seem appropriate. We find the use of such objects particularly useful for making 'mini-sculpts' of how a situation seems now, and how people would like to change. One client for example, who had a complex family relationship which included a number of children and stepchildren, as well as ageing relatives, found the use of coins a powerful aid. He was invited to use the coins to represent the people who were important to him in his current situation, and surprised himself at how he grouped individuals as far or near, and indeed he speculated what value he had given them. He was able to make instant adjustments to his coin-sculpt to represent where he would like to be in relation to everybody else, and vice versa. We were then able to work around what changes would have to occur to make this happen, and to develop both insights and strategies to facilitate such change.

These media can be conceptualised as crude forms of play therapy,[6] and sometimes the very act of doing such play offers a certain liberation. It is helpful if the counsellor is prepared to take a few risks and to venture into areas where they may perhaps feel a bit foolish, but if they can take this chance, it can help the client enormously. For the 'playful' counsellor, the use of dolls and figures can be very helpful; Lego people, rag dolls, teddy bears, all have their part to play if it seems that they might be useful to the client's ability to express themselves.

As well as the tactile sense of touch, some individuals find it useful to use movement as a form of counselling, and the two main media for such work are dramatherapy and dance therapy. Dramatherapy as a 'pure' discipline is well documented and derives from the pioneering work of Moreno, the Viennese psychiatrist,[7] and we believe that some of the simpler techniques are useful in different ways within counselling. If the counsellor is confident with their own framework and ability to 'catch' if things don't work out, then we would encourage a little experimentation. Four methods in particular seem specially useful to us.

One is that of 'sculpting', which we have mentioned in relation to the use of objects. Sculpting lends itself particularly to group sessions, where an individual can take others as representing members of the family, or of a love relationship, a work situation, or whatever is applicable. They can then position them as if they were marionettes, in relation to each other, and, of course, to the client. This can be helpful to both seeing and feeling how each position is; actors can give

'I didn't know that self-awareness could be so much fun.'

feedback on how it is to be standing over/under everybody else, and clients can be helped to take a 'third' position on what is happening in their situation.

Another way of using drama within counselling is to use the 'empty chair' technique established in gestalt work. Again, while gestalt is a whole system which can be studied alone,[8] it has only derived from that which happens between people; in other words, it is not highly mysterious, and the techniques may be used when offered with integrity, skill and purpose. The empty chair technique has two distinct uses. One is to imagine someone who you wish to dialogue with as sitting in an empty chair, and to express what you really want to to that imaginary person. You can then change places and respond in the position of that person. The exercise then serves several purposes: it facilitates expression of emotion and thought, it encourages a fresh perspective on the other person, and it facilitates self acceptance. Another possible use of empty chair is when the client is in that kind of situation where their conflict is internal; in other words, it exists only in their head, originating in the ingrained messages given in years gone by, internalised, and kept alive by the client's self-talk. This can make for all sorts of dilemmas.

A client who came for counselling following a long illness featuring depression and anxiety, told one of us (Graham) that he had become ill after the death of his Mother. Although 'empty chair' was not the only technique used to enable this client's recovery, it did feature very strongly in the 'breakthrough'. Listening to his story about the death of his Mother, and empathising with his sorrow and guilt, ultimately lead to the question 'what would you change that to if you could?'. 'Just to say goodbye and say I'm sorry', was his reply.

This answer suggested the technique of empty chair almost immediately. After explaining the technique, its purpose and its risks, (sometimes powerful emotions can be overwhelming for a client) he agreed to try it. The chair was firstly talked to by Graham, this serving the purpose of letting the client see that you are at least as 'barmy' as he is for doing this, thus paving the way for depleting any embarrassment. Then he was asked to speak freely to his Mother and see perhaps what she had to say to him. At one point he was prompted to ask her how she viewed his behaviour when she was dying, and if she held him responsible or to blame in any way. It was a relief to hear him say his mother not only forgave him, but told him off for being so silly! It needs to be said that MOSTLY this is the outcome; occasionally you could have a client whose Mother (or whoever is in the chair) is not so charitable, but even this can have the benefit of raising self awareness, although it may be more painful to hear a Mother say 'Yes, you did let me down, but then you always were a selfish little shit, weren't you?'.

A third liberating method which is on the edge of the dramatic is acting 'as if'. This can be used in two ways. One is in a situation which seem irresolute. For example, one couple who we counselled had a situation where the wife had taken a lover two years before counselling had begun. The affair had been short lived, and the couple had derived several benefits from having their rather complacent relationship. They were highly motivated to stay together, had a great investment in providing security for their children, had many things in common, enjoyed their sex life together, and respected each other. They identified some mutual goals and some disparate goals, and acknowledged that they would like more 'quality' time together. Despite the pain and jealousy which had been experienced, then, this couple had a lot of pluses on their side.

However, there was a mutual problem of trust. The woman in the relationship had a long-standing distrust of men, a distrust which had begun with her father, and which was reflected in her fairly radical political views which conceptualised most societal sins as emanating from patriarchal social relations. The man distrusted the woman; she had had one affair, who was to say she would not have another? They found that they were caught in a vicious circle: they went for days and sometimes weeks getting on very well, then one of them would start talking about the affair, or how they did not feel trusted.

There were various issues for working on with this couple, not all of which were interpersonal. However, the insecurity question acted as a barrier which inserted a step back for every hard earned step backwards. When the couple were asked how it would be different if they were secure, they identified a number of behavioural manifestations. They would not ring each other compulsively when they were away from home (both had demanding jobs which entailed travelling). They would not ask each other their every move when they were away. They would not worry about what the other was doing. They would not talk about the past hurts. What would they do instead then? Well, they would trust each other, and believe in each others love. They would ring home when away only if they wanted to express something positive to one another, or to use each other as supportive resources. They would spend free time when away on pursuits which were relaxing; reading, jacuzzi, cinema, sport. They would spend time talking about their future, and they would always know when their next 'quality' time together was coming up.

Sometimes a little imagination can go a long way.

118

We contracted with this couple that for the next three months, they would act *as if* they were secure with each other. The couple found it astonishingly easy. They had to check themselves once or twice, but they found it easier to enjoy the positives which they had. Behavioural changes led to changes in both cognition and emotion. This exemplifies the *as if* technique when applied to interpersonal relationships. It can also be applied to specific *situations*, rather than relationships. For example, we might be taking on a new training contract, in which we feel a little nervous. While some anxiety may be useful, we also want to acquire confidence. It can be quite simple to approach the situation *as if* we were our version of the greatest trainers on earth, someone who we really respected. How would they do it? How would they gain rapport? How would they introduce themselves? This can be a very simple and effective aid to personal presentation. And of course can apply to self-development. The woman had space to explore her intrapersonal issues, and both parties understood each other more freely.

If Music be the food of love . . .

The sense of sound is of great importance to our development, although its importance is often perhaps understated (and as you read this, just take a second to check out what senses you are using to do so). It is often the internal representation of sound which we allow to reinforce habits, behaviours and feelings which we do not wish to have. In other words, it is the words which we tell ourselves, the tones which we hear, and the frequency of their use which influence us. This means that we can allow our aural sense to be very confining. The best thing about knowing this is that we then have the power to make it very liberating.

'Blimey, this is loud.'

Consider the power of self-talk. Many people talk to themselves over the course of an average day. Such self-talk is relatively unresearched, although some little work has been carried out into the nature of such talk which suggests that it is surprisingly (or not) rooted in our distant but apparently not so dim past.[9] An average trail of self-talk is wonderfully illustrated by the following story.

Fred is sitting in his living room one Sunday afternoon in Spring. You can imagine the scene, he in his armchair, pleasantly sated after Sunday lunch, feeling warm and full, watching an afternoon movie. His eyes wander to the window, where he notices that the grass is long. A thought passes through his mind - maybe I should mow the lawn - yes, I think I'll do that. Somewhere inside, he knows that *it's good to keep the grass tidy.* Fred feels good. Suddenly, however, he realises that he hasn't had his lawnmower fixed. He swears, inwardly - inwardly, because *a gentleman doesn't swear.* Immediately, he wonders how to solve his problem, and it occurs to him that Jane next door has got a lawnmower - he could ask to borrow hers.

So far, Fred has gone through a commonplace process. He needs a lawnmower, Jane has one, perhaps he could borrow it. But wait - Fred hasn't finished talking to himself yet. As he rises from his armchair, he stops mid-movement. A voice in his head is whispering insistently - *neither a borrower nor a lender be - it isn't good to borrow.* He realises that he cannot possibly ask Jane for the lawnmower, because she will think *what a damn cheek, haven't you had your own lawnmower fixed yet? You really are hopeless.*

Fred sits down, disappointed. He ponders - no of course Jane won't think that; after all, *most people are only too pleased to help out.* And after all, mowing the lawn is a socially productive act, as well as being personally gratifying. *Your neighbours will appreciate the place being looked after.* He must have been wrong; he will go and ask Jane for the lawnmower. He rises again, exhaling, feeling more relaxed, and strides across his living room. He is hit by a moment of doubt - didn't he recently borrow the jump leads when he'd inadvertently run his car battery down? *Stupid fool, you're always so forgetful.* So wouldn't Jane think he really was very rude indeed, *Don't go bothering people, and don't show your weaknesses.* And so he pauses, sits and thinks some more.

You get the idea, and won't be surprised to know that five minutes later, Jane, who is feeling mellow after doing her yoga, hears a knock on the door. She sees through the glass that it is Fred, and thinks nonchalantly how nice it is to have friendly neighbours. She is shocked, therefore, to open the door to a crazed looking Fred who is red in the face and spluttering:

'Sod your damn lawnmower, I never wanted to borrow the flaming thing anyway!'

How often have you done this? This story was once told to one of our supervisees, who was agonizing over approaching her manager over a difficult issue. She battled with self-talk which consisted of limiting messages and fantasised responses. She was left contemplating her own decisions. Several days later, a card arrived through the post - Thanks, I borrowed the lawnmower.

With clients, it can be immensely useful to introduce clients to the idea that you can influence your own self-talk.[10] For now, we would just like to invite you to try some very simple ways of recognising that self-talk can be changed. Can you for example turn up the volume, or turn down the volume? Can you slow it down, or speed it up? Can you play music in the background, and bring it to the foreground? And can you change the content? Once these realisations are made, it is usually possible for people to find ways of challenging themselves through their own internalised messages.

'External' sound is also of course a source of memory stimulation. We hear a piece of music and it transports us back in time, either to a specific memory or to an emotional state related to such a memory.

'Your strategy is served, m'lud.'

In sum

We could go on and on in regard to using creative strategies when working with clients, but all good things must come to an end.

Remember that whatever you do, whatever strategies you use, it should always be at the service of the client. Just because you learned hypnosis last week, or new approaches in transcendental guruing, or have read a brilliant book called Blank Minds and Sticky Moments, does not mean that your next client has to be tried out on it. Nonetheless, we would wish you good luck in your creativity and wish you the traditional Quaker motto:

'Live life with adventure!

And finally, in a fundamentally creative way we will terminate this chapter.

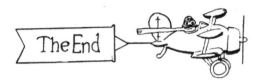

Endnotes

1. As you will know from our writing, we do not hold the position that there is one definite reality, rather it is constructed. However, neither are we total relativists. Our position then is one of realism, where we agree that individual realities are constructed, but that we have a negotiated reality with others, where, for example, six people in a room might all agree that there is a table and six chairs within it. The seventh person, who sees no table but a pride of lions instead, would, in this version of events, be experiencing a distorted reality.

2. Reyes (1995) puts this succinctly through the eyes of her heroine:-

    > There are some very intimate things which I can't write. To write them would be to condemn them to death. Certain rituals of tenderness, for example, certain laughs, certain sexual practices. As long as these things remain unwritten, we can relive them a thousand times without the feeling of repeating our selves. Often they are so small, so fragile. To speak them would be to ruin them, to repeat them having spoken them would be to copy ourselves (1995:43).

3. It is interesting that some religions guard against writing the word for their deity as this would misrepresent the concept.

4. This knowledge has been introduced through the pioneering work of Neuro-Linguistic Programming.

5. There are of course a number of specialist books on this subject, for example Bass and Davis (1988, 1993).

6. Virginia Axline's 'Dibs in Search of Self' (1964) remains a classic account of a piece of play therapy, and is a delightfully presented book which is a pleasure to read.

7. Moreno's Psychodrama is the classic innovative text in this area.

8. See Houston (1982).

9. Roma Byer. Voices in our heads ; unpublished MA thesis, University of Durham, 1995.

10. There are many ways of achieving this, largely borrowed from cognitive behavioural approaches, and Neuro-Linguistic Programming - See Beck (1976) and O'Connor & Seymour (1990).

Chapter Six. Let's get all this counselling stuff into perspective: We can only do what we can do!

Introduction

So far we have looked at themes of Blank Minds and Sticky Moments, and offered some principles and strategies for dealing with them. In this chapter we explore some specific issues which recognise that the practice of counselling, although always determined by the individual practitioner, is influenced by its context. Practitioners working within organisations are sometime constrained and find themselves frustrated or helpless because of conflicting professional codes, goals or directives. On some occasions this conflict, and the challenge which it can provoke, can be a good thing. While agencies that have been set up to help people under the auspices of counselling are mostly helpful, they can on occasion be counter-productive to helping. This may be particularly true when the organisation has grown to the extent that it has forgotten or dislocated from its original purpose. In this situation practitioners are often left in a position where they are restrained from being maximally helpful by policy or procedure.

Many helpers working for Health Trusts or Social Services will immediately identify with this comment. In similar vein, sometimes agencies and organisations may have goals which are inconsistent or which are mutually incompatible. For example, Counselling Associations may have espoused aims of promoting counselling, supporting counsellors, and protecting the public. It is not hard to see how in a situation such as the public exposure of a counsellor's malpractice these aims may be at odds with each other.

This chapter then offers discussion and analysis of a number of issues which provoke dilemmas and blanks. It is divided into two main sections. First, we look at some of the complexities and contradictions of professional and agency ethics and goals. Secondly, we have some points to make on some of the conflicts which can occur between the rights of clients to a useful and professional service, and the rights of counsellors to a useful and professional life - indeed to a life!

Ethics and Agency Goals

The state and the counsellor

It has been suggested that the state may avoid responsibility of care for its citizens by employing counselling programmes as an alternative to active intervention. If it is possible to convince the average person that they are responsible entirely for their situation, and that counselling is the panacea to enable people to marshal their resources and take self responsibility, then it may also be used as a device for maintaining the status quo. This enables those actually responsible for social conditions and resourcing active interventions, such as medical research, housing programmes, or employment initiatives, to avoid their absolute responsibilities. If social problems can be redefined by engaging counsellors and counselling programmes instead of by other means, then this

'Yes, I know you feel that you've been treated in a very sexist way, but have you ever stopped to think that if you hadn't been a woman, it would never have happened?'

may signal that counselling has become another *"opium of the masses"*.

It is easy to see how enthusiastic new counsellors embrace the activity with gusto. It is made out as something very special; its training groups have an exclusiveness for 'safety' reasons. It demands, ostensibly, of ourselves. It is easy to feel delighted in the first flush of success with clients. Thus the larger cultural and social consequences can be easily missed. Our own experience combines an interest and expertise in psychology of individuals with equal expertise in social psychology and sociology, which can help to remain a step back from our own discipline. Ideally, we would both like to see philosophy and sociology taught as components of any higher degree counselling course. An awareness, at least, that counselling can be just another agency of social control must surely be integral to the discipline. Taking these views into account, it is hard to assert that the practice of counselling is or should be "value free". On a more practical note, we invite you to reflect upon your own practice and ask yourself these questions:-

- Are my responses to the client enabling them to take action and change their life for the better, **OR** am I placating or suppressing the appropriate anger and injustice that they feel towards a society that treats them unfairly?
- Do I encourage the client to 'take ownership' of everything that happens to them, **OR** do I challenge the client to clarify for themselves and accept only what is appropriate responsibility for their situation.

Such questions invite self-challenge. Counselling is best considered to be an occupation that operates in a context. Once it is divorced from its appropriate context it becomes more difficult to justify in terms of either need or usefulness. For example, a few years ago one of our supervisees, explained that they had lost 'faith in counselling'; by this they meant that they could see no good reason for doing such a trivial thing, when people were starving, being tortured, slaughtered, and so on in other parts of the world. Even closer to home people were in great distress that required active help rather than merely talking with them about their problems! His point was well made, and since then, many students have voiced similar concerns to us. Our reply is usually one which enables the counsellor to see their own contribution to the welfare of their client.

We were faced very sharply with the challenge of considering our own contribution when, in conjunction with the University of Hull, we delivered a Masters degree in Counselling to Muslims from the former Yugoslavia. We worked hard, were invited to share extremely traumatic accounts and experiences, and became increasingly frustrated with what we were doing. The counsellors had come, but where the heck were the UN troops. Every time we flew back to Britain, we were charged up and incensed, wanted to chain ourselves to railings to *make the world listen and act,* and really felt that we were doing nothing. This, however, was not really the case. We were not stopping the war. We could not explain human-kind's destructive violence to itself. We could not give people back their homeland. Our students however let us know very clearly what contribution we had made to their lives in emotional and pragmatic terms, and to the possible choices that they now had. In a strange way, our very natural helplessness could have become a form of arrogance, by defining what is useful and wanting 'big' results. And in the end, it became fine and valuable to be two counselling trainers who offered a different kind of approach to a group of people who found it of value, and who received a lot of learning for ourselves in the process, including a humility which we would like to keep.

> **Principle: Help in the way you can, when you can, in a way which is appropriate to the circumstance and the context in which you are offering help.**

Report writing and recommendations

We have both been asked on numerous occasions to write reports on, or recommendations for, clients. These are often requested by agencies such as social services, or for courts, or in some cases organisations like the church. These may cause some concern to the counsellor, but can generally be 'negotiated' with the parties concerned with a little honesty and immediacy. One of the areas for discussion may well be whether this service is part of the negotiated contract, or if it is reasonable to ask for it at this point in the relationship? Does the counsellor feel 'pressured' or 'coerced' into providing this service? Is it antithetical to provide a report which has within its scope 'assessment' when the relationship has been based on 'non judgementalness'?

An actual example may be helpful here. A client of one of us asked if we would submit a report to the court for the purpose of supporting a lenient sentence. It was explained to the client that if such a report was to be contemplated then it would be written without prejudice. This meant that the report would be written honestly and without any intent to influence the court outcome one way or another. Once written it was handed to the client who was free to choose whether to submit it or not. Furthermore, it was explained to the client that the process of being asked to write such a report raised some issues, and some questions may need answering if counselling was to continue. i.e.-

- How long have you been thinking about asking for this report, and has it influenced your honesty of disclosure?
- Does the content of the report change the relationship we had established?
- Have you any other surprises up your sleeve, oh dear client?

Perhaps even more difficult to contemplate ethically is the ex-client who asks you to write references for employment; a report to support mitigation in court cases; or a submission in a law suit. We would strongly advise that in these circumstances you remain objective and stay strictly within your proven credentialled professional competence. If necessary, take legal advice on your position before submitting any reports or recommendations to a court (written or oral); this may be done through contact with your professional association or organisation such as BAC or the BPS, as written client waivers may be necessary for your own protection. Reports about current clients by similar agencies will almost certainly require the client's informed consent in writing to avoid recriminations at a later date.

Working for specifically focused agencies

Perhaps the most important question to consider when working for specialised agencies is whether the specialist nature will affect the way I view and work with my clients. The answer is invariably 'Yes' in some shape or form. Can I live with that? is the second question it begs. Undoubtedly, agencies with specific objectives make great impact into peoples lives and mostly this seems to be beneficial; our caution is that you should only have one client, and it is that client that has the right to determine outcome. Hence if you find yourself working for an organisation primarily concerned with helping people with alcohol problems, for example, it is useful to check out if there are any underlying policies which constrain the client, and whether you wish to co-operate in this constraint. Some such agencies may dictate that all clients must have the goal of giving up alcohol if they wish to participate in the programme. Although this may be both realistic and practical, we also have to acknowledge that it is one less option for the client to choose from. For a more extreme example to illustrate the point, would you consider working for a 'pro-life' agency that would only help pregnant women who chose to reject abortion as an option? And if so, could you consider your contribution as counselling?

The question of pregnancy counselling in all its forms raises some extremely contentious issues. Counselling in agencies where the given brief is to offer voluntary counselling to a woman who is unsure what she wants poses little problem; the general ethos of counselling is possible to maintain. Much more contentious, however, is the issue of that activity which has become known as 'abortion counselling'.

Under the current Abortion Act, women who choose to have abortions have to prove that they have good reason, within the definitions laid down, that to continue with the pregnancy would be detrimental to their welfare. In order to do this, agencies often insist that the woman see a 'counsellor'. This raises serious discrepancies:

- The counselling is non-voluntary - can it be called counselling?
- The objective of the session is to determine the woman's 'eligibility' in some way, in the terms of the Act - can this be called counselling?
- The woman is now being seen as non-autonomous - what implications does this have specifically and generally?

It can be argued that through the institutionalisation of counselling, the whole abortion issue has been diverted from a political issue into an individual one. The slogan 'a woman's right to choose' has been manipulated; the abortion is seen as the woman's problem, but she does not yet have the right to choose - she must do psychological somersaults in order to get the assent of a doctor. Should counselling be involved in this?

Our view is that anyone has the *right* to counselling. Thus if a woman considering a termination is either already in counselling, or sees this as the reason for starting counselling, so be it. Any issues which arise can be approached from a counselling ethos.

However, it is a total misnomer to call an enforced consultation on abortion, whose purpose is specifically to ensure that the termination can take place, counselling. It is a different activity. It may include elements of support, it will hopefully be facilitated with the use of counselling skills, it may even be part of a larger counselling contract. But it is essentially a necessary step in a legal procedure whose underlying tenets are antithetical to the spirit of counselling, to the autonomy of women, and it really is not counselling. Unfortunately, this rather institutionalised use of the term is one of the biggest weaknesses of the profession, who are reluctant to put any parameters on what counselling is and isn't.

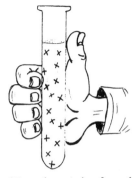

'Now that we've found that your test is positive, you realise that you are incapable of making any further decisions on your own?'

The ramifications of this are really much underestimated, and we would like very much to see a strong stance on this issue, not just for 'our' credibility, but to prevent collusion with oppressive practice and to dissociate from it. This holds true also for 'counselling' in IVF clinics, and in G.U.M. clinics - you can't have the test or the treatment till you've been counselled. What dangerous statements!

Pride and Prejudice

Then there are the agencies which overtly advertise their pride and prejudice, and expect that their workers must also share these in order to be involved with the agency's work. Gay rights organisations, the Church, and Women's Refuges immediately spring to mind as examples. Whether you are personally being discriminated against or not is not the point. And simply because you are what the organisation wants does not exempt you from considering the ethics of exclusive policies. Various questions need to be addressed in deciding whether only gay people can be allowed to help gay clients, or only women be involved in helping in women's refuges, and only those sharing the religious values of the church be employed to help those requesting counselling. There may, of course, be some argument as to the special sensitivity of counsellors who are in some way identified with the client group, but this is similar to saying that only counsellors that have had 'x' experience can counsel clients with 'x' problem.

There are of course major flaws in such an argument. If counselling is indeed a credible activity, then we need to recognise that each person is dealing with their experience, their responses, even where a practice is universal. If you are a woman who has been raped, you might decide that all men are bastards; if I am a woman who has been raped, I might decide that one man I know was a bastard, and as the mother of a son, have an agenda to negotiate and communicate with men. Even if we have exactly the same view, it should be irrelevant unless identification is seen as particularly helpful; as documented in chapter Two, actually, identification can be extremely unhelpful, and group identification carries some weaknesses as well as the obvious strengths of support.

'Stay over on your own side, you straight, you queer, you inadequate!'

Furthermore, identity is somewhat more complex than merely a celebration of my religion, my sexual preference, or my gender. Working with a particular women's organisation not too long ago, we heard the statement that any woman was welcome to become involved on the management group, but no men. The facilitator pushed the point - so, if Margaret Thatcher were to want to become a member of the Committee, with Edwina Curry as an aide, would that be alright. The resounding answer was no. Ultimately, any policy on segregation or specific cultural criteria for exclusivity needs to be carefully examined in the light of the purpose of the organisation and in terms of the interest of the client group. It would seem that much more examination of such issues could be undertaken.

Ethical Codes. Counselling, therapy, counselling skills?

Although we believe that the current ethical codes set out by BAC and BPS do an admirable job, we would draw the reader's attention to the potential of ethical codes to clash. For example, a professional nurse may discover that the disclosure s/he is hearing from another nurse during a *counselling* session is something which she is obliged to act upon according to the nurse's professional code of ethics, but not from the counselling code. For example:

Judith is a qualified health visitor who has competed a diploma course in counselling and has been accredited by BAC. She is therefore obliged to accept and observe both her health visiting and counselling codes of practice. One of her clients is a registered nurse who discloses that she is stealing sleeping tablets from the ward stock because she has had great difficulty sleeping during her traumatic divorce. She offers the explanation that her G.P. has refused her a prescription because he is concerned that she might become dependent on them. Judith now has a dilemma. Her health visiting ethic decrees that she must disclose this information to the health authority which employs her client. Under the BAC code of ethics, however, such action might be seen as breaching the client's confidentiality. Would informing the health authority also be seen as betraying the client's trust, and would Judith be seen as judgemental, disrespectful to the right of self-determination, and lacking warmth?

Similar situations will occur for counsellors who have other professional codes which determine professional behaviour. Social workers, for example, have a statu-

To tell or not to tell, that is the question . . .

tory obligation to report any incident of child abuse. On occasion, however, they might hear such disclosures within a confidential contract. Or they might have real personal and professional dilemmas about whether the client's interest would be served by disclosing the information concerned. The worker may feel that they have very good reasons, connected to the maintenance of rapport and trust, that prohibit them taking action. It is difficult to know sometimes which role should take priority.

Those professionals who are using counselling skills to augment their role are not necessarily bound by any code other than that of their own profession. BAC suggest that workers using counselling skills should follow the *ethos* of the counsellor, and lay this out clearly for those intent on using counselling skills.

It is our view that ethical codes are only developed because people transgress them; in other words, if people always had the wherewithal and motivation to act with total integrity all of the time, then there would be no need to devise such codes. We have certainly had to think seriously at some times about the conflicts which arise when becoming a professional counsellor and simultaneously belonging to another profession, and for one us, this meant leaving that profession. Currently, we are both at liberty to use the BAC code of ethics as our primary code, although even that demands unique judgement calls, of course. We have developed strategies and skilled responses to forestall some of the potential difficulties, and each of us sets a great deal of store by clear and careful contracting. This is so helpful as a baseline for avoiding clashes of interest and divided loyalties, because it allows for exceptions and conflicts to be identified **before** the counselling begins. Examples of what might go into a contract to minimise conflict and to set the limitations of the counselling might be as follows:

- My confidentiality is limited to, or boundaried by:
  The law of the land
  Disclosure of endangerment to yourself or others
  Disclosure of exploitation of vulnerable others
  My need to sleep at night
- I have to keep within the ethical codes of (Nursing, Social Work, Police, etc)
- I would have to act if .....
- I would have to say if....
- I would....
- I will not....

It is our experience that all counsellors, whether or not they are constrained by other codes, do well to consider very carefully exactly what they can and can't hear about, or be party to, **before** entering into counselling with any client. In the absence of clear guidance, it has taken a number of years for us each to evolve contracts which seem to serve the interests of the client while maintaining the personal comfort and safety of the counsellor, and part of the nature of the work is that facets are always evolving - for example the aspect of contracting which allows us to talk about our work more freely, albeit with anonymity and discretion, could not have been told us before we had experienced isolation. However, ultimately, the more that counsellors can consider these issues from the outset, the better. Each individual will still have to examine their own conscience and decided what they believe they should negotiate on, and what are their bottom lines. The professional codes only provide the crucible within which each counsellor will determine their own contracts.

I would if I could, but I can't so I won't, so you'll have to do what you can

People who have impaired or limited abilities for judgement may benefit immensely from helping activities which incorporate the use of counselling skills. However, it is unrealistic to imagine that everyone can benefit optimally from counselling, and individuals who have impaired or restricted judgement, for whatever reason, may be put at risk if they are left to self determine without support or guidance. We know that this is an immensely tricky area - who determines who has impaired judgement? However, if we're honest, we do all operate some criteria - would we let our best friend, when completely drunk, do something drastic that we know they would regret in the cold light of day, and which would have severely detrimental consequences? To use counselling as an excuse to allow such cavalier attitudes with others is not really acceptable. And although we would caution, as we guess you would, before determining that someone's judgement is impaired, we do believe that they would benefit more from guidance, suggestion, persuasion and occasional restraint, than from a counselling approach. We would certainly advocate the use of high level communication skills such as active listening, reflecting, and the use of a focused problem solving model, but believe that it is folly to commend all of counselling's philosophy and interventions to every situation. For example, the bereft woman, depressed and suicidal following the tragic death of her son, about to jump out of a forty storey window, would not much benefit from any of the following:

- It's up to you, pet, you need to decide for yourself.

- I can see that you are upset; your son is dead, you have no one left and no, you don't have anything worthwhile to stay alive for.

- So tell me, Marjory ,what would it look like if it were a little bit better?

- You feel sad and depressed because your son has died, and you feel that there is little point in carrying on.

We would suggest that empathic understanding and challenge, the urge to self-determination, and future goal setting might not be quite so appropriate as persuasion, distraction, calling emergency services, or hanging onto a leg.

So who has impaired or restricted judgement? Well, people in drug induced states, children, people with learning difficulties, people in extreme reactive states, and people with mental health problems - perhaps even Søren Kierkegaard, if assessed in today's culture.   If you are up in arms about such untrendy categorisation, we urge you to stay with us just a little longer. We would want to make it very clear that we do not believe that anyone in these categories should always be told what to do, that their judgement is never useful, or that they should never have any influence over their lives. Neither are we saying that 'the rest of us' always have full and good judgement. But we do believe that there is a matter of degree of probability of judgement being impaired, and that some factors, such as those mentioned above, will create a more likely tendency to such impairment than others. Having said that, decisions about people's lives should only be made in the interest of increasing the potential for *quality of life as far as we can best discern,* and compulsion of any degree would ideally be reserved for issues of personal safety.

However, life, as usual, is just not that simple. Children, for instance, may have difficulty making a choice between something yielding immediate gratification that has long term difficult consequences, and something which has long term benefits yet which is immediately unpleasant or irksome, or whose value cannot be seen. Going to school might fall into this category. Yet few adults would support the decision of a seven year old to abandon school because they were a bit fed up that week; some employ varying degrees of coercion and compulsion to get children to school. If the same child was unhappy at school at twelve, and was interested to find other ways of pursuing education, then they would probably find more adult support, and their decision be given more credibility as perhaps better thought out.

Much controversy has raged over the years over adults with learning difficulties or with some serious mental impairment , and whether or not they should be able to make choices about marriage, spending an inheritance, deciding to have children. Some tactics used have seemed abhorrent and disrespectful of the people concerned. In terms of helping, however, we have found that most people who we have encountered with mental limitations can, with careful listening and with effort, explain likes, dislikes and preferences, which should influence any decisions which might have to be made on their behalf. Using some of the principles and adapting some of the techniques in this book, for example, it should not be beyond a counsellor's ability to identify abstract goals, determine a person's values, and find some understanding of a person's emotional world. If *any* communication is possible, then some of *this* communication is possible. Sticky areas, and we can only do our best. We recognise also that counselling is not always the appropriate helping activity.

Informed Consent

The argument regarding whether someone has 'impaired judgement' is linked to that of whether a person can give informed consent. The idea of informed consent may be applied to processes that lead to change and where the outcomes are likely to have implications for the well being or quality of life of the individual affected. Conventionally, this is applied to treatments such as surgery or the prescription of medication or physical treatments of psychiatric disorders which involve serious, permanent or irreversible change. The law requiring such consent is very specific and clear, especially when addressed to patients who may suffer diminished judgement, such as patients with learning difficulties, mental disorders or immaturity

Whilst it is not being argued that counselling leads to serious, permanent or irreversible change of a deleterious nature, it is possible that a less extreme parallel may exist. It is perhaps easy to see that counselling may lead to change; clients are not only aware of this implication but indeed, desire change of some kind. However, if the nature and extent of change is difficult to see at the onset, then it could be argued that informed consent is required.

One view may be that in counselling there is always an implicit prescription for self reflection and this in turn will produce change. Even if that change is perceived by the client as "good", and has been freely chosen, there is still an exhortation to become more 'self aware'. It could be argued that prescribing "self awareness" is perhaps the riskiest of prescriptions, for, logically, informed consent cannot have been given.

Prescription of any kind carries with it, for the prescriber, some responsibility for the outcome. For example, General Practitioners carry both legal and moral responsibility for any drugs that are prescribed for their patients, and an investment consultant carries some responsibility and consequent damage to their reputations when their advice leads to financial losses rather than profit. The equation, it would seem, is that the narrower the choices and the greater the degree of directiveness, the more responsibility is carried. Responsibility can be seen as being mediated by the aware-ness of risk and the influence which the prescriber exerts over the choice. The argument here then is that when therapists of any description prescribe anything for their clients, they do so with considerable responsibility, and should always seek informed con-sent by offering clear explanations of the likely outcomes of the work.

Rights and Duties

Ultimately, much of the above discussion is arguing firmly for the limitations of counselling, and for a realistic approach towards the objective of counselling for client, agency, society, and indeed the counsellor. For the last section of this chapter, we would like to focus on the world of the counsellor and to suggest some limita-tions to how far they might take their role. Counsellors can easily take the view that they are more than mere mortals, that they are able to turn round in a telephone box and suddenly turn into SuperCarl, with their knickers over their tights and a nice line in Lycra. It is then quite important to look at some of the more absurd expectations which counsellors either accept or provoke and to debunk some of the myths surrounding this.

I have to be there for them - day or night

Yes, this is absolutely true. Once you become a counsellor, you have no right to any social life, any independent happiness, or any human autonomy. Such luxuries are only fit for your client. Much like entering a holy order, you must make yourself available day and night, consider your client's needs before your own, and allow any intrusion. You have total responsibility for all your clients' lives, if anything goes wrong then not only is it your fault, but you should have foreseen it and helped them to avoid it. Now that you didn't, however, and they're in this mess, you must immediately rescue them!

Although this may look ridiculous when written in black and white, it is amazing how prevalent these or similar beliefs are amongst counsellors. We do have responsibilities to our clients. One of those responsibilities is to discourage dependency. We have already mentioned how one of us spent three weeks responding to suicide notes pushed through the letter box of our home on a Sat-urday, before realising that this was not helping the client. We also know various tales of counsellors putting up with a mild version of 'stalking', outside houses or in shops, and even being publicly ver-bally assaulted, under the guise of the 'therapeutic relationship'.

Not very therapeutic for the client.

But hey, let's not pretend this is all about the client, important though their self-respect and independence is. We have rights too. We have a right to privacy, respect, free time and our own lives. Each of us must decide where our boundaries and preferences lie, what impact our work has on our private relationships, and what messages we are giving out to clients. And this may mean that we are not always 'there' for someone. Four or five years ago, one of us had a phone call on a Sunday lunchtime. We'd just had (unusually) a 'family' meal (and don't those families taste delicious!) and a couple of glasses (read vats) of red wine. The phone went. It was a prospective client to whom we had been recommended. Immediately, our response was that yes, it was the right number, but could she possibly call us in office hours. She began to tell her tale of distress. Again, we reiterated that we could be really helpful - tomorrow. We also drew attention to emergency numbers. This client never rang back. For some counsellors, this would be untenable. For the one of us concerned, however, it was important to our own health and privacy that we were persistent with not having our private world intruded upon, and we had no belief that this person's welfare was our responsibility. Everyone must make the realistic choices that they think serve their own rights and well being, as well as their duties.

My clients are small, fragile and precious flowers. If I say something wrong, they will be scarred forever

'I used to be a perfectly beautiful rose, you know, until my counsellor made just one wrong move.'

It is amazing how many students studying counselling are terrified that if they say the wrong thing it may have some dreadfully dire consequences for their clients. It has been our experience that clients wanting help are already proving just how hardy humans can be. Clients are not some hot house plant which will crumple and die at the first frost; they are hardy annuals that have already been through a lot; often they have survived more than we care to think about. To treat them as so fragile is both patronising and nonsensical. Counsellors will make mistakes, they will say the wrong thing and their clients will survive. Counsellors should respect and trust their clients enough to treat them at least as equals if not superior beings.

If I open this can of worms.............???

The fear of opening the can of worms is one of the things that prevents counsellors moving their clients forward, or exploring the 'real' issues of the client's problems. Some counsellors confess to fearing the consequences of facilitating strong emotion. Will it make things worse? Perhaps one of the fears here is that although the emotions belong to the client, they are like a genie being released from the bottle, once out maybe things will get out of control. Supposing once faced with all of these emotions, the client can't cope, becomes more and more distressed and ends up committing suicide - I mean, it is possible, isn't it?!

Yes, sometimes, although we believe **rarely,** clients opening up to their own emotions and becoming distressed can be problematic. Yes, sometimes, although we believe **very very rarely,** a client may self harm, and yes it just may be because you helped them get in touch with their feelings. But let's get real - the practice of *any* psychological technique has its risks. But be aware that this is not about counselling being risky, it is about some individuals being at risk from themselves. Having willingly elected to get to know themselves better, it remains their right to self determine from their self knowledge. The practice of counselling deliberately avoids diagnosis, therefore to assess 'can this client be trusted to be confronted with their own deeper emotions?' is not generally within the scope of the counselling practitioner. *If* we have accepted the client for counselling, we will assume with trust and confidence in our clients that they can deal with their own emotions.

O.K. but what if things do get sticky - what can be done? Over our years of experience we would have to say that all of our clients survived exposure to their deeper feelings. Although we have experienced our clients self harming on occasions, this has not been as a direct result of exposure to their deeper feeling. If clients get upset, and more rarely deeply distressed, our antidote (if one really is needed) is to allow time and quiet; to challenge their strengths; and if appropriate to move them briefly into Egan's second stage. This latter strategy hardly ever fails, providing it is done skilfully, moving the client into the arena of hope by simple prompts - 'So what would you like to be feeling instead?', or, 'what would you like the situation to change to?'. But beware, this would not work if it were appropriate for the client to stay with their distress such as in acute bereavement, for here we would reinforce our belief that the client needs to ventilate their emotion, not escape from it.

Remember also when avoiding the can of worms, it is the client's can, and they have probably come to counselling for help to open it! They may well need to open up before they can move on. Let's not waste their time simply because of our anxieties: help them get moving again as quickly as possible.

Summary: Limitations to Counselling as a Social Practice

To summarise, then, we are suggesting that there is a limitation to counselling as a social practice. Part of our objective is to state the obvious and put a little common sense back into the sometimes esoteric tripe which can be found in counselling culture.

- Change is voluntary. Unless the client is assisting this process, any change is unlikely.
  Not everyone is helped by counselling, some clients require different approaches and some clients cannot be helped!
- The client's behaviour only represents their strategies to achieve their goals. Work with their goals to enhance desired behaviour change.
- We can only do what we can do. Do your best, it is probably better than what is otherwise on offer.
- Agencies exist to serve clients, not to serve themselves.
- Know your ethical codes, limitations and areas of conflict.
- Counsellors have rights to a life too. Know your own boundaries and limitations.

Chapter Seven. Permission to think!

Introduction

In the last chapter, we began to look at the context of counselling and how it might affect practice. In this chapter, we do more of the same to try to contextualise counselling as a social practice. So be warned - don't read on if you wish to keep a fixed view of counselling!! Our intent is to challenge your thinking, and to confirm what a limited activity counselling is. We begin by exploring the ubiquitous nature of counselling and its culture specific context. We also ask the question 'who wants counselling?', and no doubt those of us whose income depends on clients will be relieved to hear the answer...everyone! We then suggest some of the *functions* of counselling in twentieth century society. Finally, we urge you to consider the status of counsellors and how this can lead to some dangerous and narrow assumptions.

We believe that it is important to have such a wide view on counselling for two reasons. One is to remember that it relies on theories which only represent one way of looking at human behaviour. The other is to remind ourselves of the myriad expectations which clients might have. Our hope is that this helps the practitioner to understand and to feel freer about what could be done in counselling.

They seek it here, they seek it there, they seek for counselling everywhere . . .

Counselling : The panacea of all ills, or a convenient way to hoodwink the voters?

Sometimes, when we hear people talk about counselling as a remedy for all ills, we step back and wonder at the narrow vision which this can create. It can be salutory to remember that the professional practice of counselling[1] is comparatively new to the world; we existed for a very long time without it, and do well to retain some humility about its potential for humankind. Counselling has emerged from diverse sources, with various roots which may be traced to practices of magic, religion, medicine, psychiatry, and experimental psychology. Not surprising, then, that there are many different 'versions' of counselling which both complement and compete with each other.

It is still difficult to describe what it is we counsellors 'do'. If an alien were to ask us, then it is much more difficult to describe than the job of a doctor, a bricklayer, a technologist, a teacher. How many counsellors have tried describing their activity to children in a way which makes sense? Indeed, to potential clients who know nothing about it. We help people - to do what? To feel better - how? By helping them understand themselves better - what do we do to enable this? We use techniques and qualities to help them explore their minds. How do we know it works? We don't. Is there a tangible end product? No, no wall, no feat of engineering. Is there research done into counselling? Yes. What does it tell us? Nothing tangible. Why do we do it? Because we believe it works.

How many counsellors does it take to change a light bulb? An infinite amount . . . but the light bulb has to really want to change.

Not only do counsellors believe that counselling is worthwhile, but, increasingly, so does society. The number of agencies offering counselling is growing, and counselling is increasingly accepted as a valid intervention to social problems. You may think it extraordinary that counselling has exploded onto the scene, despite the fact that it has no quality assurance measures, no proven cost-effectiveness and no-one can agree even on a universal definition of what it is and what it is supposed to do! However, part of the success of counselling may lie in its ability to be in the right place at the right time, i.e in a society which is embracing individualism. In 1984, Nigel Lawson spoke of 'fighting and changing the culture and psychology of two generations', and that although 'this cannot be achieved overnight...let there be no doubt that this is our goal.'[2]

Three clear examples of just how much our culture and psychology have been changed are the social responses to three of the fastest growth industries over the last ten years; i.e. counselling as a response to HIV, counselling as a response to political and economic redundancies, and counselling for post-traumatic stress disorder , which covers anything from long-term consequences of abuse or shock, to sudden and critical incidents such as the Dunblane shootings.

The most recent innovation which we heard of was that presented at an International Conference of Psychologists in Canada, which detailed the development of traffic accident roadside counselling services. And it would seem that the counselling culture is only too keen to help us and apply itself to virtually any life experience ranging from traumatic sexual abuse to winning the lottery the week you didn't put your pound on. Indeed only last season, we considered setting ourselves up as relegation counsellors for York City fans, but fortunately, or unfortunately

for our pockets, our local team stayed up. Very soon after the 1997 disastrous election defeat for the Tories, we heard the Bishop of Leicester suggesting that they were in too much of a 'grief 'state to yet start contemplating their future. Counselling was perhaps just what they needed! Counselling, whether we like it or not, seems here to stay: have problem, will counsel.

Counselling ideologies and theories are also demonstrated in 'folklore' understandings. It is widely accepted and understood at some level, for example, that the bereaved need to mourn psychologically rather than (or as well as) ritualistically. Many people have some concept that there is a grief cycle and while in Britain this is becoming increasingly acknowledged in terms and conditions of some work contracts, in the United States, some private health insurance covers for a finite number of grief counselling sessions.[3] Many stages of human development are accepted as transitional within the life cycle, and expressions like 'finding myself', or 'working through' are common to everyday discourse.

From Agony Aunt to Doctor of Divinity

'I know just what will help you deary.'

Not too many years ago, people who saw themselves as needing help turned to the agony aunt in the local or national press for consolation. They were helped with advice, guidance, and periodically they would receive some minor admonishment for their immoral or deviant behaviour. Not so now; we have developed to such a sophisticated degree that it would seem that only counselling can really help. Advice, guidance and admonishments are no longer acceptable; never again are we to be told that if we just put it all behind us, and get a new dress, my dear, it will all be alright. Instead we must have warmth, genuineness and empathy with large helpings of non-judgementalness, the bedrock of skilled counselling, rather than agony aunting.

We also now think that we know how to teach counselling. A record number of training courses are now available in counselling, and if it's difficult to attend, well, there are always distance learning packages. 'In-house' training is on the increase, within social services, health trusts, industry, voluntary agencies and the church. Counselling bodies are currently in a process of professionalisation, with courses and individuals vying for accreditation from recognised organisations. Moreover, the teaching of counselling and counselling skills is being increasingly recognised as an academic discipline, with some universities now developing departments of counselling, and the first Chair of counselling being well established. Counselling can now be studied to Masters level, and indeed to Ph.D level, at most universities. An extraordinary and extremely rapid achievement for a discipline so much in its infancy.

. . . and when they've found it, what's it do?

By and large, then, the counselling movement sees itself as a 'good thing'. This of course might not necessarily be the case, and some of the assumptions which underpin counselling will be challenged later in the book. What *is* clear, however, is that counselling is being used to fulfil a number of different functions, some of which might previously have been served through magic, religion, and medicine. Enumerating and understanding these functions may help to explain why counselling has become such a prevalent social practice, and yet why it seems so difficult to pin down precisely.

Fromm[4] Here to Eternity . . . the quest for the meaning of life

Sometimes, people who ask for counselling are grappling with philosophical and theological issues, and they see counselling as offering a method to help them make sense of what is happening in their everyday lives. Such issues are often to do with the meaning of life, the distinction between right and wrong, questions around how much of life is under individual control, and personal questions which go along the 'why' lines:

- 'why do I get so depressed'?
- 'why did this awful thing happen to *me'*?
- 'why do my relationships not work'?

Such questions embody several fundamental issues for the individual: the search for causal explanation; the question of morality and values; the dilemmas of naturalistic man; spirituality and self-determination.[5]

Counselling may also be seen as helping the individual in their quest for *existential* meaning, providing answers about the very state of being. Not only is the meaning of life up for exploration, but the meaning of *my* life. Sometimes people feel that they are uncertain in their existence, and that they want to 'get in touch' with their 'real selves'. Feelings of frustration that they are not living life authentically and to the full may influence their decision to seek counselling. Much humanist and existential counselling depends on a layer of the onion version of self; wherein the real person is found to be within layers, waiting to be peeled. It is thought that counselling can offer the arena for the client to discover themselves in this sense.

'Am I there yet?'

Such questions would at one time have been answered through different media. 'Why me', for example, might have invited an answer which had to do with astrological forces, or curses from external sources. Questions of selfhood might have been answered through religious discourse.[6] We need to remember, then, that the language and metaphors of counselling psychology are more than a method of treatment; they are a whole system of ideas which pervade society at every level Thus, they present a socially and culturally specific paradigm of understanding and explanation to both ordinary and extraordinary events.[7]

By way of illustration, consider eating disorders. There are many accounts of young women not eating in centuries gone by, one such being the tale of two women, Sarah Wright and Anna Trapnel. In the 1650's , both Sarah and Anna fasted for over ten weeks while in their early teens. One ate and repeatedly vomited ,and made suicide attempts, the other simply stopped eating. While delirious in their beds, each were visited by strangers and their words listened to for wisdom and guidance. Both were hailed as prophets, later to be accused of witchcraft. In the 1650's, the condition was interpreted and understood within a frame of reference revolving around the idea of the saving of souls and within a system of religious politics. Today, it would likely be construed as anorexia nervosa, which is seen as a psychological disorder associated with issues of power, control and self-esteem.

Change is here to stay - with gusto!

Counselling, then is ambitious. In a rapidly changing world order, its theories and practices seek to explain phenomena which would previously have been explained in terms of other social practices. Within this context, counselling is also seen to offer a *cure* for the malaises from which individuals and society suffer. In individualist terms, malaise might originally be equated with Freud's idea of neurosis, where the focus is on the idiosyncratic circumstances of the client's development and life. In wider terms, however, it is commonly suggested that modern living has entailed a loss of purpose to life, a loss of freedom, loss of tradition, loss of morality, loss of norms and security of social relations[8] resulting in a fragmentation or loss of a sense of self.

The notion of the experience of loss as a significant part of the individual's development is increasingly common within counselling approaches. While loss as an experience is an obvious enough focus where experiences of bereavement and separation are involved, the more vague sense of loss experienced by some clients is most clearly signified by the idea of *hidden loss*[9], a concept increasingly used to inform counselling practice. A survivor of sexual abuse, for example, is commonly conceptualised as having lost aspects of childhood and self. Members of culturally diverse families may describe feelings of alienation from each other, loss of control, or loss of role. Such issues refer to cultural as well as individual malaise.

Mary Mary, quite contrary, how does your story flow?

Within this context, counselling is also increasingly seen as offering a means of understanding our life *narrative,* or life journey. In the complexities of everyday life, some clients want to take the time and effort to review not only their identity, but to make sense of their past and present and to feel that they have some control over their future. It can be suggested that many critical life experiences are separated out from public life, leaving the individual with a sense of lack of continuity and security. Death, for example, once a very public and open experience, is largely sanitised and dealt with behind closed doors. We now know that there are many experiences of abuse which are hidden away, sometimes for many years. Issues of sexuality are also relegated to the private sphere of life, with many partners feeling sexually cold or exploited, and with many individuals keeping sexual preference a secret for fear of repercussion. The narrative of the self is the assembly of sequential life events and moments in a way which provides some sense of order, security and

'Well I know where I'm going.'

continuity This idea is especially relevant to any kind of counselling which see the world as 'constructed'. Through sharing the details of one's life within a counselling relationship, it is deemed possible to reconstruct a narrative which makes sense of events.[10]

Within the 'narrative of self' purpose to counselling, it may also be seen that counselling psychology offers a means of making sense of life stages and transitional periods, through infancy, childhood, adolescence, adulthood, 'mid-life crisis', and old age, stages which were once known as 'rites of passage' . This idea has been widely taken up, with books like Gail Sheehey's *Passages* being major best sellers in the Western world. Indeed, it is now difficult to imagine the Western world without conceptualisations of life stages, so prevalent are terms like adolescence and mid-life crisis.

OK, so now I know who I am, where I've come from, and what's happening to me. . . what's next?

'Hubble bubble toil and trouble, how does my practice grow?'

Counselling does not end with making sense of the past and the present. It can have a decidedly future-oriented aspect to it in terms of the individual being encouraged to make choices and envisage what they would like in their life. This is seen as a part of 'life planning' . It is partly illusory, in as much as it is clearly impossible to predict or to control the future, and partly a recognition of the fact that given this limitation, the individual may benefit from taking responsibility for those choices which *are* under their control. This process becomes a part of identity. We use visions of the future to make sense of current situations, feelings and decisions; strategies involving the amount of work we undertake, for example, are influenced by desired outcomes for next year, five years on, retirement, or whatever. We also use visions of the future to create an inner goal to the identity one would like to become.[11]

I've hurt my psyche, can you make it better?

Counselling is, of course, often embarked upon at periods of distress or disturbance. Individuals may want to break behavioural patterns, such as drug addiction, or violent outbursts to self or others. Events might have occurred which have caused sudden distress such as separation or bereavement or coming to terms with serious illness. Or a series of events might occur which 'accumulate' to produce intolerable levels of stress or depression. Or relationship problems might lead to couple counselling, sex therapy or family therapy.

In these instances, people want very varied kinds of help. One woman we know who chose to have bereavement counselling following the death of her father describes the main benefit, which she valued highly, as that of support. Another friend describes the preferred route of changing her excessive drug habit as one of management and behavioural programmes. Some people discover that on facing loss, they rekindle other experiences of loss and choose to explore their past to help resolve the present. Still others wish to commit themselves to long-term therapy in order to make new meaning of their life in the belief that this will aid the current feelings and processes.

That hat looked good on her, why doesn't it suit me?

We can see that there are several functions, then, which counselling fulfils. Coping with loss and transition, specific or general, searching for meaning, making sense of the past, resolving painful feelings, and taking some charge of the future. Does this then mean that every counsellor can help every client, at any time? Not quite!

'Well, I can't understand it . . . it worked on the Gorilla.'

When we remember that there are many different reasons which propel people to become clients, and a whole range of counselling and psychotherapies available, this should make us and our clients very selective about our work. Counselling is a *purposeful* activity, and it is well worth spending a considerable time understanding the purpose of each counselling contract before agreeing to and beginning the work.[12] The counsellor who has only one way of conceptualising what is 'really going on' is at risk of imposing a journey which might not have been requested, or which may not be appropriate.

It is important then to consider whether our own particular form of counselling is appropriate to the client and their purpose. This is not always easy. For example, few counsellors receive mental health training within their courses, unless they are already trained in psychiatric nursing or social work. Although we have advocated that clients can by and large handle their own emotions, there are definite mental states where this is not necessarily helpful, for example where there is a tendency to psychosis. Undergoing other treatments may preclude counselling. For example, one of us was once approached by a client who manifested symptoms usually associated with forms of psychosis, and in the course of negotiating our alliance, it discovered that she was on high levels of medication. During our negotiations, it was felt that her expectations of counselling were unrealistic, and that the effects of the particular medication were incompatible with the counsellor's orientation. The kind of counselling on offer was not appropriate at this stage, or , to put it another way, this client was not appropriate to the counselling approach. This is not to say that other forms of help were not available or appropriate.

Counselling covers a lot of ground, and serves many functions, but let us not get over ambitious. It is good to help, but not everyone needs our help in our way. Even more serious is the realisation that not everyone will benefit from counselling. The cynic in us may see some of its practice as self-serving. In its most helpful mode counselling may be seen as a humane response to personal distress, which demonstrates a social understanding of the trauma experienced. But it must also be appreciated that bringing in the experts can also have the effect, or contribute to the sequestration , or cordoning off, of life events. For example, dealing with grief in counselling might limit the form in which grief is dealt with within families and communities.[13] Little is yet really known about such consequences.

Counsellor or God, that is the question

So where does all this leave the status of counsellors? Our heading may be flippant, but sometimes we wonder just how omnipotent counsellors can believe themselves to be! At this point perhaps we can suggest another important principle of counselling which we would like to introduce, namely;

Principle: Never travel without your humble pills

It is apparent that the discourse of counselling addresses some fundamental philosophical questions about the self, particularly in terms of identity and purpose, as well as offering a forum for dealing with personal distress or unhappiness. If we accept that there are many different reasons why people come for counselling, we will know that to decide that we know the way to help clients after an hour's airing of their story is a decision that needs to be taken with respect and caution. We once heard the tale of the counsellor who saw her (female) client for the first time accompanied by her (the client's) father. Within minutes, she had 'diagnosed' suspected sexual abuse. An extreme example, but how often do we think we know what the work is going to be from the briefest of introductions? Counselling is not a panacea for all evils and neither is it always appropriate. There are complex reasons why people approach counselling, and there are always consequences to embarking on a counselling relationship. We do our best, and our best is enhanced by humility.

If, like us, you don't feel too Godly yet, then the question of status may not arise for you. However, beware, for it has got us in the past and it has this nasty habit of sneaking up on you when you're not looking. We allude here to the tendency of counsellors to grade the problem or the work. It is quite common to hear a certain tone of distaste at the notion of 'problem solving', as if it is in some way superficial, or not as meaningful as 'proper' (and for proper you may read long term) counselling. Yet we find this bewildering. For some people, a problem consists of having to make a choice about whether or not to change jobs. This may be surprisingly straightforward; or it may uncover all sorts of dilemmas about upheaval, relationship, loss, or self-esteem. For some people, a problem consists of their fear that if they don't get something changed soon, then they are going to become violent towards their children. For some people, a problem hinges around identity, or depression.

All of these occurrences are problems - they are problematic to the person experiencing them. It is not the role of the counsellor to make a hierarchy in terms of importance of issue, or 'depth' of work. Who is anyone to say that, for instance, working with young adults who are sexually abused, working with a woman terrified of molesting her daughter, in short intense contracted counselling, is any less 'deep' than working in a counselling relationship that spans months, or years. Not everyone has months or years; not everyone wants to spend that much time on counselling; some people are as incapacitated by the prospect of changing job as others are by the prospect of living with life-threatening illness. To scorn problem solving is to narrow our choices considerably, and shows a misunderstanding of the term. It is all to easy to become the superior expert and to begin to assess the worth of counselling purely from a quasi-professional viewpoint, and not that of the client.

Moreover, it is well to remember that every person is different, with the attributes, abilities and qualities which make them who they are. Just as there may be a difference in learning styles and abilities in conventional educational settings, so in counselling which, after all, is a process of self-education. One or two sessions may be enough for some people, others might want much more. We learn and process at different rates, and of course much goes on outside the counselling session. Therefore people's needs are different, and the means of fulfilling them really should not be exposed to a rating of 'depth' or 'significance' by the counsellor.

Finally, there is the rating scale which has been covertly developed to grade the 'realness' and 'depth' of cognitive versus emotional counselling. For many counsellors, the cognitive is seen as lacking depth and status. This is a curious state of affairs. In our understanding of personhood, cognition, emotion and behaviour are all interlinked. There can be as much value in identifying and changing cognitive processes as in experiencing emotion - actually, we don't really believe that either occurs without the other, it's just that counsellors seem to feel more self-satisfied if they can release the emotion first, and indeed, many counsellors lack competence in cognitive challenge. The effect of cognitive challenge has a tremendous range and potential depth. It seems that the modern counsellor puts such incredible value on the expression of emotion that other forms of being and expression are devalued. You can discern this in the snobbery which is apparent between say 'professional' counsellors and psychiatric nurses. The psychiatric nurse may help people through suicidal, depressive and destructive episodes with the help of cognitive and behavioural approaches, yet they are usually seen as not doing 'proper counselling'.

So duck soup or suck dupe? What's on the menu from here?

So where does this leave us? With something of a professional haggle over what can and can't be used in counselling, not always to the benefit of the client. Part of the reason for this is that the counselling movement has problematised the fact that we do not really know how the human mind works. In other words, rather than simply accepting this, counselling is part of an approach to the world which seeks to explain human behaviour in all its forms, when actually, such explanations are not really forthcoming. This is not to say that we don't have observations, ideas, information. But it is well to remember another principle which is rarely admitted:

Principle: Counselling psychology is no more than informed speculation

We don't have answers, we cannot make blanket statements, and we tread a challenging tightrope between applying what is known without excluding ourselves to new possibilities. However, one of the errors which the counselling movement makes is to try to monopolise a knowledge which it doesn't really have. It would be helpful to say, we don't know how the mind works, we have some ideas, we constantly test them. Some things work in counselling and we can't always extrapolate reasons or universally held theories.

But the profession chooses otherwise. Consider this next argument, presented to us by a senior figure within the counselling profession when we first mooted this book:

> The authors will need to be clear about whether they are being pragmatically eclectic or whether there is some overarching integration. Current trends in counselling are towards integration rather than syncretism. This is particularly important for the trainee counsellor or the counsellor seeking accreditation/registration. A pragmatic eclecticism would not be considered acceptable to most of the existing schemes.

Note that the priority here is for counselling to fulfil an academic standard rather than serve an effective function. Integration helps to make sense and order of things and demands theoretical understanding, whereas pragmatism allows of some ad hoc interventions. It also admits of not knowing. Professions don't like not knowing. Living with not knowing however can be immensely liberating, and leads us to a further principle which we believe to be in the interests of the client:

Principle: Within the context of a counselling philosophy . . . if it works, and its ethical, then use it

Ultimately, we believe that counselling has developed through different modes and orders of human communication. We believe that it is a mistake to become precious or territorial then about what will be counted as acceptable on the basis of what the profession demands. If people are to be excluded from accreditation or recognition on academic rather than pragmatic grounds, then we embark on an extremely precarious route. In other words, if proficiency is determined more by knowledge of limited theory, than by measuring counsellor competence, we are in trouble, and have lost client focus. This does not mean that we advocate an entirely ends justify the means approach. And perhaps we need to answer the question:

So its OK to do anything that works is it?

This isn't quite what we said or quite what we meant! Before we can have some concept of what's expedient in relation to counselling, we have to have some conceptual notion of what counselling is. We will elucidate this point in Chapter Eight. A key concept in most definitions of counselling is that of facilitation, which is seen as a central technique of self-development. Facilitation is used to describe a particular type of help to the individual, specifically without influencing, directing or subjectively contaminating through the values or advice of the counsellor. Through this process, the client is helped to develop a new perspective on them selves or their situation, hence to be able to experience self and events in a different way, and thus to make decisions about their present and their future.[14]

Technically, facilitation entails the use of a range of skills which are essentially reflective in nature. It is hypothesised that such skills are non-contaminative communication skills, i.e. the counsellor's thoughts, views, wishes or anxieties will not be expressed to the client. Reflection is thought to offer a summary 'mirror' of what the client seems to be saying and an opportunity for them to vent the accompanying emotions. Through such expression, the client is helped to develop insights and an opportunity to craft a considered and clearly goal-oriented future, within their own value system. Hence the client is thought to reach their own solutions, rather than those suggested by the counsellor.

This emphasis reflects a cultural shift to the meaning of counselling, which may be seen as having changed from telling someone how to solve their problems, to listening and reflecting in order to help them solve their own problems. As an activity associated with mental health and well-being, it invariably refers to a process wherein people are helped not only to solve problems, but to develop insight, in order ultimately to shape their lives in a less stressed or more fulfilling way. Insight is assumed to be a desirable attribution, as is fulfilment. The concept of fulfilment is grounded in the client's own value system. Thus any activity to help clients move needs to both purposeful and facilitative to stay within the ethos of counselling.

Summary

Hopefully if you've got this far then we have at least caught your attention. We believe that counselling is grounded in purpose and principles, not in theoretical definition or pure skill delineation. Counselling also operates within a cultural context, and has implications for that culture. Although it is difficult to put our views and questions in a nutshell, key points of this chapter have revolved around the following:

- Counselling has infiltrated just about every pore of our society....is this a good or a bad thing.....not sure yet, it's probably both.

- It used to be OK to give advice, but now it's a definite no no. Even advice agencies seem to frown on advice. Although advice is not a good idea in counselling, has counselling infiltrated too far into advice?

- If we (society) can't solve a problem, or it's inconvenient or too expensive to try, then we can throw counselling at it: is this really what we want?

- Clients, clients everywhere, did we need so much counselling ever before? Does this indicate we are transforming into a society of namby pamby wimpy wallies?

- In this age of quality assurance, performance indicators and essential empirical research, how on earth has something as nebulous as counselling thrived so well....could it be magic, or is it????

- The functions of counselling are amazing.....to know who you are, to narrate your present, identify where you've come from, to support you in crisis, and to solve your problems. How did we manage before??
- Does everyone need counselling? In whose interest is all this proliferation of counselling activity? The clients we hope!
- Do counsellors consider enough whether their method best suits the client's needs?
- The status of the counsellor needs to remain humble and egalitarian. There is a lot that we don t know; counselling psychology is mere informed speculation. Spare us from more gods.
- Counselling should be helpful, let us beware of becoming too precious. If it works for the client then let us use whatever is available within the proviso of the professional ethic.

Endnotes:

1. To say that professional counselling is new to the world is not to deny that human beings have given each other counsel for time immemorial. There are however significant differences between the professional practice of counselling which sees counselling as a non-advisory activity which helps with intra personal issues, and forms of counselling which are more the offering of guidance, support, and wise counsel, and which existed in a world order where all phenomena were not explained in terms of internal processes.

2. See Paul Heelas (1991), for an interesting exposition of the relationships between individualism and the human growth industry.

3. Worden,(1993) and Morgan-Jones, (1993) provide classic texts on the subject.

4. Eric Fromm is noted as one of the great writers on existentialism, as is Carl Rogers. For more contemporary writings, see the work of Emmy van Deurzen-Smith (1988).

5.   See Bridger and Atkinson (1994:18-19) for elaboration on this list. Carl Rogers conceptualises the question which he believes is fundamental to clients in therapy thus:-

It seems to me that at bottom each person is asking, "Who am I really? How can I get in touch with this real self, underlying all my surface behaviour? How can I become myself? (Rogers, 1961).

6.   The interested reader may appreciate the work of Keith Thomas (1977) for his historical documentation of changing social discourse to address questions of meaning. The work of David Smail relates such change to the counselling culture.

7.   See Smith (1989:45-53)

8.   See Smail,(1987) ; Taylor,(1991) and Giddens, (1991:49-51).

9.   This is said to be characterised by a loss of sense of self, of security, of continuity, of trust, of safety, and of freedom, milder version of the ontological uncertainty described by Laing (1964) in his existentialist approach to mental health.

10.   MacIntyre (1981) queries whether it is rationally justifiable to conceptualise the self as such a unity, which resides in the unity of a narrative which links birth to life to death as a narrative beginning to middle to end; (1981:189-191). Such sequestration is described in more detail by Clark (1993) and Giddens (1991)

11.   See Peter Berger, (1973:72).

12.   We are constantly surprised at how contracts are seen as a somewhat perfunctory or superficial part of counselling. Perhaps it is the language which inhibits people from addressing it more thoroughly. From our perspective, however, a well negotiated contract is the first foundation block for effective and ethical counselling.

13.   See Sennett (1977, 1988).

14.   The process is undoubtedly informed by the view that the self has several aspects e.g. self- esteem (how one experiences oneself in terms of value), self-awareness (how one perceives oneself acting and the effects of their actions), and self-actualization (the notion coined by Maslow (1987:66) meaning 'the intrinsic growth of what is already in the organism, or more accurately of what is the organism itself').

Chapter Eight. Talk, Talk, Talk: What is all this about?

Introduction

On current evidence, then, it would seem that whatever the social consequences of counselling, it is currently here to stay. Its very diverse functions and models make for something of a minefield for the individual who wants to be involved with this emerging profession. There is no doubt that there are a number of activities which constitute some form of counselling. There are also a number of arguments surrounding what should be allowed into counselling, who should control it, who should accredit it , and who should make money out of it. Such arguments deserve mention, although the full debates will be simply acknowledged and the interested reader referred elsewhere for further discussions. This brevity is partly expedient; this book is designed as a slim volume, not as a three volume tome. But it is also in recognition that the arguments can become extremely convoluted and precious, and at times can forget what we think is a fundamental principle of counselling, namely, that:

'Counselling is a specific service aimed at helping clients fulfil their potential, when, where and how they choose to! Ya!'

Principle: Counselling is for the client

You may be wondering why this even needs saying - after all, we're all client-centred - aren't we? We all respect our clients - don't we? We always have the client's interest at heart -don't we?

We never overestimate our own importance - do we?

Well, in name, most counsellors would say that they are client centred, although most would also admit that there are times when they forget this and become preoccupied with other matters. However, it is worth keeping an ear or an eye on just who we think counselling is for as we follow some of the debates currently underway within the profession of counselling.

In this chapter, then, we will explore the following. We will review the professional debate as to what counselling actually is, and the difficulties of definition. We will then offer our own definition which underpins this work, and offer a means of differentiating counselling from psychotherapy. Counselling will then be contextualised alongside other interpersonal activities, and, finally, we will introduce some issues regarding the exclusive consequences of the current push to professionalisation of counselling.

So what is counselling?

The central British body committed to the professionalisation of counselling, which has provided a forum for the exchange of ideas and practices, is the British Association for Counselling (BAC). The BAC is unique in being established, in the mid-seventies, in order to associate and co-ordinate diverse bodies of people concerned with the development of counselling, and to further the profession. It is currently rivalled by the British Psychological Society who have a professional resistance to the notion of lay counsellors, and who have instituted a charter system for counselling psychologists in order to retain professional identity and status. Their definition of counselling, and the development of their code of ethics and practice, has nevertheless been strongly influenced by those of the BAC. Likewise, the United Kingdom Council for Psychotherapy also stands in both negotiation and competition with the BAC, and has a national register for Psychotherapists. There is currently a new national register for counsellors, which has been developed 'in the interests of the public', although there is as yet no evidence that such a register will achieve higher quality or more competent counselling, in either an ethical or a practical sense.[1]

The BAC Code of Ethics and Practice for Counsellors states:-

> The overall aim of counselling is to provide an opportunity for the client to work towards living in a more satisfying and resourceful way. The term 'counselling' includes work with individuals, pairs or groups of people, often, but not always,

referred to as clients. The objectives of particular counselling relationships will vary according to the client's needs. Counselling may be concerned with developmental issues, addressing and resolving specific problems, making decisions, coping with crisis, developing personal insight and knowledge, working through feelings of inner conflict or improving relationships with others. The counsellor's role is to facilitate the client's work in ways which respect the client's values, personal resources and capacity for self-determination. (BAC Code of Ethics, 1990:2)

Well, that certainly seems straightforward enough, but of course it does get complicated within common parlance because of the advisory meaning to the word 'counsel'. 'Counsel' originates from the Latin *consilium,* meaning consultation, advice, judgement or deliberating body. The advisory aspect of counselling is perhaps its oldest and most traditional meaning, a tradition still evidenced in legal, medical and, to some extent, religious circles. The term 'counselling' however has undergone an expansion in meaning over the last three hundred years, as counselling has developed as a practice of psycho-social intervention. The Oxford English Dictionary now recognises such a shift, and defines counselling as both advice and as a form of psychotherapy in which the counsellor is supportive and permissive of the client in their own problems solving. Again, this seems rather straightforward.

Yet there are difficulties in defining counselling as an activity independent of any advisory meaning. Firstly, there are historical factors in which advice is very strongly linked to counselling, as mentioned: barristers are still referred to as Queen's Counsel, financial experts are still seen as offering wise counsel on pecuniary affairs, and more recently, a whole host of beauty counsellors, fitness counsellors, have developed. In the public arena, then, the advisory meaning is not only located in the past. Secondly, there is no doubt that the counselling profession wants to define its terms in order to identify areas of *exclusive* expertise. This may or may not be helpful to the client in the long run; it is certainly seen as necessary *if* counselling is to be a fully fledged profession. However, since there are different professional bodies at work, definitions inevitably become part of the game. Take counselling psychology, for example. We used to think that counselling psychology referred to all those theoretical underpinnings of counselling practice, but no, we failed to recognise that according to BPS, only graduate psychologists can be counselling psychologists. Whose interests are being served here?

There is another reason why counselling is difficult to define, and this is that individuals have unique reactions to particular language.[2] Some counsellors for example despise the phrase 'problem solving', some understand 'goal' as a useful concept which is flexible and may be abstract, whereas

'Oh those sort of goals!'

some understand it as a rigid constrainer. There is a tendency for the individual to associate the meaning of an activity with an emotional reaction to the words used to describe it. Those for whom counselling has a comfortable 'feel' to it because of it being described as non-directive will understand the activity differently from those who feel uncomfortable with a lack of clearly defined steps within the activity. In the end, it may not be possible to reach a consensual definition of counselling. So where do we go from here?

One route is to try to distinguish counselling from that which it is not. However, as the *ethos* of counselling, with its emphasis on client self-determination and the facilitative role of the counsellor, is reflected in other 'helping activities', delineation becomes increasingly difficult. In a recent study aimed to differentiate between the activities of advice, guidance, befriending, counselling and using counselling skills, it was found that practitioners in all five activities found the notion of giving the client direction to be undesirable, and seen as incompatible with helping them make appropriate choices and decisions.[3]

It is likely that there is a process of mutual influence between these activities. It is noteworthy that they are all seen as being fuelled by high level communication skills, known as counselling skills when they are used within the values and ethics ostensibly associated with counselling. The notion of interpersonal skills as being a set of activities which individuals can learn, and then apply in the interests of desired outcomes, introduces factors to relationships which are perhaps specific to modern life. Interpersonal relationships become a *reflexive* venture, with individuals consciously considering their utterances before making them, and relating them to what effects they wish to stimulate. What is more, they become a subject, a topic to be learned, to be graded and improved through the use of feedback, itself a reflexive process. This is a move which is quite unique culturally and historically.

Our own belief, based on our experience and research, is that there is an identifiable difference between counselling and other activities. Our definition, which is rather simple and flexible, should be seen in context to the following debate in regard to 'Counselling versus Psychotherapy';

> Counselling is the process by which the client is helped to develop insight into themselves, identify their goals, and construct realistic and appropriate strategies to achieve them. This is done using whatever skills are useful; *without* offering advice, suggestions or guidance; with respect for the client's self determination; and using whatever challenge is required to ensure that the client moves towards their valued outcomes.

With this in mind, we throw the following considerations into the melting pot of current debate.

Counselling and psychotherapy : Won't anyone tell me which is which??

While some professional disagreement is evident in distinguishing between the activities of counselling and the uses of counselling skills, the argument is generally settled to some extent by the notion of how the activity is contracted.[4] More controversy is evident in the clinical distinction between counselling and psychotherapy, and while the dictionary (and perhaps even the layperson) might be content to see them as forms of each other, the professionals have no clear distinctions between the two, claiming substantial similarities and differences within a rather vague context of no committal.

Rogers' fundamental principles have formed the main exemplar of what has become understood as 'counselling'. This term is now used to indicate a therapeutic process which for the most part does not include advice, prescription, or direction. Rogers[5] reported that therapists taking his non-directive approach changed their responses from interpretive, diagnostic, questioning, reassuring, encouraging and making suggestions, to responses that demonstrated understanding of their clients' feelings and attitudes.

From the original idea of counselling as a replacement for medicalised therapy and to today's multiple approaches[6] which flourish and prosper under the umbrella term 'counselling', the differences between counselling and psychotherapy have become blurred. It is now the case that many students and practitioners find the whole business of sorting out counselling from psychotherapy both confusing and tiresome. Time and time again when in the company of student counsellors or at conferences or meetings of qualified and experienced counsellors, this issue arises. It would almost seem that the profession (if we are yet that) has given up on trying to distinguish the two and instead has decided, much like Rogers, to use the two interchangeably.

Even the more obvious distinctions between counselling and psychotherapy seem to have lost their definition. At one time the simplest contrast might have been that counsellors dealt with the more practical everyday problems of people and their relationships, and psychotherapists dealt with the more esoteric, 'intrapyschic' dimensions of the human condition. Today, with counsellors increasingly experimenting with techniques to elicit 'deeper' understanding and to help reconstruct identity , and with psychotherapists becoming increasingly concerned to incorporate skills models into their therapeutics, there appears to be little or no consensus amongst practitioners on definitive distinctions.

It is possible, however, that this move to not distinguish between the two activities is premature, and misses some extremely important distinctions between counselling and psychotherapy which might, just, be of great interest to potential clients. It is also our sense that such a move is more easily acceptable to counsellors than to trained psychotherapists. It is true that both have in common the expressed intention to aid the client's capacity to self-determination and to self-understanding, or insight. Both claim to abstain from advice-giving by the counsellor or therapist. Both claim a facilitative aspect in terms of the process required. They are rendered distinctive, however, both by their method and the theories and philosophies which inform them. The clinical debate will no doubt continue, and may be seen as representing issues and arguments of professionalism within expert systems. In the meantime, however, clients may suffer from not having a clear idea of the range of options open to them, and the demands of any one approach.

Each professional body will make its differentiations when credentialling and examining its own brand of product, and in selling it to the client group, although interestingly the British Association for Counselling declines to demarcate:-

> It is not possible to make a generally accepted distinction between counselling and psychotherapy. There are well founded traditions which use the term interchangeably and others which distinguish them. Regardless of the theoretical approaches preferred by individual counsellors, there are ethical issues which are common to all counselling situations.[7]

It seems then that either the profession really believes that there is no difference, or else it has given up because the issue is so complex. If the latter is the case, then shame on us! Surely it is imperative that the client has some understanding that the type of help they receive might demand quite different things of them, especially with the 'deep' intrapsychic exploration and potential change that some psychotherapies insist upon. Moreover, we might recognise that the motivation of clients to enter any kind of therapeutic activity may be very diverse. And as we mentioned earlier, some people want help with a specific issue, some wish to confront issues of identity or existentialism. It would seem helpful if they could have some information as to whether they are in the right place!

Directive and non-directive

Will you tell them what to do or will they do what they want?

However, we recognise that it is not surprising that the terms counselling and psychotherapy are used interchangeably, for counselling is certainly about 'a person's well being' which when liberally interpreted could be described as 'therapy'. Also the work is usually focused upon 'self awareness and insight' which is, of course, a mental process - thus in line with the prefix 'psycho'. However, the difficulty may be in the therapy part, which carries with it so many connotations of 'doing to' someone, rather than some process that has an egalitarian ethos. It can, of course, be argued that therapy, or the process of therapeutic change can be done by oneself to oneself, and undoubtedly this is the way Rogers perceived it.

Rogers'[8] view was that although there was a therapist present who 'facilitated' the process, it was the clients who, given the necessary conditions, developed their own insight, healed themselves, solved their own problems and became fully functioning. Despite counter claims arguing that even Rogers himself was directive,[9] it is clear that it was his *intention* to be non directive.

One way out of this confusion may be to think of counselling as a process of helping which could be categorised as 'non directive' or 'directive'. But this sits very ill at ease because when Rogers coined the term 'counselling' as a means of professional demarcation, he used it to specifically exclude directiveness. Another alternative might be to see psychotherapy as the umbrella term and simply have 'non directive psychotherapy' and 'directive psychotherapy', and our hunch is that currently, implicitly, this is what we already have!

Will you tell them where to go or just how to get there?

Another factor, just to make the complicated more complex, is that there are both degrees and different *types* of directiveness. One type of directiveness refers to the advisory role of the therapist who will suggest a specific technique to try such as fixed role therapy in Kelly's Personal Construct Theory.[10] The direction of the fixed role therapy will be dictated by the client, and there is no directive from the therapist or client to discover *why* the client is faced with particular problems. Another type of directiveness is linked to advice, in terms of the therapist suggesting strategies, or ideas of what might be done.

Other psychotherapies follow a cause and effect model of psychic development, and seek to explain behaviour. Such therapies are directive through their insistence on the theoretical framework driving which developmental issues need attention; moreover, such theory also directs the focus of the relation-

'That way I tell you . . . no that way.'

ship between therapist and client. Hence the directiveness is channelled through the theoretical framework.

In all types of directiveness, there is a range of *degree*. The
therapist who is directive of strategies or techniques might impose
their view through the raised eyebrow which shows some disap-
proval, or an encouraging nod, to the fully frank 'no you mustn't',
or 'that sounds really good'. The theoretically rigid therapist will
make sure that the client makes specific intrapsychic explora-
tions, e.g. the relationship with a particular significant other,
whereas the theoretically flexible will be more experimental.

'Pure counselling', on the other hand, claims to be non-directive
in both senses. No single model of human development underpins
the process, though various skills are recognised as essential for
its conduct; listening, attending, empathic understanding, focusing, challenging, summarising.[11] Additionally, counsellors espouse
a philosophy wherein particular personal qualities are seen as essential to the counselling process, as are the adoption of specific
attitudes.[12] The counsellor is seen as having to be genuine and
respectful, to offer a 'congruence of self'. S/he is expected to suspend judgement of the counsellee, to adopt an attitude of unconditional positive regard, no matter what the behaviour of the client.
Moreover, s/he must be able to convey such personal attitudes
and qualities to the client.

Such complexity makes it difficult to be clear. An added
complication is the reluctance of some professionals to define counselling at all, as each counselling relationship is 'unique' as a human interaction.[13] However, we believe that counselling can be
defined in terms of purpose and principles, and in the spirit of
inquiry, we propose the following differentiation between counselling and psychotherapy.

I can see clearly now the fog has gone!

Firstly, let us take 'counselling' to mean something close to Rogers'
proposition of meaning 'non advice', 'non-directive', 'non-
interpretive', 'non-suggestive', 'non-reassuring', 'non-prescriptive',
'non-diagnostic', but for absolute clarity we label this type of
psychotherapist a 'non-directive, person centred counsellor'. And
we take something approximating the opposite type of practitioner
who is 'directive', 'advisory', 'diagnostic', 'controlling', 'prescriptive'
and 'interpretive' and for absolute clarity we call this person a
'directive psychotherapist'. We can then compose an axis which
would be helpful to measure where we fit on it, help us describe

our preferred way of working and therefore how we intend to work. Again, we would suggest that this is useful to the client.

Whereas counselling embraces eclecticism, psychotherapy often embraces a 'cause and effect' theoretical model of human development. The therapist has access to the theory being applied and offers interpretations of the client's feelings, experiences, thoughts or behaviour, in direct correlation to the specific ideology. For example, a therapist who embraces feminist versions of psychotherapy might suggest that her female client is depressed because of the patriarchal system in which she has been placed by society. A Freudian psychotherapist may interpret dreams about trains and tunnels in direct association to sexuality.

The traditional psycho-analytical model of psychotherapy is a lengthy and intense process wherein the client is encouraged to relate present day feelings to past influences and relationships, notably those within the family. The therapeutic relationship is seen as central to the process, and is used systematically to explore relationships, express 'repressed' feelings and produce changes in ways of relating.[14] Here it is clear that the therapeutic relationship is analysed in terms of transference and countertransference, projection and projective identification. Within this theoretical framework concepts such as stages of bonding, dependency, confrontation, integration and separation may be also be identified, speculated upon, and suggestions for change made.

Why . . . Psychotherapy? What . . . Counselling?

In crude terms, then, it could be suggested that the major distinction between the two activities is that while psychotherapy is concerned with the question why, with definite notions of cause and effect being inherent in the theory, counselling may be seen as addressing the question what, for example:

> What are you experiencing, what are you feeling, thinking, and doing, what do you want instead, and what is your best way of achieving it?

Although we believe this is helpful in underlining one of the biggest distinctions, we are only too aware that all the distinctions are not as clearly silhouetted. For us, however, counselling and psychotherapy need to be clearly differentiated in order for the client to receive a better service, to provide the client with a clearer choice, and to help the practitioner to work more purposefully. To this end, we have developed a practical axial model of differentiating counselling from psychotherapy which we hope will be helpful to the reader, or at least prompt some further thought.

A proposed 'Axis Model' Differentiating Non Directive Person Centred Counselling and Directive Psychotherapy.

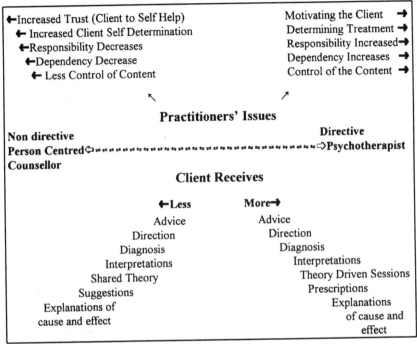

←Increased Trust (Client to Self Help)
← Increased Client Self Determination
←Responsibility Decreases
←Dependency Decrease
← Less Control of Content

Motivating the Client →
Determining Treatment →
Responsibility Increased→
Dependency Increases →
Control of the Content →

Practitioners' Issues

Non directive
Person Centred⟵~~~~~~~~~~~~~~~~~~~~~~~~~⟶**Psychotherapist**
Counsellor

Client Receives

←Less   More→

Advice   Advice
Direction   Direction
Diagnosis   Diagnosis
Interpretations   Interpretations
Shared Theory   Theory Driven Sessions
Suggestions   Prescriptions
Explanations of   Explanations
cause and effect of cause and
                  effect

The diagram reflects some of the central concepts which we believe fundamentally separate the two extremes of counselling and psychotherapy. In addition to the diagram we would add notes on the following issues.

Responsibility

Issues of responsibility have been discussed in Chapter Six. Basically, we are suggesting that prescription of any kind carries with it, for the prescriber, some responsibility for the outcome. When choices of which issues to explore, what strategies to take, are limited in any way by the practitioner, then the greater the degree of directiveness, and the more responsibility is carried. In other words, when therapists prescribe anything for their clients, they do so with considerable responsibility and should always seek informed consent by offering clear explanations of the likely outcomes of the work.

Dependency

My client's very wealthy, she comes to see me eight days a week!

Prescription and advice, inherent in some of the approaches labelled psychotherapy, carry with them the greater possibility of dependency. Some approaches even embrace dependency as an inevitable and helpful part of the therapy; by some it is considered in much the same light as transference, that is, to be employed gainfully in the helping process. We have no doubt that the majority of clients who experience dependency are initially undaunted by it and indeed welcome it, after all, to be given clear direction and answers to questions that have previously eluded one, is a relief. However, it is our view that in the longer term, dependency can be debilitating to the individuals' prospect for self determination, for the client has only learned to be thankful for the therapist's good suggestions and blame them for the ones that didn't work!

Control

Let's move on or tell me about your sex life

Another way of distinguishing the difference between counselling and psychotherapy is to examine how much and what type of control is exerted over the client by the therapist. It would seem to us that when the therapist takes complete charge of both the process and the content of the clients session, then considerable control over the therapy has been exerted - this we would consider to be at the 'directive therapy' end of the continuum. Towards the counselling end of the continuum, it would seem that the control of the process would be more evident, but hardly ever the content. For example, using Egan's framework, the counsellor might ask the question, in stage two 'so what would you like instead', or in stage three 'how many ways can you think of that would enable you to achieve your goal', but never 'tell me about you sex life'. There is still inherent expertise here, in terms of the counsellor being able to understand and apply any framework, but it is an expertise in helping the client find their own solutions via their own routes. It is never telling someone what to do, or which areas it would be useful to explore.

Counselling and other interpersonal activities

Oh my God there's more

The debate and distinctions between counselling, psychotherapy and other activities is deeply enshrined within the establishment of professional boundaries and the development of systems of expertise. There is another set of distinctions and similarities which bear brief visit, namely, those between the activities of counselling and relationships of friendship.

'Yes, but will you still respect me after the ses-

Friendship is apparently very little discussed within most clinical and counselling literature, although it is frequently posited that loneliness and isolation, or lack of intimacy, are common reasons for entering into counselling. Friendship and counselling enjoy a complex and paradoxical relationship. On the one hand, counselling claims some of the qualities we might normally associate with friendship, such as unquestioning support and acceptance, genuineness and empathy,[15] to be available to the client all the time, although whether or not this is actually possible is of course a debatable point. On the other hand, counselling is also seen as very definitely different from friendship in its contractual nature, and it is ethically required that counsellors make it explicit that they will not transgress their own boundaries by becoming friends with their clients, although in practice we know a substantial number of counsellors, ourselves included, who will use their skills and understanding with friends within a contracted counselling period.[16]

There are identifiable similarities and differences between counselling and friendship. For example it is commonly supposed that the counsellor has more power than the friend, in a specific kind of way; the counsellor works to a professionally, and sometimes legally, enforceable contract; the counsellor offers promises of virtue and reliability; and the counsellor is especially employed to foster the client's self-esteem. The friend, however, although offering some similar qualities of warmth and acceptance, is likely to have a more equal relationship in terms of power and status, and will expect a

169

mutuality in quality and activity in a two way process. Friends might offer advice, be judgemental, share their flaws as well as their insights, and negotiate their relationship in an ongoing way which recognises that it does not have pre-determined, or specifically anticipated, outcomes.

There are activities which seek to transgress the differences between contracted helping activities and benevolent helping relationships, the most prominent being befriending and co-counselling. References to befriending go back to 1879, when missionaries 'befriended' offenders and their families.[17] More recently, befriending has been commonly associated with the Samaritans, and with agencies dealing with HIV and AIDS, such as the Terence Higgins Trust. Befriending schemes in this context are often referred to as buddying. Befriending is defined by practitioners as providing a high quality level of support to individuals in periods of distress, its purpose being both to help the befriended (friend? client?) to develop appropriate coping skills, and to lessen the person's sense of social or personal isolation. Befrienders might also take on an advocacy role at times, in order to help the client-friend to have access to all available resources.

Befriending is specifically associated with countering social isolation, and befrienders actively resist the move to make it a profession. This becomes more difficult as the activity takes on more and more the use of counselling skills. There is an inherent paradox being highlighted in this resistance, which hinges around the apparent incompatibility between human closeness as an informal and "natural" activity, and as a "skilled" activity, as detailed above. Countering isolation implies some sort or level of intimacy, perhaps, while there is suspicion as to whether this is genuinely possible if the emphasis is on skills.

In practice, of course, not only do some counsellors counsel their friends, but they might also feel the urge to make friends of clients. One counsellor divulged recently that she had twice said to a client that she *felt like* saying, 'Oh for God's sake, let's just stop this counselling and go down to the pub for a drink and a talk'. What is unusual about this counsellor is her level of honesty and her insight to make of that some appropriate interventions with the client, but the feeling is not unique to her and happens not infrequently - 'if only we'd met in different circumstances, we could be friends'. A curious and contentious profession that legislates for (or against) human relationships. No wonder this is not always easy.

So after all of that what is proper counselling?

So who does proper counselling? Apart from the disputes between counsellors and psychotherapists, three main arguments exist over this question. One is over the status of the problem of the client, and another the intervention style of the counsellor (cognitive v. emotional, for example), both of which have been addressed in Chapter Seven. The third regards the battle of the barefoot counsellor versus the mighty shod, which deserves brief mention.

I'm terribly distressed, but first show me your certificate

The barefoot counsellor is usually highly experienced and counsels in situations where all that stuff we're taught on our training courses to Masters level doesn't apply. The barefoot counsellor counsels through letter boxes when women are not allowed out for either personal or cultural reasons: s/he counsels in corridors and crowded rooms, with children running around; s/he counsels on the bus, in the car, on any moving object with wheels (well, they do say that counselling is like taking a personal journey!) ; s/he counsels people who are short of a fix, or about to get one; s/he counsels in situations of crisis, and has to deal with the unexpected. This is not the type of counselling where two people sit in a peaceful room and work solidly together for fifty minutes out of an hour. This is on the hoof work, rapid response work, with individuals often developing their skills alongside their nous; not everyone can afford to undergo the highly expensive training programmes which are currently cornering the market and defining counselling, and not everyone wants to. One of the consequences of the current training movement and the accreditation movement, which is not competence based, is that it is producing a highly value laden and culturally specific notion of what counsellors should do. As well-shod counsellors shout louder for their value, command higher fees, and persuade organisations that their counsellors should be accredited/trained, so the value of the barefoot counsellor is reduced. Moreover, training courses become more and more expensive, and more and more academic, with insistence on an understanding of counselling theory which becomes exclusive and which may be quite unnecessary. The barefoot counsellor can however take some comfort from the fact that none of the distressed people we've helped have ever asked for a look at our certificates. Just as well, really! However, they have asked for and been offered information regarding our experience and our approach. Perhaps these are after all the most important aspects of our credibility.

Summary

In sum, then, we are suggesting that currently, there is some disarray within the counselling profession about what activity it is they offer. There is particular dissent between what differentiates counselling and psychotherapy. There is also a degree of snobbery about who should be 'proper' counsellors. Our own perspective is that it is important to distinguish between counselling and psychotherapy as they are informed by different theoretical approaches, and therefore require different activities and commitments from the client. This differentiation seems much more important than the distinction between qualified/unqualified practitioners. Ultimately, competence should be defined in terms of client outcomes within a counselling ethos.

Endnotes:

1. It can be argued that the registration of practitioners is more for the good of the profession than the safety of the public, which is the usual justification. There is no evidence of standards of work being increased through such moves. See Russell and Dexter (1993), and Pilgrim and Teacher (1992).

2. This realisation was made during an exercise in differentiating counselling from other activities (Russell et al, 1992), and is also made eloquently by Colin Feltham, (1995:6).

3. See Russell et al (1992:17).

4. The BAC Code of Ethics and Practice, (1989) states that:

   The term 'counselling skills' does not have a single definition which is universally accepted. For the purpose of this Code, 'counselling skills' are distinguished form 'listening skills' and from 'counselling'. Although the distinction is not always a clear one, because the term 'counselling skills' contains elements of these two other activities, it has its own place in the continuum between them. What distinguishes the use of counselling skills from these other two activities are the intentions of the user, which is to enhance the performance of their functional role, as in line manager, nurse, tutor, social worker, personnel officer, voluntary worker etc. The recipient will, in turn, perceive them in that role.

5.   Rogers (1942) in his early book highlighted an entirely new way to offer help without taking an expert position, and emphasized that there was no need for advice . His faith in the client's ability to help themselves if the right conditions existed was a theme he vigorously pursued throughout his life-time.

6.   Karusu (1986) and Feltham (1995) suggest somewhere between 3 and 4 hundred approaches are currently operated under the guise of counselling or psychotherapy .

7.   This is an interesting statement as it is grounded in ethical rather than practical discourse, and avoids totally the questions of what each activity is. Doubtless there are ethical issues which counsellors share with doctors, although their activities are quite different. See BAC (1992).

8.   Rogers (1957) classic article setting out his necessary and sufficient conditions for change using a counselling approach is well worth the effort to read first hand. Also available in Kirschenbaum & Henderson (1990).

9.   Rogers and B. F. Skinner, debate the possibility that non verbal prompts gestures and smiles may well be considered to be directive see: Kirschenbaum and Henderson (1990).

10.   George Kelly (1955, 1955a) used many different approaches in his work with clients: very little could be inconsistent for him, as his consumate theory, from a cognitive frame, allows a refreshingly flexible approach without excessive directiveness.

11.   See Russell et al (1992), Egan (1994), Culley (1991), and Carkhuff (1987).

12.   See Rogers (1951), Egan (1975,1990 &1994) Truax and Carkhuff (1967), and Corey (1996).

13.   This seems to be rather a copout. Any 'helping' profession, including teachers, social workers, foster parents, nursery nurses, psychiatrists, establish human relationships of a higher or lower calibre. Their professions can all be defined though in terms of what they are there to do.

14.   One short description of psychotherapy is :

     ..the systematic use of a relationship between therapist and patient- as opposed to pharmacological or social methods - to produce changes in cognition, feelings and behaviour. Holmes and Lindsey (1991:.31)

15.   See Feltham, (1995:19).

16.   Feltham (1995:20) makes the same point that although there may be hallowed rules which divorce counselling from friendships, in practice it is likely that some counsellors do contract counselling with friends much more commonly than is currently admitted.

17.   See Hagard et al (1987)

Chapter Nine. Philosophy, Psychology, Faith, and Goodwill: Aimless prattle or just common sense?

Introduction

The underpinning philosophy and values of counselling are based on some rather flimsy and somewhat superficial consideration of debate on the nature of self. For example, despite the rich philosophies of self available to us from both Western and Eastern philosophies over hundreds of years, counselling has almost unquestioningly embraced that of Kierkegaard. In other words, it exhorts us to be that self who one truly is . There is an increasing philosophical and sociological literature challenging the wisdom or credibility of such exhortation, literature which argues that the metaphorical 'wearing of masks' is in fact both useful and necessary to 'healthy social relations'. Such acknowledgement is so far missing from the counselling literature.

This is not to say that counselling literature does not talk about self all the time. Indeed, the wide range of counselling literature depends on all kinds of grand claims; the self is tripartite (id, ego, superego), the

A rather gloomy man called Kierkegaard thought we'd better drop all masks, so I guess we'd better . . .

self is in constant mental conflict, the self is ultimately good, the self exists as a self-contained (sic) unit, the self is an essential attribute, the self is layered, and so on. However, the legitimacy of these assertions seems somewhat taken for granted, rather than contextualised or questioned within relevant discourse. Therefore, the philosophical speculations which they represent are sometimes presented as truths. So once again, some humility and careful considerations would be much welcomed into the counselling world on these issues.

There is much theoretical exploration to be had here, and hopefully the next few years will see more of it in print. For issues of practice, it is useful to examine the philosophical foundations which currently inform the practice of counselling. These can be usefully summarised by looking at the assumptions which inform the core conditions which have come to be accepted as legitimate principles of successful counselling. What beliefs underpin such conditions and are presented as truths within the counselling world? Consider the following:

- People are intrinsically good
- People, given the right conditions, move toward 'self-actualization'
- There is such a thing as self-actualization
- Self-actualization is intrinsically social
- Counselling can provide the right environment for self-actualization to occur.

Sometimes, these are presented as such absolute and unchallengeable beliefs, so fiercely held, implicitly trusted and so assertively espoused as to render any doubt or scepticism almost sinful in some circles. However, *they are only beliefs.* This does not render them useless, but in order to enhance our understanding of the possibilities and limitations of counselling, it is necessary to analyse or deconstruct them.

It is our view that a healthy dose of critical subjectivity, or scepticism, is of great value to the counsellor. We do not believe that students (and we use this term in its broadest sense) should accept without reservation all that they have been told. Good counsellors are social scientists, and as such should be able to step back a little from their discipline to critique it. So, in this chapter, we invite you to look carefully at some of the concepts which are perhaps too readily accepted in training courses, and to determine for yourself whether all of the ideas first adopted in your training still hold for you the same magical entrancement when they are demystified. Through offering a critical appraisal of the core conditions, we are also suggesting that some of the philosophical doctrine in counselling is not simply constructed from an altruistic stance, entirely for the benefit of the client. Indeed our conclusion is that many of the value bases of counselling have very pragmatic purposes.

The core conditions and associated concepts

We are informed by the research that empathy, warmth and genuineness[2] are the necessary pre-conditions which must exist for the client to benefit from any form of therapy or counselling. Eminent authors[3] argue other essential counsellor attributes, i.e. non judgementalness, unconditional positive regard, and respect for self determination, as enhancing the process of therapeutic personality change. These are widely, although not universally, accepted as central concepts of counselling. Indeed, it is mooted that these are the conditions which are so mighty that they can transform whole personalities, even inter-state relationships. What are these conditions then which are claimed to make counsellors the 'strong men' of the Western world?

Empathy

Empathy is defined in most counselling texts as the listener's ability to thoroughly understand the client's world without contaminating that understanding with their own thoughts or feelings. Empathic listeners are said to be able to perceive the client's thoughts, feelings, behaviours and experiences "as if" they were one's own.[4]

This would seem to represent a difficult task for any human being. There are four points which make it so. Firstly, this quality of understanding needs to be communicated effectively by the client either in the form of language, which in itself has its own limitations,[5] or by non verbal messages which are open to interpretation.[6] Secondly, the negotiation of accuracy is mediated by the motivation of the client to allow such intimacy with the counsellor. The relationship between the counsellor and the client will be a significant variable in this latter respect. Intimacy requires a relationship of trust which may not be in place immediately. This would rather point to empathy being a state that exists as a process rather than a moment to moment event. Thirdly, if this special understanding is possible, and all these difficulties can be surmounted, there still remains the potential for contamination in regard to the cultural contexualisation of the client's experiences which may not instantly be available to the counsellor. For instance, the class, status, education, and race of the two people engaged in the interaction may have significant influence on the accuracy and depth of understanding between them.[7]

Finally, feelings, and their interpretations, represent a formidable barrier to understanding. Precise understanding would require very skilful negotiation between client and counsellor to ensure accuracy, and this would rather preclude the *"moment to moment"* immediacy that some authors propose. After all the counsellor has only his/her own perceptions of verbally labelled emotions to gauge the client's world. To elucidate further, it is only possible to understand what jealous, hateful or relaxed mean, in terms of one's own psychological and physiological state; an individual has no way of knowing the intensity that is currently occurring for another. It is only possible to approximate from observations, and be corrected by the other. This will invariably take time, and therefore cannot be an instant or spontaneous event.

This does not logically mean that empathy cannot occur. It simply means that if, or when it does, it is an uncertain event. Neither party can be sure that a state of empathy has existed. This assertion is in regard to the inability of any person to be positive of what is occurring in the other's world.

'I know that you believe you understand what you think I said but I'm not sure you realised that what you heard is not what I meant!'

Clients, for their part, may simply be unable to communicate their complex worlds adequately to the counsellor, either verbally or non verbally, or they may withhold some private elements of their world from the counsellor, either consciously or unconsciously, deliberately or accidentally. Neither the client nor the counsellor can be absolutely certain. It is perhaps more sensible to look at empathy as a difficult skill which is evidenced by the development of understanding between two people.

Empathy as a skill then will also depend on the proficiency of the counsellor, and the way that they articulate their empathy will have different effects upon the client and the subsequent relationship. There is no doubt that empathy is understood variously, and practitioners think that they demonstrate empathy while relating their understanding in very different ways. For example, possible differences may take the following forms:

Client: Last night I had a heavy row with my lover and said some terrible things. (Sighs) And this morning I wish I hadn't.

At least three possible responses may occur here, for argument's sake, which might have different effects.

C.1.   So last night it seems as if you were angry with your lover, and now it sounds as if you feel some regret.
C.2.   (Nodding copiously) I feel the sadness in you.
C.3.   I think you've done something which you wish you hadn't and I think it's brave of you to admit that. I think you've done really well.

The first response is purely reflective to help the client identify the emotion. It combines 'there and then' empathy along with 'here and now empathy'. There is no attempt to merge with the client or to offer opinion. The second attempts some kind of statement of 'altered selves' and some display of merger. The third offers 'empathic challenge', in noting the hidden strength of the client, but within the framework of the therapist's opinion and offer of approval. Each may have different consequences in the quality of the emergent relationship as perceived by both parties. While we would only call one of these responses empathic, we know full well that others might argue that the other two would create the state of empathy. A complex area then.

To summarise, empathy may or may not be possible, but it would seem that its existence is always doubtful in any interaction. The existence of empathy rests largely on the ability of the two parties to willingly negotiate complete understanding. Many factors play a potential part in making this difficult, i.e. language, and its intrinsic potential for misinterpretation; cultural, educational, and individual incompatibilities; the motivation of the individual to communicate honestly and completely; the ability and willingness of the counsellor to hear accurately all of the client's disclosure and not to listen selectively ; and the accurate understanding of non verbal communication with its inherent cultural identity. We doubt that it is some God given intrinsic ability or gift that only some of us can have, or some mysterious artistic magic that defies description. We believe that it would serve the interests of the profession to be very honest and describe empathy as hard work requiring full concentration, sensual acuity, rapid data collecting and plain common sense.

A further question exists however; is empathy actually necessary to therapeutic change, to counselling? Do I actually have to be understood by the counsellor to feel respected by them enough to benefit from their expertise? While the automatic answer is yes, it could be argued that as long as the counsellor enables me *somehow* to better understand *myself,* then why do *they* need to understand me at all? What if I don't want you to understand me, but I desperately want to be challenged in my thinking to help me make an important decision - and I'm confident enough that we don't have to have an empathic relationship to achieve this? Empathy can only ever be instrumental to the counselling goal, so it is by no means *absolutely* certain that it is per se necessary to all counselling. However, from the evidence of our own experience and of available research, we do conclude that it is helpful for counselling to occur effectively.

I'm telling you sincerely, folks, that what you see is what you get. . .

Genuineness is possibly one of the most abused terms in counselling discourse. It is used to incorporate congruence - is the counsellor acting in a way which demonstrates their immediate thoughts and feelings: transparency, can the client discern this: or authenticity, a concept which refers to the counsellor being that self who they truly are without masks or role. All these terms have been used to refer to the helper's effective avoidance of posturing, playing a role, or erecting a façade or a barrier between the client and her/himself. In essence, it is the counsellor being "real". Two common misinterpretation occur, one that the 'role' of counsellor demands nothing more or less than being how you usually are, and the other that if you adopt postures of any kind, then you are erecting façades. There are some very tenuous links made in these equations which are not necessarily either true or helpful, and which have resulted in two weak developments. One is the extreme emphasis placed on counsellor self-development, and the other is on the spurious belief that the genuine nature of the relationship is more important than the level of skill or competence. Additionally, some authors[8] point to a lack of genuineness or authenticity as a source of client dissatisfaction and lack of effectiveness in therapy. So what is this really all about?

'I'll show you who I really am . . .'

Firstly, let us examine whether genuineness is feasible. Is it possible to be completely genuine with clients whilst trying to establish a climate approximating the pre-requisite core condition of warmth , which is discussed later in this chapter? Only, it would seem, if the individual can genuinely feel warm toward the client. We may ask the reader if it is always possible or indeed prudent to express *genuine* warmth when clients disclose certain types of behaviour?

For example, where would the reader be warm and where would they be genuine when faced with the following:

- A woman who discloses her contempt for all men;
- a man who discloses his contempt for all women;
- the client who relates the actions involved when helping their sick mother with her suicide;
- a client's joy at the death of their partner;
- indifference of a mother towards the welfare of her children;
- the racist comment of the client relating their acts of discrimination.;
- the HIV+ive/hepatitis B client carelessly exposing others to infection;
- the therapist abusing their trust with their clients.

These situations can sometime take the counsellor by surprise, when we guess genuineness will take care of itself; but what of a deliberately chosen response for the second time this situation is disclosed - what then? Genuineness, unconditional positive regard, or warmth? Maybe such dilemmas herald a blank mind or sticky moment.

As this book seeks to inform as well as stimulate your thoughts, we'll answer these questions in this way. **We believe that to abandon your own values in order to be able to be genuinely warm towards a client holding values that would normally be abhorrent to you is not acceptable or helpful!** The price is too high, and the risk of colluding with offensive and antisocial behaviour is too great a risk. The philosophers and theorists who suggest that it is OK to remain warm towards the person and still condemn the behaviour are at odds with the practicalities of everyday life. The idea that the client, or the counsellor for that matter, can separate them'selves' and their behaviour, and thus make sense of this idea, is unrealistic. Most clients that we have worked with have a clear union of them'selves' and their behaviour. They are proud of, or down on, them'selves' because of their behaviour. Even if we are able to genuinely respect the person in front of us and separate her/him from their behaviour, doing so carries with it a great risk that the client will not be able to differentiate so easily.

To illustrate this we invite the reader to imagine what they would do if they had two clients, each of whom recounts a story about them losing their temper and hitting their partner. If client A relates this in a tone of deep regret and client B without any remorse, how do your responses differ? If for example, both are responded to with empathic responses such as "It seems as though when you remember hitting your partner you do so with deep regret" and "You feel satisfied about hitting your partner because they irritated you", what might be the effect upon each client? We could suppose that in the worst case scenario of each example client A would feel more guilty, and client B may feel that his behaviour was accepted as justifiable in the eyes of the counsellor. The way in which the empathic response is delivered may have immense potential for tonal innuendo; if the counsellor is extremely careful to avoid judgement in their voice, they may inadvertently produce a tone of assent. Too much sympathy in the tone may indicate an opinion that the behaviour was acceptable or they too might have been violent in these circumstances. It is because of the potential for inadvertent messages such as this that we would advocate clarification of the counsellor's position in any circumstances where there might be confusion. To place emphasis on the "you" in "you feel" in these circumstances is extremely important. This then carries with it the correct inflection indicating that this is the counsellor's *neutral* demonstration of understanding of the client's world and not the counsellor sharing an opinion about the behaviours or experiences disclosed.

On the other hand, we can only remain neutral if we really are. It can be argued that we should do our upmost to avoid inadvertently colluding with anti-social behaviour, malevolent thoughts, or in any way contaminating the client's ability to review and assess their own true feelings being related. We have no doubt that in the reality of the counselling situation your values will inform your natural warmth towards clients, and this will differ depending on the personality before you. We know that it is useful for the client to encounter warmth, and yet we can also see that on some occasions it is necessary for clients to see genuine reactions to their behaviour, their personalities, and their physical presence. Indeed, feedback via the counsellor's personal responses to the client's behaviour, as in immediacy, is sometimes a part of helping the client see themselves more neatly. The counsellor may decide to use their own judgement in such circumstances, and choose to contextualise their reactions and inadvertent opinions disclosed. When this contextualisation is carefully implemented the fundamental underpinnings of the philosophy of client self-determination is more likely to be preserved.

More trivially perhaps but equally pertinent, can we always be genuinely at ease and display warmth when confronted with disfigurement, looks which we perceive as plain ugliness, or lack of charisma in our clients? Do any of these give rise to greater concern for you? Does the reader recognise themselves in any of the following examples?

- The sudden exposure to physical disfigurement stimulates an involuntary shudder or wince directed to the vision rather than the person exhibiting it.
- Counsellor finds eye contact and interest more difficult with the 'ugly' client?
- Lack of charisma is confirmed by the counsellor's excessive distraction and lack of concentration.

None of these appear to be particularly damaging to a relationship over a long term, but each in its turn demonstrates the absence of warmth - yet they are genuine. Equally, if we did feel warm towards a client and found them immensely attractive and charismatic, would we disclose this to the client?.

We would assert that to recoil at the client who for the first time reveals their disfigurement, to be angry and disgusted by some recounted behaviour, or demonstrate your feelings towards some prejudiced remark can be both natural and helpful (For more on this see Chapter Three). We would be quick to qualify this by also saying that **the therapeutic process is only enhanced and pursued if the counsellor is able to contexualise their reaction.** The client has the benefit of knowing that her/his therapist is genuine, and that despite what was disclosed they want to be helpful. It is important that the counsellor finds a way of being able to demonstrate their feelings toward a disclosure and simultaneously inform the discloser that it is the client's feelings which are under review. They need to know that disclosure of themselves in any form will meet with some human reaction, but should that reaction be perceived as negative, it does not mean they, they are judged to be a 'nasty' person without hope of help if they wish it. In this way the counsellor can remain genuine and real, whilst remaining supportive to the helping objective and accepting of the person as having potential for change.

'Yes, I've got my empathy and my warmth, I'm going for genuineness next.'

So, we might conclude that genuineness is possible though complex. The second set of questions regarding genuineness are to do with its nature and its worth. Is it always a good thing, what impact might it have on the client, and is it the same as authenticity?

The counselling profession has almost automatically accepted that being genuine is a good thing. Although we as individuals have come to this conclusion ourselves, it has not been automatic and does rest on some pragmatic reasoning rather than idealism. Genuineness is important because it may have strong influential properties. One possibility is that genuineness is an instrumental agent in the client's change. The client's perception that the counsellor is genuine will have the tendency to validate the counsellor's skilled responses, whether they are attitudinal, i.e. demonstrating warmth, positive regard, or whether skilled empathic responses or challenges. Because the *counsellor* is perceived as genuine their responses are also perceived as genuine. The client, then, may experience a powerful influence, in terms of feeling understood, valued, or if we were to be prescriptive, encouraged to take a particular direction or course of action. In other words, genuineness encourages credibility, apart from anything else.

Further, therapy is acknowledged as having the potential to be persuasive and powerful,[9] with potential for exploitation.[10] Moreover, the counsellor will, in behavioural terms, be modelling genuineness and thus, if the client is susceptible to this influence, it is possible that the client will move towards becoming more genuine him/herself. Taking this theme of genuineness even further, we are obliged to register what the behaviourist school of psychology add to this debate. The effects of modelled behaviour described within social learning theory suggest clear possibilities that it is possible for clients to manifest a behaviour or behaviours that were first portrayed by the counsellor.[11] The likelihood of this occurring is enhanced by factors such as admiration or respect for the person exhibiting the behaviour.

It can be seen then that counsellor behaviour, especially if the counsellor is in some way charismatic, may well be mimicked by the client. Thus, behaviour observed in the client may have been originally instigated or modelled for the client by the counsellor. This tends to suggest that there is potential for the process of counselling to be more directive than initially suspected or intentionally proposed . The reader at this point may want to consider the advantages to the counsellor of the client becoming more open and genuine and contemplate the practicalities of 'modelling genuineness'. We might also want to stop and explore the cultural ramifications of exalting genuineness as a *desirable* quality to emulate.

Finally, you will have gathered that we largely agree with the concept of genuineness as helpful, although we would stress that our agreement only holds when genuineness as a practice and a concept is purposeful and contextualised. We do not understand genuineness to necessarily mean the same as some understandings of authenticity. We feel free to consider our responses, and to not share all our thoughts and feelings with the client. Being genuine does not for example mean saying everything that occurs to one, voicing your opinions without thought for the reactions and impact upon others; although this may be genuine, it would seldom be either helpful, skilled or caring. The withholding of an opinion, reaction or thought, when motivated by regard for the client, does not make the counsellor ingenuine, simply more tactful and sensitive to potential adverse reactions. There needs to be a distinction acknowledged between genuine in terms of motive, choices made, responsibility taken, and genuine in terms of "I make my every inner thought and feeling transparent to you". A thorough knowledge of your own beliefs and clearly held values, congruent with what you espouse, would be closer to our contextualised definition of genuineness and therefore helpful in a therapeutic relationship.

In addition to the above qualities this genuine person would be someone who is not afraid to disclose facets of her/himself when it is appropriate to helping, but is capable of differentiating what is purposeful disclosure and what would be fruitless. This genuine person would know the difference between privacy and tact, and secrecy and indiscriminate comment. As a final note, it is perhaps important to make clear that these comments are not intended exclusively in regard to counsellors. The client may also have good reasons for avoiding certain disclosures which would not automatically indicate non-genuineness. For example, a client may avoid talking about essentially pertinent issues, simply because it involves talking 'disloyally' about someone they feel protective, supportive or lovingly toward. This does not mean that their desire for help is not genuine. 'Genuineness' does not exist in a vacuum - genuine for what end, within whose framework, and in what context; such questions inform us to a more realistic quality rather than some ideal mumbo jumbo.

'Let me give you my whole self on a plate, my dear.'

In summary it can be argued that the therapist's genuineness can exert a considerable effect on the client in relationship to potential influence; that genuineness and warmth are unlikely to be consistently congruent unless the counsellor is accepting of others values; genuinely displayed negative reactions, although not always associated with warmth are not only acceptable but helpful if contextualised; and genuineness is purposeful and thus should not be confused with tactlessness and indiscriminate comment.

Even though you are a sleazy, greasy, slimeball with the morals of an alleycat and the manners of a pig, I prize your very being - or the myth of unconditional positive regard.

Carl Rogers described this concept as a warm caring and acceptance for a client which is not possessive, demands no personal gratification, and sets no conditions on the thoughts, feelings or behaviours of the client.[12]   Clearly, his clients were more on the Gloria side of the human continuum than the Adolf Hitler side. In coining unconditional positive regard, Rogers merges three concepts already being used in the practice of "client centred therapy"; warmth from the therapist, the unconditional basis for that warmth, and acceptance. It has to be noted that acceptance is not the same as unconditional positive regard, as it has a connotation of neutrality, i.e. I can tolerate or accept a person's behaviour; this does not mean I prize it, as unconditional positive regard implies.[13]

Rogers ideal is the "prizing" of the client's feelings irrespective of them being "good" or "bad". This then goes beyond an acceptance or tolerance of the client as a person. The more pragmatic counsellor might read Rogers as reserving the concept to describe the feelings of the client, and this enables them to address the concept without appearing to condone anti-social or "bad" behaviour of the client. However, this is not precisely what Rogers wrote. In his book "On Becoming a Person: A Therapist's View of Psychotherapy", published in 1961 he is very clear that this regard for the client includes behaviour;

> "By this I do not mean that he [the therapist] simply accept the client when he is behaving in certain ways. It means an outgoing positive feeling without reservation, without evaluations." (p. 62)

Without reading this with extreme care, it is easy to see how a counsellor may be misled into believing that they need to suspend all of their moral judgements during counselling. Implicit in Rogers writing is the belief that people have the ability of being good , and his philosophy is one that prizes the person *despite* the behaviour, this does not necessarily mean that he would approve of some behaviours as the last quote may indicate.

Another difficult question is whether adopting a position of unconditional positive regard is possible or valuable. Rogers' idea of *"a fully functioning person"* is his description of a person 'potentiated' in personal growth. The use of this term enables him to describe a person fully potentiated without having to label that end point as "good" or "bad". However, there is no doubt that it is seen as both individually desirable, and of a social nature. In other words, there is a checklist which is to do with whether we are fully-functioning or not, so that there is a very clear and value laden directive as to how and when personal growth is realised.

Moreover, Rogers does hold an implicit belief that all human beings are capable of becoming "good". In his writings there is the flavour of the evangelist, a fundamental belief that there is no innate evil, and if each infant was surrounded by the core conditions, i.e. they were cared for by real "genuine" people, in a climate of warm regard, empathically understood, and prized for their feelings and behaviours, they would evolve into the inherently good person.

Taking Rogers' hypothesis to its furthest end, does he mean that if society accepts unconditionally any behaviour an individual manifests, and also prizes them for it, that each individual in society will develop into a "fully functioning" person? Would society's "problem behaviour" exist no longer? Without being too critical of this idea, the variables appear somewhat difficult to control. Although it can be argued that extinction of non reinforced behaviour can be rapidly reversed in controlled conditions, these conditions would be hard to replicate in today's society, and within a person's cultural reality.

If society is to accept *any* behaviour and prize it, where would society's values stem from? The reality is of course that they derive from history and context. In some war-torn countries, where violence may be a second generation norm, the ability to be effectively violent might be prized. This does not differentiate the individuals concerned from the rest of the human race, it merely illustrates that society's terms of fully functioning may be wide and varied. Therefore "fully functioning" *per se* is a questionable ideal. In Western society, the drive towards 'fully functioning' which idealises authenticity and self fulfilment is perhaps really only helpful if it takes the individual to a point of understanding self, which includes a heightened awareness of their (social) values and morality. This in turn needs to be contextualised into their dialogue with others and society to prevent it becoming self defeating for them. If the route to self fulfilment does not take account of significant others and society, e.g. relationships are simply instrumental to self actualization, the ultimate result is a degeneration to selfishness without any intrinsic value for the individual.

If the counsellor then is relentlessly practising unconditional positive regard, in behaviourist terms this would be the ideal to be modelled to future generations as "normal" learned behaviour. The difficulty then arises from the task of producing the *environment* which will establish "fully functioning" people as counselling ideology decrees. If we adopt a Rogerian view, and simply take one case at a time, then the task is a great one, for it cannot easily be seen how, in periodic sessions with a client, the influences of peers, significant others and society in general can be reversed. Can the application of unconditional regard by a single therapist reverse the extremes of "bad" behaviour where the formative roots are in childhood behaviour. The practical application of the idea appears to be seriously flawed.

This leaves only five logical explanations for believing that unconditional positive regard is helpful to clients in counselling. These are:-

1.) Counsellors only take clients that are already "good" people that can have that "goodness" enhanced.

2.) Counsellors must operate some judgement as to the proposed outcome of change and influence this throughout the counselling process.

3.) Counsellors disassociate the client as a person from their behaviour. This would give freedom to the counsellor to respond congruently to the behaviours from their own value orientation, whilst still maintaining unconditional regard for the person.

4.) Counsellors begin by operating on a basis of unconditional positive regard, which changes to conditional positive regard in the light of relevant disclosure.

5.) Combinations of all of the above.

If these conclusions are correct it may explain some of the other interpretations of unconditional positive regard in the literature. For example, Gerard Egan's preference for the term 'respect' allows the counsellor more scope to use their personal judgement of a client's behaviour, whilst still holding a neutral position in regard to their client's values.[14]

Warmth

Warmth is itself difficult to define without contrasting it with coldness. Objective, logical and calculating individuals more concerned with fact than emotion are often perceived as cold. However, counsellors may need to have just such qualities in order to see the client's world without becoming subjectively engaged in it, and losing their effectiveness. Thus counselling appears to require the ability to stand back objectively and perceive rationally what is going on.

However, somehow, in some way, whilst operating this 'objectivity', the counsellor must be perceived by the client as being 'warm', i.e. as having some [15] caring toward them.

'My counsellor is so warm and tropical, I just melt . . .'

How is this feat achieved? We would suggest that the non verbal behaviour of the counsellor is 'read' by the client as warm, rather than the words spoken necessarily demonstrating agreement or a positive regard. This is really rather important, because we believe some counsellors perceive 'warmth' towards their clients to be conveyed by demonstrating that they are 'on their side', that they agree with them or by commiserating with them about their predicaments and problems. In this understanding, warmth is presented as a feeling rather than an attitude. We strongly disagree! If this were the case then a considerable amount of the criticisms levelled at counsellors in regard to them being prescriptive and directive would be confirmed. It is most important that counsellors do not collude with their clients view, but instead reflect back the stated view to the client for further contemplation.

An illustration of this may help here. Some time ago whilst working with a client who was regularly beaten by

'I envy you, darling, mine has all the sensitivity of a snowman.'

her husband, one of us (Graham), was confronted with the client's desire to be supported with regard to the way she felt towards her husband. This was easy to spot because her descriptions of events and her opinion about such behaviour was permeated with 'isn't he' and 'shouldn't he'. The client was not only seeking understanding of her situation and how it affected her, but reassurance that her perception of her husband was correct. The easiest course of action in this type of situation is to agree, to say "yes, your husband is a bastard, yes I don't blame you for wanting to kill him, yes of course you should......." but, of course, for those of us who respect the principle of self determination, this would be falling into a very deep trap. On the other hand to withhold some judgement of the husband's behaviour may leave this woman in confusion, or worse, confirm to her that her suspicions are correct - it really is her fault!!

So here we have a situation where the counsellor may feel outraged by what they are hearing, but cannot express this, for fear of influencing the client in which direction she takes. The counsellor's caring instincts may be a powerful desire to convey their personal warmth for her, to hug, comfort, protect or in some way make it better for this woman. All of these approaches are unacceptable to the counselling approach for reason of non interference, yet to suppress these emotions and desires may lead to non-genuineness, another no no. The professional who wants to be able to negotiate around all of these issues, stay client focused, demonstrate warmth and genuineness, has a difficult job. Without wanting to sound trite or glib we suggest this possible way around this logical impasse:

- Remain empathic - "As you are telling me about these events I notice you tremble, I guess even remembering makes you feel unsafe and upset."

- Use appropriate self disclosure - "Simply listening to you recounting your story stirs a lot of emotion in me."

- Contextualise the self disclosure - "However, what I may think and feel is unimportant, what I really want you to do is examine your thoughts and feelings about these events, so eventually you can decide what is best for **you**".

- Challenge dependency and potentially distorted thinking - "Rather than me tell you what I think, ask yourself this question - What is your part in perpetuating this situation?"

■ Inappropriate or impulsive action plans (I want to kill him) can be avoided by challenging the client to identify her goals - "What would you achieve by killing him? Are there other ways of achieving what you want?" or "What would be the consequence of doing that?"

In this way the best hope for some critical distance is preserved and potential for influencing the client is minimised. The client should still perceive you as warm because it has been demonstrated that you are understanding, that you have feelings about her story but that you are consciously (some may say professionally) resisting superficial sympathy in exchange for a positive approach which promises to be centred on what it is she wants to achieve for herself.

One of the essential and different ingredient of this approach which is often undefined is that here we have warmth which is selfless. By this we mean that counsellors' ability to express regard toward the client in this way does not depend on the client reciprocating this regard. In other words the counsellor does feel warm towards the client, and as a pragmatic it would be helpful if the client knew this, however the counsellor is not dependent on the client for self worth or positive regard. It is often this absence of need in the counsellor that will allow the client to be open and honest expression of their thoughts and feelings.

Warmth is an issue that often bewilders students on counselling courses. The same non verbal behaviours that are used to communicate warmth in close personal relationships and friendships are required to be differentiated in some way when used in helping relationships. Both Carl Rogers and Gerard Egan suggest that the helper should have no personal motive for communicating warmth, other than to facilitate the helping process. However, it can be envisaged that both counsellors and clients may have some difficulties operationalising this principle on occasions. It may be postulated that clients finding themselves listened to empathically; addressed with unconditional positive regard; and responded to positively and warmly, irrespective of their disclosures, may find this situation confusing. It may be argued that clients who disclose, for example, foolishness, criminality, selfishness or anti-social behaviour and so on, and meet warm responses, may be forgiven for believing that the counsellor has more than a professional interest in them.

To be non judgemental

The idea of a non judgemental approach is connected to the ability to be warm and to adopt positions approximating unconditional positive regard. However, the idea is reviewed separately because it would appear that it often substitutes for the absolute condition of unconditional positive regard and non possessive warmth. The concept of non judgementalness can be see as:

- a value orientation for practitioners;
- an exemplar of good practice;
- a measure to seduce clients to engage in an intimate climate of self disclosure to further the purpose of counselling.

As a value orientation, it serves to advise counsellors that the client has as a right or entitlement to his/her own view of the world, their own behaviour within it, and their choices for their own self determined changes. For instance, the client who is currently considering an abortion; reducing their alcohol intake; giving up smoking; using drugs; taking out private health insurance; sending their children to private school, etcetera, will all have some impact upon the value perspective of the counsellor. It would not be of particular relevance or serve a therapeutic end for the counsellor to make known their view on the subject. Most counsellors would probably have no difficulty seeing this as logical if they were pursuing a non directive approach. This is not to be confused with making no judgements at all; clinical judgements, and judgements about how we communicate, operate throughout.

Where judgement is suspended, however, this does not amount to unconditional positive regard or non possessive warmth. The absence of judgement is a neutral stance, not to adopt an affirming or prizing of the client s choices or values. This adoption of a non judgemental approach is therefore a half way house for the therapist, one which allows him/her to proceed with a client towards some degree of self-determination without having to either condone or challenge the client's perspective. This approach appears to be the safe moral ground for most, but breaks down when the value ascribed to by the client is diametrically opposed to the one adopted by the counsellor. This is especially the case in situations when the course of action, or the value attached to such ideas, are extreme, counter cultural or in some way threatening to the value integrity of the counsellor. An example of this might be the client who reveals that they are intent on committing murder, rape or some act that contradicts the "norm" of legal, moral or ethical behaviour. In these instances, the counsellor may be forced to resort to an evaluative stance based on their own value orientation in deciding whether they can continue to be non-judgemental, or indeed whether they must act independently to prevent the exploitation or endangerment of other people.[16]

Counsellors who purport to address the qualities of respect and caring for the human individual would be identifying a conflict of interest if they were confronted with a choice of encouraging self determination and protection of the life or liberty of another human being. It is theoretically possible to dispute responsibility for client actions on the grounds that without the conditions of intimate disclosure, they would not be forearmed with the knowledge of such intent, but this serves little logical argument in terms of the contradiction of acting upon one's values in such situations. On a very practical note this situation can often be avoided by clearly demarcating the lines of confidentiality and potential 'post disclosure interference' by specifically contracting these areas before counselling commences.

A further, more contentious, view of non-judgementalness takes the rationale that, when adopting this approach, it will have the effect of seducing the client into honest self disclosure. As a device, it precludes the need for the client to fabricate or try to deceive the counsellor, as the counsellor will adopt a neutrality of evaluation in each subsequent disclosure. The counsellor adopting this approach does not respond in any moralising way to what the client discloses, so the client learns that it is their responsibility to evaluate what they say and do. The counsellor simply becomes a passive recipient of the person's disclosure, so that to lie, elaborate or deceive is to do so to one's self. The latter position adopts a pragmatic view rather than a moral one. It is not adopted from any philosophical value orientation, but simply from the practical position that it is likely to further the aims of counselling.

There is a third possible outcome of such absence of judgement, which is that the client will, in fact, self-delude, and that the counsellor becomes party to such delusion. To put this simply, the client, in the absence of judgemental feedback, decides that the behaviour, thoughts or feelings disclosed are acceptable or appropriate. This is justified by the lack of negative feedback that the 'untrained' client may be expecting from the professional helper. Thus the false belief is affirmed as correct! It is logical to assume that this potential as described would occur more often in counselling than in the more overtly moral and prescriptive therapies which might analyse disclosures and make determinations about them.[17]

In sum, then, we regard non-judgementalness as a *temporary suspension* of opinion and moral values for as long as that is tenable in the context of the counselling. It seems that at one time counsellors accepted it as a quasi-value to be aspired to at all times, and that now, current (welcome) critiques make it an impossibility. We would argue that all human beings are capable of making a temporary suspension of judgement while they replace such activity with something else, such as a willingness to understand another perspective; if they weren't, then our arguments, morals and perspectives on life would never develop. However, in any context, including counselling, information might come our way from either external or internal sources which interrupts our ability for such suspension. This to us is the realistic view, and we have no doubt that the tendency towards purposeful non-judgmentalism within counselling is both useful and feasible.

Self-Determination

Finally, a central philosophical belief underpinning counselling theory is self determination. Although few authors write specifically about it, it is a condition connected to respect and unconditional positive regard. The belief that each client has an absolute right to choose which direction s/he wants to go, to select goals from his/her own value orientation, and to determine behaviours for him/herself is strongly held in counselling circles. The central precept of counselling hinges on this concept. The preferred stance of the counsellor is one of an egalitarian relationship; one which asserts the position that the client is just as able to solve problems and gain insight into themselves as the counsellor. This differs slightly in psychotherapy, where the therapist may suggest treatment programmes and régimes from their particular theoretical framework, from which the client will work.

'Where there's a whale, there's a way!'

The reality of self determination as an achievable objective is perhaps debatable. Although within the practice of counselling it has become a valued aim, in practice it could be argued that the evidence for its existence is scarce. To elucidate further, it can be seen that to maintain self determination, the client would have to be offered unconditional regard; be resistant or immune from the influence of the therapist; and fully understand and choose their own goals and behaviour. In the light of previous arguments, it would appear that all of these conditions are unlikely. Unconditional positive regard is likely to be positive regard from the counsellor's own value orientation; to be resistant or immune from the influence of the counsellor is hardly what most clients seek a counsellor for, nor would their awareness of the implications of influence prepare them for resistance. And if self awareness is to be achieved through the counsellor's most often chosen strategy, empathy, then the difficulties highlighted earlier make this also a somewhat unlikely proposition.

Taking a less absolute approach to this issue, it is quite possible to see self determination as a matter of degree rather than an unequivocal state. From the arguments presented so far, it would seem that counsellors probably do influence client outcomes to some extent, in either their intentional or unintentional interventions in the world of another person. This does not mean that the notion of self determination has to be rejected. In some ways, it may be viewed in the same way as the other core conditions. The concept is powerful and conceived from an altruistic perspective, yet it may be impossible, and even undesirable, to achieve it in pure form. An acknowledgement of the practical difficulties, and an alertness to them, may be a better position for counsellors to adopt.

It can be argued that encouraging self determination is a somewhat self indulgent approach, and denies the existence of the greater aspects of self within a society. The individual, at some point, may need to be reminded of the cost and consequences of reaching their goals. It is possible that in the process of striving for and attaining one's own fulfilment, others and society can be damaged. For example, individuals who express their smoking behaviour may deny other individuals, in their presence, their right to a smoke free environment. Taking a more global perspective, the individualistic society based on consumerism may be encouraged to possess such 20th-century paraphernalia as the motor car, at the expense of the damage to the environment that others have to live in. Every action has some kind of reaction, and one person's freedom may, as a reaction, create another's imprisonment. Over the past few decades in this country, the individual has been encouraged to be self-reliant, to be less dependent on the state. Specific examples of this phenomenon are not hard to identify; privatisation of health care, education, and pensions are all pointers to the gradual withdrawal of central government's provision to the average person, and a trend for individuals to provide for themselves. This general attitude tends to have the effect of enhancing individuals' idea of self identity, and individualism at the cost of a more moral awareness of the common well being of the collective society.

When we look at the practice of counselling and its doctrine of self determination in this context, then it can be viewed as an amoral or an antisocial activity. Although we would agree that self fulfilment in itself is not a bad thing, and that its pursuit does not have to mean the dereliction of responsibility for the collective good, we would also want to highlight that any pursuit of self indulgent goals without consideration of their effect upon others may eventually lead to a serious erosion of collective human values, and a limited perspective on the world.

If it is possible to convince the average person that they are responsible entirely for their situation, and that counselling is the panacea to enable people to marshal their resources and take self responsibility, then it may also be used as a device for maintaining the status quo, and enabling those actually responsible for social conditions to avoid changing them. If social problems can be consummately addressed by engaging counsellors and counselling programmes instead of by other means, then this may signal that counselling has become another *"opium of the masses"*. Counselling in this context could therefore be labelled amoral as it takes the virtue of "unconditional positive regard" and of "self determination" without reference to the wider view of society's needs or the effect that the self-determining person will have on another.

In consideration of this latter position, it should be made clear that the position of counsellors can be attacked from either direction. If counselling takes the position of non directiveness and an amoral approach it may be damned for colluding in an individualist society that may be damaging to the collective good. On the other hand, the counselling approach that "selectively" attends and responds to the client from the value orientation of the counsellor could equally be attacked for perpetuating a biased approach from whatever position the counsellor holds. Equally this latter position suggests that, as counsellors are largely recruited from the educated, white middle class, this situation offers simply another agency of social control, supporting the status quo and perpetuating the trend towards an individualist society. Taking these views into account, it is hard to assert that the practice of counselling is or should be "value free". The principle of self determination in counselling practice is therefore an ideal that may well be fatally flawed, even though on face value it would appear to be desirable.

In Sum

In reviewing the whole of the last section on core conditions, it can be seen that their study is somewhat complex. It would seem that counsellors need to develop self awareness in order to be genuine; engage with clients in order to understand them intimately; offer acceptance without judgement; respect the clients right to self determination ; and be aware of their own prejudices and discard them. In addition, the counsellor has to develop these attributes and attitudes irrespective of any conflicting client values or behaviours that they may encounter. We wish you luck!

However, it is our belief that an acceptance of the complexities makes for better, rather than impossible, practice. Principles and values are guidelines which can help a lot of the time: do you remember learning to drive, and being told don't worry about getting on that motor way, people would let you in. This is true for ninety-nine percent of the time, but we always keep an eye out for when the principle doesn't operate. Because in practice, it can't operate a hundred per cent. Perhaps counselling is a bit like that - let's not make its principles sacrosanct, or mystical. They are an aid towards achieving our purpose, not some immutable ideals of themselves. Ultimately, we need to be in constant negotiation with our clients - *have* I understood you, I'm having difficulty with this bit and I *want* to understand, I find it difficult to work with this attitude, but I know I can suspend my difficulty, or I know that I just cannot accept this and so am not the person for this particular job. Core conditions are approximations and useful devices; it's only when we hold them up as rigid imperatives that we begin to make impossible and saintly claims which are no good for either the counsellor or the client.

Endnotes:

1. See for example Richard Sennett's masterly exposition of 'Destructive Gemeinschaft', in which he argues that the drive to maskless relations is producing a tyranny of self and emotion. Also, Alasdair MacIntyre's work on 'emotivism', wherein moral judgement is replaced by the ethical preferences of the unmasked self, offers some provocative viewpoints on the role of the Therapist in modern society.

2. These are the three core conditions, identified by Anthony Truax and Robert Carkhuff (1967), which are suggested to be an essential precursor for clients to perceive the therapy as a positive experience helping to resolve their problems. These conditions were asserted as necessary components of successful therapy, irrespective of whichever therapeutic approach was being used. It was postulated that when these conditions are not present any therapy has a greater chance of failure. This research helped explain the rather random results of success and failure across a range of therapeutic approaches and pointed to the relationship between therapist and client as being as important as the particular therapeutic approaches used by any therapist.

3. Carl Rogers , is the most prestigious, prodigious and classic source of much of the common wisdom and beliefs held by counsellors today. His work (1957) suggests not only that the core conditions are *necessary*, but also that they are *sufficient* for successful therapeutic personality change. His writings span a period of over forty years and have been criticised and applauded by generations of counsellors and psychotherapists from all branches of the field of helping. Much of this chapter is informed by the studying of his works and his critics . See also Egan (1994), Feltham (1995), Gellner (1985), Krumboltz and Thoresen (1976), Strong (1968)

4. Rogers (1990) description of empathy is as follows:

    "The ability of the therapist to perceive experiences and feelings accurately and sensitively, and to understand their meaning to the client during the moment to moment encounter of psychotherapy...Accurate empathic understanding means that the therapist is completely at home in the universe of the client...It is a sensing of the client's inner world of private personal meanings as if it were your own, while never forgetting it is not yours...The ability and sensitivity required to communicate these inner meanings again to the client in a way that allows them to be "his" experiences are the other major part of accurate empathic understanding. To sense the client's fear, his confusion, his anger, or his rage as if it were a feeling you might have (but which you are currently not having) is the essence of the perceptive aspect of accurate empathy. To communicate this perception in a language attuned to the client, which allows him more clearly to sense and formulate his fear, confusion, rage or anger, is the essence of the communicative aspect of accurate empathy". (p.15-16)

5. Extended and elaborated code studied by Bernstein(1962) and many other sociologists, make the significant point that culture, social status, and ethnicity will have a profound effect on mutual understanding. Bandler and Grinder (1979) also make the point that "Neuro-linguistic" compatibility will have an important impact on meaningful communication between individuals. i.e. "I *see* your point of view" can be framed "I *hear* what you are saying, I'm in *touch* with your meaning, or I can *feel* your discomfort," or even "that *smells* fishy to me".

6. The interpretation of body language and non verbal communication is the subject of continued study. The complex nuances and subtle variations of messages are determined by culture, ethnicity and specific societal influences, making universality of interpretation extremely difficult for the individual therapist. See Argyle (1975), Seigman and Feldstein (1987), and Sue (1990).

7. There is increasing interest in cross cultural counselling and specifically whether there are particular differences in cultures that make counselling and psychotherapeutic approaches inappropriate. As already mentioned earlier in this book, certain cultures view empathy for an individual's emotions an 'intrusion' into their privacy. See chapter Two and also Sue (1990).

8. Truax and Carkhuff (1967) suggest this as a definition of genuineness:-

    "Genuineness implies most basically a direct personal encounter, a meeting on a person-to-person basis without defensiveness or a retreat into façades or roles, and so in this sense an openness to experience." (p. 32)

9. Research in the 1960's argues that it is impossible to have a strong supportive relationship without exerting some social influence. Whether this is inadvertent, unconscious, accidental or deliberate is not necessary to determine. It is argued that our opinion is frequently given in our non verbal postures and language, even if there are no clues in our spoken words. See Frank (1961).

10. It is unfortunately the case that many incidents of exploitation in counselling and therapy have come to light. Some of these are unintentional errors of judgement and simple cases of a deep relationship being misinterpreted by both clients and therapists, but others are more malignant examples of deliberate exploitation for purposes of therapist gratification. See Russell (1993)

11. Albert Bandura(1977) has amassed significant research evidence that observed behaviour may be mimicked or learned by others in everyday interactions and experience.

12. Rogers (1961) building on the work of Fiedler (1950) and Standal (1954), first described the concept of unconditional positive regard thus:-

    "...the therapist experiences a warm caring for the client - a caring which is not possessive, which demands no personal gratification. It is an atmosphere which simply demonstrates " I care"; not "I care for you if you behave thus and so"...... I have often used the term acceptance to describe this aspect of the therapeutic climate." (p.283*)

13. Some might argue that Roger s meaning here needs to be contextualised in relation to his own life and his experience of receiving highly conditional approval within family and educative institutions.

14. Egan's (1994) view of respect is perhaps exemplified best through these quotes from the "Skilled Helper" :-

    "Your manner should indicate that you care in a down-to-earth, non-sentimental way. Respect is both gracious and tough minded." (p. 54)

    "Challenge clients to clarify their values and to make reasonable choices based on them. Be wary of using challenging, even indirectly, to force clients to accept your values." (p.195)

15. We use this term advisedly. Caring does not have to mean that we personally have an investment in how the client's life turns out; it means that we care in this counselling that the client is treated both professionally and 'with care', with respect which is driven towards their attaining the changes they want.

16. Some attempt to give guidance on these issues are reviewed in Tim Bond's book and are addressed within the British Association for Counselling code of ethics. See BAC (1992) and Bond (1993).

17. Gerard Egan the great pragmatic genius in helping, offers a gem of common wisdom in regard to non- judgementalness:

    "Suspend critical judgement. You are there to help clients, not to judge them. Nor are you there to shove your values down their throats. You are there, however, to help them identify, explore, and review the consequences of the values they have adopted." (1994:.53).

Chapter Ten. Blank Minds - Hardly Ever Sticky Moments - Not any more!

Introduction

This final chapter is a short organisation of the important issues attended to in the previous chapters. In much the same way as the component parts of a painting often seem important but random until the whole picture emerges, chapter ten is designed to enable the whole story to be seen.

Principles, theory, philosophy, skills and techniques may provide some food for thought, and in themselves can provide significant help for the practitioner and then subsequently the client. However, it is our strong belief that practitioners who are largely familiar and competent in these areas, yet still suffer from stuckness and experience blank minds from time to time, would benefit mostly from using an organising framework. Frameworks are never rigid. To have some organising framework should not serve to straight jacket or constrain the practitioner, but simply prevent them getting lost. The success of the framework depends on how flexibly it is used.

We believe a framework or system should act like a map, offering signposts, possible routes, and clearly marked destinations, it should not tell one how to travel or what speed to go at. This chapter offers such a framework, firstly in an unsophisticated and rugged form, easy to remember and instantly available. And secondly the same framework with a little more detail, referenced back to the appropriate chapters and sections so as to prevent repetition.

Using a framework - not counselling by numbers

We are, as most of you probably know, great advocates of Egan's problem solving model. We believe that those practitioners who balk at Egan's work as simplistic, and counselling by numbers, are often those who have not had it taught to them with the complexities and intricacy that it deserves. On the other hand some antagonists refuse to employ it because it is too cumbersome to 'hold in one's head' whilst doing so many other things. It is for these reasons that we propose practitioners take the Dexter and Russell look at Egan, and see how the complex can be made easier, and the too simple can be employed intricately. We are at this point, to some extent, taking some liberties with another author's work. However, we do this with the greatest respect for Dr. Egan's ingenuity, and out of a desire for his work to be more available to a greater number of practitioners than it is currently. We are proposing modifications to Egan's work, as additions and simplifications which have worked for us in practice. We know that Gerard Egan would be the first to recommend creativity, flexibility and enhancement at the service of the client. For the full unexpurgated and original work we commend all readers wholeheartedly to his comprehensive book 'The Skilled Helper'.

The Simplest of Models

For a simple model to prevent the practitioner getting lost, thus reducing at least one source of blank minds and sticky moments, we offer you the following simple formula to remember:

Contract	Empathy & Challenge	Goals	Strategies
Why are we here?	*What's up and what's really up?*	*What do you want instead then?*	*How are you going to get what you want?*

If you are stuck, then one of these requires more attention! If your mind has gone blank, then check your contract - what did I agree I would do if I got stuck? Or check your goals - what is it I'm trying to achieve? If neither of these seems appropriate, use empathy and challenge as a strategy to get moving again!

The more complex version of the simple model

Contract

During the course of this book we have been very clear that contracting with your client in the first instant is very important. We suggest the following as essential parts of the contract which will help your mind stay clear and prevent you getting stuck:

- Contracts should remain flexible and open to renegotiation by each party.
- Say what service you are offering - counselling and what it is, psychotherapy and what speciality accompanies it, or a mixture which is proactive according to the clients needs.
- How non-directive, non-judgemental, active or passive are you intending to be - the client may like to know that you will remain silent without explanation, before they agree to pay you!
- Do you have any boundaries to your respect for confidentiality - what are these? Ensure your client knows before you begin.
- How long is the session, and do you really mean 'x' minutes or is this just a rough guide. Will you break this boundary if something 'really' important or dangerous comes up at the last minute?
- How many sessions are you offering, is there some possibility of renegotiating the number of sessions later on, or is the number fixed? Is it an open ended contract – 'I'll be here for you whenever, forever?'
- What are the boundaries of contact? Can the client ring you at any time? Do you expect a friendship or love affair to develop? How will you respond if you meet socially?

Empathy and Challenge

The emphasis on this stage is to engage with the client in whatever ways possible that enable an advanced state of understanding (essentially one way) to exist. The purpose of this is to permit the practitioner to know the relevant thoughts, feelings, and general situation of the client in order to demonstrate their comprehensive understanding. With this display of uncontaminated perception into the client's world, the practitioner will create the necessary trust and rapport in order for the client to continue disclosing sufficiently to enable a clearer view of themselves to emerge. This usually will not require any questions, any opinions or any direction from the practitioner. The use of simple skills such as reflecting, paraphrasing, clarifying, and summarising (or similar non linguistic skills as employed by art or drama-therapists) should be entirely sufficient.

If the client's world is not clearly visible after such simple empathy, then challenging skills will be required (see Chapter Four).

All sorts of potential challenges may be helpful for different clients in different situations and no one particular approach appears to be uniquely advantageous in all situations. This is perhaps where the study of differing approaches may be helpful to practitioners. Taking a didactic approach and pointing out the blindingly obvious, or subtly inviting the client to reconsider some entrenched position which is unhelpful are interventions which develop from differing philosophical viewpoints, but both may be helpful for some clients on some occasions. It is the principle of being helpful to the client that should influence your choice of challenge, not some intractable philosophical dogma.

Goals

Ubiquitously misunderstood, goals often provide the most powerful of levers of helpfulness. They are in the main the most positive of challenges that can be issued. They are looked at in more detail in Chapter Four, but for the purposes of this précis, they can be divided into the following:

- Abstract Goals

    The hidden goals and values of the person that need to be accessed in order for the client to be able to make more sense of their existence. The words extracted from clients in this work will be emotions and states such as: More...peace, excitement, independence, freedom, stimulation, challenge, control, choice, a sense I've done my best, contentment, happiness, fulfilment, satisfaction, justice, or equality.

- Abstract behavioural pictured goals

    The abstract goals have to be translated into portraits of what would be happening if the client's life was better. Slightly more tangible imaginings that have some connection with their ideal existence need to be elicited. It is important to remember that much of what has been fantasized can be realised, but in order to do so it has to be specified in more behavioural terms:
    What do I really want from my life; if I could choose, how would I spend the rest of my life? If I had a magic wand what would I really like to be happening in my life? Who would be with me, what emotions would I be experiencing more of, instead of the ones I currently have? Where would I really like to be, what would I really like to be doing?

■ Concrete behavioural goals

Out of the picture created by the clients imagination, what is worth trying for? And what is something that could be achieved? If the client could describe in realistic terms a day, an hour, or a situation where they would be achieving their goal, what would it look like? This sometimes will require a detailed description of what would be happening to others, what each person would be saying and doing. However, it is most important here to remember the practitioner is asking 'what would' not 'what will' to ensure the client remains clarifying what they want, NOT what they intend to do!!

■ Fitting goals in context

Once the client has elicited their goals, a final check as to how they fit in with their personal environment and value system is desirable. What will be the consequence of my pursuing more peace/revenge/ more relaxation? Of leaving my partner and children? Of not leaving? Clients need to check this in relation to themselves or others; this acts as a safety net on impulsive action.

Strategy

Strategies are forms of action which help the client to achieve their preferred goals. Practitioners are often tempted to start at this point in the process instead of ending here. Why should this be? Basically, it seems that human beings are so arrogant that they believe that if they listen to someone's problem for a few minutes they can automatically solve it for them - more quickly and more efficiently than the other person ever can. This involves an incredible amount of expertise, wisdom, and, of course, conceit. What always amazes us is that, it would seem, some counsellors think that this can be achieved *without ever ascertaining what it is that the client actually wants!*

The most effective and respectful of practitioners will patiently negotiate through a thorough understanding of problems and wants *before* helping the client discover what resources, strategies and plans are needed to help them achieve their chosen goals.

So the strategy stage is important to ensure that goals are achieved, and we agree there are many ways of helping clients to get in touch with their best resources and strategies. We also believe that it is much better for the *client* to generate their own strategies, rather than be served with the practitioners best suggestions. There are a number of ways that practitioners may proceed in engaging in the strategic stage with clients, for example:

- Prompting clients to explore their own resources such as:

- Who might be helpful in achieving your goal?
- What ways can you think of that would help you to reach your goal?
- How many organisations, agencies or groups can you think of which might help?
- In your day to day life do you pass or visit any places such as parks, shops, libraries that might help you achieve your goal?
- Are there any things or places that might help you get to where you want to be?
- Think of as many wild or crazy ideas as possible that might be helpful in achieving your goal.
- How many people can you think of who have had your problems - what did they do?
- Some therapeutic approaches may stimulate clients into exploring their resources. Some examples such as:

- Rehearsing through role playing and role reversal techniques. - Gestalt and Dramaturgical approaches.
- Conducting small and safe experiments such as those involved in Kelly s fixed role therapy. - Personal Construct Therapy.
- Trying out different ways of behaving through sensory reprogramming and seeing what different outcomes occur - are they better? -Neuro-Linguistic Programming.
- Identifying thoughts or ideas that prevent goal achievement and replacing them with more goal conducive ones. - Cognitive Behavioural Therapy.
- Changing one's inappropriate 'Ego' states during interpersonal exchanges. - Transactional Analysis.

All of these are possible ways of stimulating the client into exploring their own resources and discovering their own wealth of creativity. They are then simply a list of strategies themselves.

Some are better than others in some situations, some are more directive or didactic than others. Some involve more exploratory work, of past or present; to achieve peace of mind, perhaps someone needs to work through some unresolved grief, or to confront (metaphorically or otherwise) an important figure in their lives. Strategies are not merely lists of superficial actions, they are *everything that the client does through the process of counselling.* So it is very helpful to have them directed to the client's goal, and to remember Egan's principle that strategies should always be *'directed to the service of the client'.*

Summary

To sum up, not only this chapter but the whole book, is therefore rather simple. Whether the client's problem is some deep seated misery conceived in some traumatic childhood history, some existential issue requiring engagement through a lengthy contemplation of the meaning of life, or a plea of desperation by someone who is unable to pay next weeks rent, they all represent symptoms of the human condition, and all require the practitioner's unhampered assistance once the contract is accepted. The practitioner, no matter what approach is being used, is required to utilise all their skills with integrity, practice their arts and science ethically, and serve the clients' needs not their own. To do this, it is important that they remain focused, that their perspectives remain grounded, and that their mind stays with the client; thus the process remains freed up.

While counselling is an extremely useful social practice, it is not the be all and end all. It operates many paradoxes, which once admitted, can aid rather than prevent realistic work. And finally, practitioners are people too, who have their own needs and limitations. We wish you all, therapists, counsellors, analysts, and practitioners of all descriptions who stay within the above parameters -

A Concentrated Mind and Unfettered Moments

Graham Dexter and Janice Russell
August 18th. 1997.

Bibliography

Argyle, M. (1975) Bodily Communication. London, Methuen.
Argyle, Michael (1987) The Psychology of Happiness London: Routledge.
Axline, Virginia (1964) Dibs: In Search of Self Harmondsworth: Penguin.
B. A. C. (British Association for Counselling) (1989) Code of Ethics and Practice for the Supervision of Counsellors, Rugby : British Association for Counselling.
B. A. C. (British Association for Counselling) (1992) Code of Ethics and Practice (3.3)
Bandler, A. and Grinder, J. (1979) Frogs into Princes, Moab, Utah: Real People Press.
Bandura, A. (1977) Social learning theory, Englewood Cliffs, N.J. : Prentice-Hall.
Bass, E. and Davis, L. (1988) The Courage to Heal London: Cedar Press
Bass, E. and Davis, L. (1993) Beginning to Heal London: Cedar Press
Beck, A. T. (1976) Cognitive Therapy and the Emotional Disorders, New York: New American Library.
Berger, P. (1973) The Homeless Mind Harmondsworth: Penguin.
Berne, E. (1964) Games People Play: the psychology of human relationships Harmondsworth: Penguin.
Bernstein, B. B. (1962) "Social class, linguistic codes and grammatical elements", Language and Speech, 5, 221-24.
Berry, C. R. (1991) How to Escape the Messiah Trap: A Workbook for when Helping You is Hurting Me San Francisco: Harper Collins.
Bond, T. (1993) Standards and Ethics for counselling in Action, London : Sage.
Bridger, F. and Atkinson, D. (1994) Counselling in Context: Developing a Theological Framework London, Harper Collins.
Carkhuff, R. (1987) (6th ed.) The Art of Helping Amhearst, Massachusetts: Human Resource Development Press.
Carroll, M. (1996) "To the Point" Counselling News, 24, December.

Clark, D. (ed) (1993) The Sociology of Death Oxford, Blackwell/
Sociological Review Monograph.
Corey, G. (1996) (5th ed.) Theory and Practice of Counselling and
Psychotherapy Monterey: Brooks/Cole.
Culley, S. (1991) Integrative Counselling Skills in Action London:
Sage.
Deurzen-Smith, E. van (1988) Existential Counselling in Practice
London: Sage .
Dexter, L. G. "A critical review of the effect of counselling training
on trainees" Unpublished Ph.D. thesis, University of Durham,
1997.
Dryden, W. (ed) (1989) Key Issues for Counselling in Action
London: Sage.
Duck, S. and Pond, C. (1989) 'Rhetoric and Reality' in Clyde
Hendrick (ed) Close Relationships London: Sage.
Duck, S. (1988) Relating to Others London: Sage.
Egan, G. (1990) The Skilled Helper: A Systematic Approach to
Effective Helping, (4th. Ed.) Pacific Grove, California: Brooks/
Cole.
Egan, G. (1994) (fifth edition) The Skilled Helper: A Problem-
Management Approach to Helping Monterey: Brooks/Cole.
Egan, G. (1975) The Skilled Helper: A Model for Systematic
Helping and Interpersonal Relating, Monterey, California:
Brooks/Cole.
Ehrenberg, D. B. (1992) The Intimate Edge: Extending the Reach
of Psychoanalytic Interaction New York: W.W. Norton & Com-
pany.
Ellis, A. (1962) Reason and Emotion in Psychotherapy, New York:
Lyle Stuart.
Falk, D. and Wagner, P. N. (1985) 'Intimacy of Self-Disclosure
and Response Processes as Factors affecting the Development of
Interpersonal Relationships' in The Journal of Social Psychology,
125(5), 557-570.
Feltham, C. (1995) What is Counselling London: Sage.
Fieldler, F. E. (1950) "The concept of an ideal therapeutic rela-
tionship", J. of Consulting Psychology, 14, 239 -245.
Foucault, M. (1987) The Use of Pleasure: The History of Sexuality
Volume II Harmondsworth: Penguin.
Foucault, M. (1981) The History of Sexuality: An Introduction
Harmondsworth: Penguin.
Frank, J. D. (1961) Persuasion and healing: A comparative study
of Psychotherapy, Baltimore: John Hopkins University Press.

Fromm, E. (1979) To Have Or To Be? London: Abacus.

Fromm, E. (1982) Greatness And Limitations Of Freud's Thoughts, London: Abacus.

Fromm, E. (1984a) The Fear of Freedom, London: Routledge, Ark paperbacks.

Fromm, E. (1984) On Disobedience and other essays, London: Routledge.

Gellner, H. (1985) The Psychoanalytic Movement, London: Paladin.

Giddens, A. (1991) Modernity and Self-Identity Cambridge: Polity Press

Goffman, E. (1959) (1971) The Presentation of Self in Everyday Life Harmondsworth: Penguin.

Grosch, W. N. and Olsen, D. C. (1994) When Helping Starts To Hurt : A New Look at Burnout Among Psychotherapists, London : Norton & Co Inc.

Hagard, M. and Blickem, V. (1987) Befriending- a sociological case history Cambridge: Oleander Press.

Heelas, P. (1991) 'Reforming the Self: Enterprise and the characters of Thatcherism', in Keat, R. and Abercrombie, N. (eds) Enterprise Culture London: Routledge.

Holmes, J. and Lindley, R. (1991) Values of Pscyhotherapy Milton Keynes: OU Press.

Houston, G. (1982) The Relative-Sized Red Book of Gestalt London: Rochester Foundation.

Howard, A. (1996) Challenging Counselling and Therapy. London: Macmillan.

Howard, A. (1990) "Counselling plc" in Counselling Vol.1, No. 1 pp15-17.

Ingram, D. H. (1991) "Intimacy in the Psychoanalytic Relationship: A Preliminary Sketch" in American Journal of Psychoanalysis Vol:51 No.4 pp 403-411.

Karusu, T. B. (1986) "The specificity versus non-specificity dilemma: Towards identifying therapeutic change agents.", Am. J. of Psychiatry, 143, 687-695.

Kelly, G. A. (1955a) The Psychology of Personal Constructs. Volume Two: Diagnosis and Psychotherapy, Norton, New York.

Kelly, G. A. (1955) The Psychology of Personal Constructs. Volume One: A Theory of Personality, Norton, New York.

Kirschenbaum, H. and Henderson, V. L. (Ed.) (1990) The Carl Rogers Reader, London.

Krumboltz, J. and Thoresen, C. (eds.), (1976), Counselling Methods, New York: Holt, Rhinehart, and Winston.

Laing, R.D. (1969) The Divided Self Harmondsworth: Penguin.

Lerner, H. G. (1989) The Dance of Intimacy London: Pandora Press.

MacIntyre, A. (1981) After Virtue: a study in Moral Theory London: Geral Duckworth & Company.

Maslach, C. (1982) Burnout : The Cost of Caring, Englewood Cliffs, N.J. : Prentice-Hall.

Maslow (1987) (3rd ed.b) Motivation and Personality New York: Harper & Row.

Mearns, D. and Dryden, W. (1991) The Client's Experience of Counselling in Action London: Sage.

Morgan-Jones, R. (1993) "Social Anthropology and Counselling" in Thorne, B. and Dryden, W. (ed) (1993) Counselling: Interdisciplinary Perspectives Milton Keynes: Open University Press.

O'Connor, J. and Seymour, J. (1990) Introducing Neuro-Linguistic Programming: Psychological Skills For Understanding And Influencing People. London: Thorsons.

Pilgrim, D. and Treacher, A. (1992) Clinical Psychology Observed. London: Routledge.

Rashid, H. M. (1992) "Human Development Theory: Islamic vs Western Perspective", in Muslim Education Quarterly, Vol. 9, No. a4, pp 4-13.

Reyes, A. (1995) When You Love, You Must Depart London: Minerval Paperbacks

Rogers, C. R. (1942) Counselling and Psychotherapy: New Concepts in Practice, Boston: Houghton Miflin.

Rogers, C. R. (1951) Client Centred Therapy Constable: London.

Rogers, C. R. (1957) "The Necessary and Sufficient Conditions of Therapeutic Personality Change.", Journal of Consulting Psychology, Vol. 21, No. 2, 95-103.

Rogers, C. R. (1961) On Becoming a Person: A Therapist's View of Psychotherapy, London, Constable.

Rogers, C. R. (1990) In Kirschenbaum, H. and Henderson, V. L. (Eds.), Carl Rogers Dialogues. London: Constable. Rowe, D. (1991) Wanting Everything London: Fontana.

Ross, P. and Lwanga, J. (1991) 'Counselling the Bewitched: An Exercise in Cross-cultural eschatology ' in Counselling Vol. 2 No. 1 pp 17-19.

Russell, J. M., Dexter, G. and Bond, T. (1992) Counselling, Advise, Guidance, Befriending and Counselling Skills: Differentiation Report, London: Department of Employment.

Russell, J and Dexter, G., (1993) 'Menage a Trois: Accreditation, NVQ's and BAC'. Counselling, 4 (4), 266-69.

Russell, J. (1993) Out of Bounds; sexual exploitation in counselling and therapy London: Sage.

Russell, J. (1996) 'Feminism and Counselling' in Bayne, Rowan (ed) New Directions in Counselling London: Routledge.

Rutter, P. (1990) Sex in the Forbidden Zone London: Mandala.

Seigman, A. W., and Feldstein, S. (eds.) (1987) Nonverbal Behaviour and Communication, (2nd. ed.) New Jersey: Erlbaum.

Sennett, R. (1977) The Fall of Public Man Cambridge: Cambridge University Press

Sennett, R. (1988.) 'Destructive Gemeinschaft' in Bocock, R., Hamilton, P., Thompson, K., Waton, A. (ed) An Introduction to Sociology: a reader Milton Keynes: OU Press.

Smail, D. (1987) Taking Care: an alternative to Therapy London: J.M Dent & Sons

Smith, N. (1989) Perfection Proclaimed: Language and Literature in English Radical Religion Oxford: Clarendon Press.

Standal, S. (1954) The need for positive regard: A contribution to client-centred theory, Unpublished Ph.D. thesis, University of Chicago.

Strong, S. R. (1968) "Counselling : An interpersonal influence process", J of Counselling Psychology 15, pp. 215 -224.

Sue, D. W. (1990) "Culture-specific strategies in counselling: A conceptual framework", Professional Psychology: Research and Practice, 21, 6, p.424-433.

Taylor, C. (1991) The Ethics of Authenticity Cambridge: Harvard University Press

Thomas, K. (1971) Religion and the Decline of Magic London: Peregrine Books.

Truax, C. B. and Carkhuff, R. R. (1967) Towards Effective Counselling and Psychotherapy, Chicago, Aldine.

Weeks, J. (1990) 'The Value of Difference' in Jonathan Rutherford (ed) (1990) Identity: Community, Culture, Difference London: Lawrence & Wishart.

Worden, J. W. (1993) Grief Counselling and Grief Therapy London: Tavistock.

Index